The Photoshop 6 Toolbox

W9-BUX-780

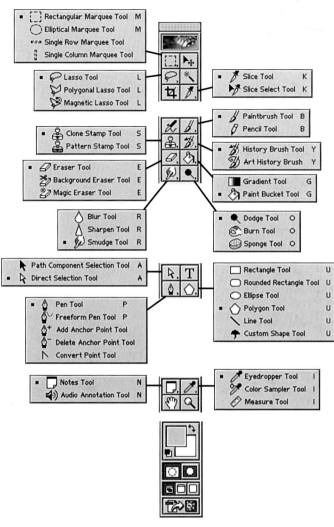

Teach Yourself Adobe® Photoshop® 6 in 24 Hours

- Keyboard shortcuts shown in pop-ups.
- Shift+keyboard shortcut cycles through multiple tools if available.

Photoshop 6 Keyboard Shortcut Quick Reference

Top-level menus have keyboard mnemonics (accessed by pressing Command+*underlined hotkey*) for Macintosh users. Windows users should use the Control key instead of Command except where indicated and the Alt key instead of Option.

PHOTOSHOP COMMAND	KEYBOARD SHORTCUT
FILE MENU	
New	Command+N
Open	Command+O
Open As (Windows only)	Option+Control+O
Close	Command+W
Save	Command+S
Save As	Shift+Command+S
Print Options	Option+Command+P
Save for Web	Option+Shift+Command+S
Page Setup	Shift+Command+P
Print	Command+P
EDIT MENU	
Undo	Command+Z
Step Forward	Option+Command+Z
Step Backward	Shift+Command+Z
Cut	Command+X
Copy	Command+C
Copy Merged	Shift+Command+C
Paste	Command+V
Paste Into	Shift+Command+V
Free Transform	Command+T
Fade	Shift+Command+F
Color Settings	Shift+Command+K
Preferences	Command+K
IMAGE MENU	
Adjust→Levels	Command+L
Adjust→Auto Levels	Shift+Command+L
Adjust→Auto Contrast	Option+Shift+Command+L
Adjust→Curves	Command+M
Adjust→Color Balance	Command+B
Adjust→Hue/Saturation	Command+U
Adjust→Desaturate	Shift+Command+U
Adjust→Invert	Command+I
Extract	Option+Command+X
Liquify	Shift+Command+X

LAYER MENU	
New→Layer	Shift+Command+N
New→Layer Via Copy	Command+J
New→Layer Via Cut	Shift+Command+J
Group with Previous	Command+G
Ungroup	Shift+Command+G
Arrange→Bring to Front	Shift+Command+]
Arrange→Bring Forward	Command+]
Arrange→Send Backward	Command+[
Arrange→Send to Back	Shift+Command+[
Merge Link	Command+E
Merge Visible	Shift+Command+E
SELECT MENU	
All	Command+A
Deselect	Command+D
Reselect	Shift+Command+D
Inverse	Shift+Command+I
Feather	Option+Command+D
FILTER MENU	
Last Filter	Command+F
VIEW MENU	
Proof Colors	Command+Y
Gamut Warning	Shift+Command+Y
Zoom In	Command++
Zoom Out	Command+-
Fit on Screen	Command+0 (zero)
Actual Pixels	
Windows	Shift+Control+0 (zero)
Macintosh	Option+Command+0 (zero)
Show/Hide Extras	Command+H
Show/Hide Rulers	Command+R
Snap	Command+;
Lock Guides	Option+Command+;
HELP MENU	
Contents	F1

OTHER SHORTCUTS	
Move view up/down	Page Up/Down one screen
Nudge view up/down	Shift+Page Up/Down
Move view left/right	Command+Page Up/Down one screen
Nudge new left/right	Shift+Command+Page Up/Down
Previous History Entry	Command+Shift+Z
Next History Entry	Command+Option+Z

Carla Rose

SAMS
Teach Yourself

Adobe®
Photoshop® 6

in 24 Hours

SAMS

201 West 103rd Street, Indianapol

Sams Teach Yourself Adobe® Photoshop® 6 in 24 Hours

Copyright © 2001 by Sams Publishing

International Standard Book Number: 0-672-31955-1

Library of Congress Catalog Card Number: 00-105617

Printed in the United States of America

First Printing: October 2000

02   01   4   3   2

Trademarks

Warning and Disclaimer

ACQUISITIONS EDITOR
Jennifer Kost

DEVELOPMENT EDITOR
Jon Steever

MANAGING EDITOR
Charlotte Clapp

PROJECT EDITOR
Dawn Pearson

COPY EDITOR
Mary Ellen Stephenson

INDEXER
Greg Pearson

PROOFREADER
Daniel Ponder

TECHNICAL EDITOR
Peter Bauer

TEAM COORDINATOR
Amy Patton

INTERIOR DESIGN
Gary Adair

COVER DESIGN
Aren Howell

Contents at a Glance

Contents

About the Author

Carla Rose started her photography career at the age of 8 with a Brownie Hawkeye. A graduate of the School of the Museum of Fine Arts in Boston, she has been a TV news photographer and film editor, as well as an advertising copywriter and graphic artist, before discovering the Macintosh. She has written all or part of over two dozen computer books, including *Maclopedia*, *Sams Teach Yourself Digital Photography in 14 Days*, *Sams Teach Yourself Photoshop 4 in 14 Days*, *The Whole Mac*, *Managing the Windows NT Server*, *PageMaker 6.5 Complete*, *Sams Teach Yourself Photoshop 4 in 24 Hours*, *Sams Teach Yourself Photoshop 5 in 24 Hours*, *Mac Online*, *The First Book of Macintosh*, *The First Book of PageMaker 4 for Macintosh*, *It's a Mad, Mad, Mad, Mad Mac*, *Turbocharge Your Mac*, and *Everything You Ever Wanted to Know About the Mac*. She is a contributing editor to *digitalFoto* magazine and has also written for publications ranging from the *Atlantic Fisherman* to *Adobe Magazine* to the *New Yorker*. She lives near Boston, Massachusetts, with her husband, audio guru Jay Rose, and two large, friendly cats. She welcomes email addressed to `author@graphicalcat.com`.

Dedication

This book's for Vicki Shore, and for Hacker and Alfie. Thanks for the love and the laughter.

Acknowledgments

No project this big could ever get started, much less completed, without help from a lot of wonderful people. I'd like to thank the folks at Macmillan, especially Mark Taber, Jennifer Kost, and Amy Patton. Thanks to Peter Bauer for a good technical edit, Jon Steever for a strong development, Mary Ellen Stephenson for copy editing, and Dawn Pearson for keeping it all on track. Thanks also to Christie Evans and the Adobe folks for providing beta software and for coming up with a wonderful product. As always, thanks to my friends in the ABC's for their moral support as I worked 20-hour days to meet the deadlines. Thanks to Village Smokehouse, Rainbow Noodle House, Quan's Kitchen, and Village Pizza for keeping us fed.

Apologies and a hug to everyone I had to ignore or chase away while I worked, especially the cats. And the biggest hug and deepest gratitude of all to my wonderful husband, Jay, who always does what needs to be done.

Tell Us What You Think

As the reader of this book, *you* are the most important critic and commentator. We value your opinion and want to know what we're doing right, what we could do better, what areas you'd like to see us publish in, and any other words of wisdom you're willing to pass our way.

You can fax, email, or write me directly to let me know what you did or didn't like about this book—as well as what we can do to make our books stronger.

Please note that I cannot help you with technical problems related to the topic of this book, and due to the high volume of mail I receive, I might not be able to reply to every message.

When you write, please be sure to include this book's title and author as well as your name and phone or fax number. I will carefully review your comments and share them with the author and editors who worked on the book.

Fax: 317-581-4770
Email: graphics_sams@mcp.com
Mail: Mark Taber
           Associate Publisher
           Sams Publishing
           201 West 103rd Street
           Indianapolis, Indiana 46290 USA

Introduction

Photoshop 6 is the latest and greatest version of a program that has set the standard for image manipulation since 1987. The new version has lots of new features, including a Tool Options bar that places all of your tool options right next to an image so that you can set them quickly and easily. The Type Tool has been totally reworked, and you can now set type right on a picture and even set it on a path! Additional type and paragraph controls give you the ability to kern and adjust line spacing and much more. There are new Vector Shape Tools that let you create shapes and shaped paths with a mouse click.

If you've used an earlier version of Photoshop, you'll be amazed at how much more powerful this one is. If this is your first experience with Photoshop, you'll be blown away. It's that good! The big surprise for first-time users is that it's really not as difficult to work with as it looks. If you have used any other Adobe software, the Photoshop interface will be immediately familiar to you. If this is your first step into creating digital graphics, you'll find the going easier if you work on the chapters of this book one at a time and don't skip the activities or exercises.

I've provided many of the source images for the book's exercises on the Macmillan Web site dedicated to this book. To download the images, point your Web browser to http://www.mcp.com/sams/detail_sams.cfm?item=0672319551.

Once the main book page has loaded, click the Downloads link to get to the files.

There's honestly no way to become an overnight expert, be it in Photoshop or anything else, but *Sams Teach Yourself Adobe Photoshop 6 in 24 Hours* will get you up and running in 24 hours or less. It's divided into two dozen, one-hour "lessons," rather than chapters. Each one should take you about an hour to complete. Some lessons may need more time; others, less. Please don't try to do it all in one 24-hour day, even if you could. The best way to learn is to take an hour or two between the lesson sessions to try out what you've learned. You'll want to simply poke around, and see what's on the menus and what happens when you click here and there.

Here's one for you to start with: Open the About Photoshop window and wait for a minute. You'll see it start to scroll through the list of all the people who worked on the program. Watch carefully for the very last name on the list. It's a pleasant surprise...

Ready? Let's get to work.

HOUR 1

The Basics

Photoshop is *still* the ultimate graphics program, though it's far different from the first version released about 10 years ago. Although it's mainly used for photo-retouching and image manipulation, you can also use it to create original art, either from scratch or based on a photograph. You can even use it to set type! It's more fun than a video game and much less difficult than you might think.

Finding Your Way Around

When you first open Photoshop, you'll see its toolbox on the left side of the screen, the new Tool Options bar just under the menu headings at the top of the screen, and four sets of windows on the right. (You'll also see your desktop, or whatever else is open at the time, if you use a Mac.)

You won't see a work area, because Photoshop, unlike most graphics programs, doesn't automatically open a new page for you. This actually makes sense, because most of your work in Photoshop will be done on pictures that you have brought in from some other source. Maybe you'll be using digital images from your digital camera or scanner. Possibly you'll work on files you've downloaded from the Internet or on photos from a CD-ROM. In

Hour 2, "Opening and Saving," you will learn all about opening these pictures. Right now, let's open a blank page so you can try out some of Photoshop's tools.

Starting a New Page

File→New is the first item on the first Photoshop menu. When you select it, you open the New File dialog box, shown in Figure 1.1. You can enter a title for your new file at the top of the dialog box, such as My New Page, or leave it untitled for now. The following sections will give you a brief overview to get you started setting up a new file.

FIGURE **1.1**

Use the New file dialog box to start a blank page.

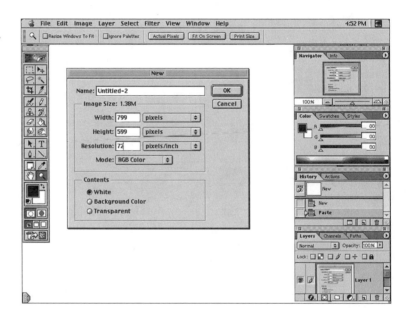

Image Size

In the Image Size area of the dialog box, you specify the size of your image—width and height—in pixels, inches, centimeters, points, picas, or columns across. These measurements are available in drop-down menus that you can access by clicking the small arrow next to the unit of measurement. For now, choose inches. Make your page big enough to work on comfortably. The page in Figure 1.1 is six inches by five inches, which is a convenient size to display on a typical screen.

Resolution

Resolution refers to the number of dots-of-ink-per-inch (if you're printing) or pixels-per-inch (if you're looking at the computer screen). It's important because the resolution of

1

the image determines the quality. Higher resolution gives you a better quality image but uses more memory. Most images that you see in print have a resolution of 150 dpi to 300 dpi—or dots-per-inch.

Your computer's monitor, on the other hand, has a dpi of 72, which is substantially lower. Therefore, you always set the resolution depending on what your output will be. For now, keep the resolution at 72 dpi because we're just looking at the screen. For the same reason, set the Mode to RGB Color, as shown in Figure 1.1. RGB Color is the kind of color that monitors display. (You'll learn all about color modes in Hour 5, "Color Modes and Color Models.")

Click the button to set the page contents to White. This gives you a white "canvas" to paint on.

If you intend to publish your images on the Web, ignore resolution completely. Rather than thinking of an image as "so-many-inches by so-many-inches at 72 dpi," think of the image as being "this-many-pixels by this-many-pixels." Consider how much of the Web page the image will cover. If, on the other hand, you are printing to a high quality color inkjet or laser printer, set the resolution to 200 dpi. You really would use 300 dpi only if you need to create professional color prints.

After you click OK in the New File dialog box, you see a new window. This is the *active window*, and the *canvas* is the large white square within it. Figure 1.2 shows the canvas. You can have more than one window open within Photoshop at the same time, but only one can be the active window. The active window is always in the foreground. This is where you create and edit images.

Set your mouse cursor at the lower-right corner of the window, and then click and drag. The window expands, but notice that the canvas size stays the same. After you have created a new file, you can only change the size of the canvas by selecting Image→Canvas Size. This command enables you to specify a new height and width for the canvas, as shown in Figure 1.3. The Anchor section lets you specify the base area from which the canvas expands or shrinks, by clicking any of the eight white squares. (Changing the image size, obviously, changes the size of the canvas, too. The difference is that changing the canvas size gives you more room around your existing image.)

FIGURE **1.2**
This is your canvas.

FIGURE **1.2**
This is your canvas.

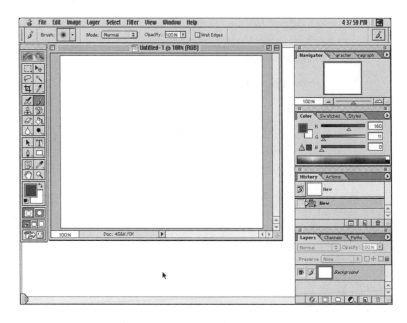

FIGURE **1.3**
Click a white square in the Anchor graph to locate your current canvas in the corresponding part of the new canvas.

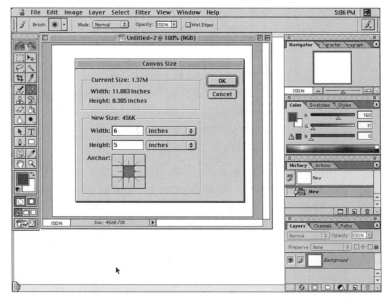

The Toolbox

The toolbox, like an artist's work table or paint box, holds all the tools you'll use to draw, paint, erase, and otherwise work on your picture. If you've used a previous edition of Photoshop, you're in for a few surprises. Some of the tools have changed locations, and gained new capabilities, and there are some very nifty new ones. There's also a new Tool Options bar, replacing the Tool Options palette from previous Photoshop editions. There are four categories of tools in Photoshop's toolbox:

- Selection tools
- Painting tools
- Path, Text, and Shape tools
- Viewing tools

Let's take a quick look at these tools. (We'll talk about them in detail later.) Figure 1.4 shows the toolbox with the tools labeled.

FIGURE 1.4

In the Photoshop tool-box, the tools are grouped by type.

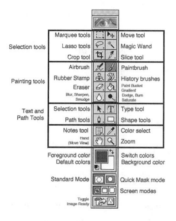

 Notice that some of the tool icons have a tiny black triangle in the lower-right corner of their icons. This means that there are more tools of the same general kind available on a pop-out menu. Point to any tool that has a triangle, click, and hold down the mouse button to see what other tools are available.

Selection Tools

At the top of the toolbox is a group of tools called Selection tools. They are used to select all or part of a picture. There are three kinds: the Marquees, the Lassos, and the Magic Wand. A selected area is indicated onscreen by a blinking selection border, called a Marquee after the movie theater marquee lights that flash on and off. Click and drag the Marquee and Lasso tools over the part of an image you want to select. Figure 1.5 shows the pop-out menus for the Marquee and Lasso Selection tools.

The Magic Wand selects by color. You can set the amount of similarity it demands, and just click to select all pixels of that color, or all adjacent pixels that match. The final tool in this set is the Move Tool. After you have made a selection, use the Move Tool to move the selected area to another place on the page.

Painting Tools

Within the set of Painting tools are an Airbrush, Paintbrush, Pencil, and Rubber Stamp. These all apply "paint" to the screen in one way or another, just like the real tools they imitate. The Airbrush, Pencil, and Paintbrush can change width and angle. The Pencil Tool and Paintbrush Tool share a space in the toolbox. There are also various Erasers that, as you might expect, take away part of the picture. You can use a block eraser, or erase with any of the paintbrush or airbrush shapes. There are two special-purpose erasers that automatically erase a selected color or background.

The History Brush is a very useful tool that, combined with the History window, gives you the ability to selectively undo and redo as many of your changes or individual brush strokes as you want. The Art History Brush lets you imitate different painting styles.

The Gradient Tool lets you create backgrounds that shade from one color to another, or even all the way through the rainbow. The Paint Bucket, which shares space with the Gradient Tool, pours paint into any area you select.

Finally, there are tools that move, blur, and change the intensity of the image. These are the Blur/Sharpen/Smudge Tool and the Dodge/Burn/Sponge Tool. The second and third options of each set are found on pop-out menus. These tools will be covered in detail in Hour 7, "Paintbrushes and Art Tools;" Hour 8, "Digital Painting;" and Hour 9, "Moving Paint."

Path, Type, and Shape Tools

These tools aren't as easy to classify as the Painting tools or the Selection tools. They do different, useful things. The letter T represents the Type Tool, which puts type on your picture. The Path Tools, represented by a pen icon, draw paths, which are a means of drawing a line or shape. After you have drawn a line or shape, you can use the tools to select a portion of your path and reshape it. Path Tools can be used as both Selection tools and as Painting tools. In Hour 13, "Paths," you'll learn how to work with all of the Path Tools.

NEW TO VERSION 6 The Shape Tools are a new feature in Photoshop 6. They can draw both filled and unfilled shapes, including rectangles, ellipses, polygons, and "custom" shapes. The Line Tool, formerly sharing toolbox space with the Pencil Tool, has been moved to this pop-out, too. The Line Tool draws straight lines which, when you hold down the Shift key, can be constrained to 45- or 90-degree angles, just as if you had used an artist's or architect's T-square and triangle. Figure 1.6 shows the Shape tools and some of the custom shapes.

FIGURE 1.6

You can create your own custom shapes, too.

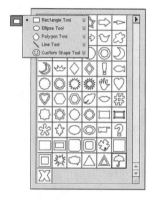

NEW TO VERSION 6 The Notes tool is also new to Photoshop 6. Use it to place "sticky" notes on your documents while you're working on them. The note can go either on the canvas, or in the area adjacent to it. You can even use voice annotations, if your computer has a microphone plugged in.

Viewing Tools

There are two Viewing tools: the Hand Tool and the Zoom Tool. The Zoom Tool is shaped like an old-fashioned magnifying glass, and the Hand, not surprisingly, like a hand. The Zoom Tool lets you "zoom in," by clicking the tool on the canvas to see a magnified view of your picture, or "zoom out," by pressing Option (Mac) or Alt (Windows) as you click the image. You can also click and drag the Zoom Tool to enlarge a specific part of the image. When you zoom in, the picture is usually too big to see all at once. The Hand moves it within the window and is helpful after you use the Zoom Tool to enlarge the picture. Use the hand, as shown in Figure 1.7, to slide the part of the picture you want to see or work on into a convenient spot.

Within this category, we can also include the Eyedropper Tools and the Measure Tool. The Eyedropper Tool picks up a sample of any color on which you click, making it the "active" color, so you can paint with it. The Measure Tool can be used to measure dimensions and angles in the picture. Click and drag a line to measure a distance between two points, and see it displayed in the Info window. To measure an angle, first create a measured line. Then, place your cursor on one of its two endpoints. Hold down the Option (Mac) or Alt (Windows) key while clicking and dragging from the endpoint of the first line in the direction of the angle.

Hand in the Navigator window

FIGURE 1.7

The Hand moves an image within its window. You can use the Hand either on the main screen or, as seen here, in the Navigator window.

Tool Shortcuts

Every one of these tools can be selected by clicking its icon in the toolbox, but Photoshop gives you another, even easier way to access the tools. Instead of clicking the tools you want to use, you can type a single letter shortcut to select each tool. To toggle through the available tools where there are pop-out menus, press Shift plus the shortcut letter until you reach the tool you want. Table 1.1 lists the tools with their shortcuts. Dog-ear this page, or use the tear-out card so you can refer to the table until you have memorized the shortcuts.

TABLE 1.1   Tools and Their Shortcuts

Tool	Shortcut	Tool	Shortcut
Marquee	M	Move	V
Lasso	L	Magic Wand	W
Crop	C	Slice	K
Airbrush	J	Paintbrush/Pencil	B

Tool	Shortcut	Tool	Shortcut
Rubber Stamps	S	History /Art History Brush	Y
Erasers	E	Gradient/ Paint Bucket	G
Pencil	B	Dodge/Burn/Sponge	0
Blur/Sharpen/Smudge	R	Type	T
Path Selection	A	Shape	U
Path	P	Eyedropper/Measure	I
Notepad	N	Zoom	Z
Default Colors	D	Hand	H
Switch Colors/ Background/ Foreground colors	X		

Some of these tool shortcuts have changed since the last version of Photoshop. Use the reference card until you get used to the new keys.

Tool Options Bar

NEW TO VERSION 6 In my opinion, the new-in-version-6 Tool Options bar, is one of the best additions to Photoshop. Previously, tool options were found on a palette usually buried behind two others. The bar keeps your tool options available at all times. The bar changes according to the tool you select. The different items on the bar have pull-down menus that let you set the options for that tool. Figure 1.8 shows the Brush Tool Options bar, with the brush shapes menu open.

FIGURE 1.8

Any tool bar compo-nent with an arrow has a pull-down menu.

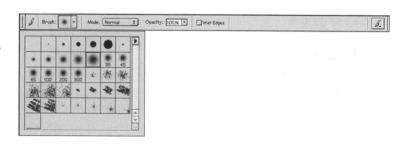

You can drag the Tool Options bar to the bottom of the screen, if you prefer. If it's been turned off, click Show Options in the Window menu, or simply double-click any tool to open it.

What's on the Menus?

The menus across the top of the screen contain the commands that enable you to open and manipulate files. They are accessed just as you would access any other menu, by clicking to open the menu and selecting the desired command from the list. Whenever you see an arrow or an ellipsis off to the right of a menu command, it indicates that there is either a subcommand, in the case of the arrow, or a dialog box, in the case of the ellipsis.

File and Edit Menus

The first two menus are File and Edit. Photoshop's File and Edit menus will be mostly familiar to anyone who has used other Macintosh or Windows programs. The File menu lets you work with files: opening, closing, saving, importing and exporting, and printing them, and, of course, quitting the program. There are also several time-saving Automation features that you'll learn about in Hour 18, "Special Effects and Useful Tricks." The Edit menu includes all the editing commands you're familiar with from other applications: Cut, Copy, Paste, Clear, and the most important one—Undo. It also contains the Transform tools, to scale, skew, distort, and rotate selections. Finally, it's where you go to manage color settings and set Preferences.

The menus that you might not be as familiar with (unless you've spent a lot of time working in other graphics programs) include

- Image
- Layer
- Select
- Filter
- View
- Window

The Image Menu

The Image menu, shown in Figure 1.9, has several submenus. The first of these, Mode, enables you to select a color mode in which to work. Most of the time, you will be working in RGB mode because that's what your monitor displays. Color modes are discussed in detail in Hour 5.

The Image menu also has tools to adjust the colors and the lightness and brightness of your picture. You will learn how to use the tools on the Image, Adjust menu in Hour 6, "Adjusting Color."

FIGURE 1.9

The Image→Mode menus.

When you want to make a picture bigger, smaller, or turn all or part of it sideways, you'll use the Image→Image Size and Image→Rotate Canvas menus. To separate the subject of a picture from the background (especially useful for catalog photography), you'll use the Extract command. The Liquify command, new in PS6, lets you treat your image as if it were completely liquid. You can do all kinds of smears, swirls, and distortions. In Hour 4, "Transformations," you'll learn how and when to use all these tricks.

The Layer Menu

Arguably the most powerful feature of Photoshop is the capability to work on different layers. This enables you to combine images, create collages, and make corrections without fear of damaging the original picture. Think of it as working on sheets of transparent plastic. Each layer is totally separate from the others. You can paint on a layer, change its opacity, or do whatever you want with it without disturbing the background or other parts of the picture on other layers.

The Layer menu opens dialog boxes to create new layers. It also has many commands to merge and work with layers, including several that are new in Photoshop 6. Figure 1.10 shows what's on the Layer menu. Hour 6 and Hour 11, "Layers," will teach you about working with layers.

The Select Menu

You have Selection tools, so why do you need a Select menu? The Select menu works with the tools to let you modify areas you have selected. You can grow or shrink the selected area by as many pixels as you want, or feather its edges so the selection appears to fade into a background on which you have pasted it. In Hour 3, "Selection Modes," you'll learn all the tricks for selecting and working with selected parts of a picture.

FIGURE 1.10

The Layer menu.

The Filter Menu

Filters are the tools that make Photoshop fun. The Filter menu lists more than a dozen different categories of filters: Some blur or sharpen the picture, some distort it, and some turn it into imitation paintings, colored pencil drawings, or neon light sculptures. There's so much for you to do with filters that we'll spend Hour 14, "Filters That Improve Your Picture;" Hour 15, "Filters to Make Your Picture Artistic;" and Hour 16, "Filters to Distort and Other Funky Effects," applying them to your pictures.

Photoshop filters are plug-ins, and many work with other graphics programs as well. If you install third-party filters, such as Alien Skin's Eye Candy or Corel's KPT, they'll appear at the bottom of the Filter menu.

The View Menu

Like the Zoom Tool, the View menu has commands that let you zoom in and out on the picture. As you can see in Figure 1.11, it also has the commands governing rulers, guides, and grids that enable you to measure and place objects precisely within the work area. The Show command opens a submenu that gives you access to grids, guides, notes, and slices.

Rulers can be set to measure in pixels, inches, centimeters, points, or picas, or by percentage. Choose the measurement with which you're most familiar. The setting is done in a Preferences dialog box; open the dialog box by selecting Edit→Preferences→Units

& Rulers. The unit of measure selected with the Units & Rulers preference also determines the unit of measure for the New dialog box (refer to Figure 1.1). When creating for the Web, consider setting your rulers to pixels.

FIGURE 1.11

The View menu.

NEW TERM *Guides* are lines that you place over your picture to position type or some other element that you're going to add to the picture.

To Do: Placing a Guide

To place guides, follow these steps:

1. Select View→Show Rulers. This makes the rulers visible at the edges of the canvas.

2. To place a horizontal guide, put the mouse pointer on the ruler at the top of the screen and drag downward. You'll see a line scrolling down the canvas as you drag. The left ruler shows you the position of the line.

3. To place a vertical guide, put the mouse pointer on the ruler at the left of the screen and drag across. You'll see a line scrolling across the canvas as you drag. The top ruler shows you the position of the line. See Figure 1.12 for an example.

   To switch the orientation of a guide as you drag, hold down the Option (Mac) or Alt (Windows) key.

After you have placed a guide, you can't move it unless you use the Move Tool. (You can place a guide regardless of what tool is selected.) You can hide it by choosing View→Hide Guides or using the keyboard shortcut in step 2 to toggle back and forth. To get rid of the guides, choose View→Clear Guides. To lock guides in place, type Option+Command+;(semicolon) (Mac) or Alt+Control+; (Windows).

The Show Grid command, which is also found on the View menu (View→Show→Grid), places an entire grid of guides over your image, rather like a layer of transparent graph paper. The Snap To commands make it easier to position an element, such as a block of type. In effect, they make a guide or gridline "magnetic," so that when you place the element near it, the line pulls the element right up against it.

FIGURE **1.12**

Guides let you place or type things right where you want them.

The Window Menu

Most of Photoshop's commands can be accessed in several different ways. The palettes at the right of the Photoshop screen give you information about your picture, character and paragraph controls for the text tool, options for many of the tools in the toolbox, a choice of brush sizes and shapes, colors, and access to the Actions and History palettes as well as Layers, Paths, and Channels. The Window menu (shown in Figure 1.13, with the History/Actions palette) shows and hides these palettes. If there are some palettes, such as Actions, that you're not ready to use, close them to keep your screen uncluttered.

The Help Menu

The final menu is the Help menu, which gives you access to Photoshop's comprehensive help screens.

FIGURE 1.13

*You can also click the
tabs on the palettes to
bring them forward.*

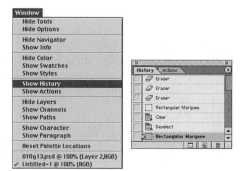

Setting Preferences

As you become more familiar with Photoshop, you might want to change the ways it
handles certain tasks. You might want to use the System Color Picker instead of the
Photoshop version. You might decide to measure in inches for one project and centimeters for another. You might need to change the color of the guides because they're too
close to the background in your photo. All these changes and many more are made in the
Edit→Preferences menus. The General preferences dialog box is shown in Figure 1.14.

FIGURE 1.14

Set preferences here.

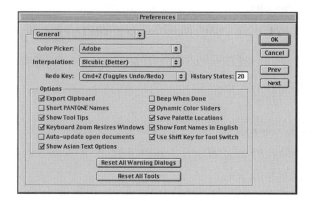

Use the Next button to scroll through the Preferences dialog boxes. You might encounter
some Preferences that you don't understand. For now, leave the default settings. As you
learn more about the program, you can come back and change Preferences as necessary.

Summary

You are starting to learn your way around the Photoshop screen, and you learned how to open a new page during this hour. You've looked at the toolbox and Photoshop's menus, and learned about grids and rulers. Finally, you learned about setting Preferences.

Q&A

Q What are foreground and background colors?

A The foreground color is the uppermost of the two colored squares in the toolbox. It's the color the brush applies. The background color is the lower square. It's the color you see when you erase the canvas.

Q What's the purpose of the picture at the top of the toolbar?

A It's the Adobe Photoshop logo. If you have an Internet connection, clicking the logo will take you to Adobe Online, a place for ideas, tips, and late-breaking Photoshop news.

Q Why are there trash cans at the bottom of the History and Layers palettes?

A Clicking the trash can for the Layers palette deletes a selected layer. Similarly, clicking the trash can for the History palette deletes an action. You'll learn more about this later.

Q How can I draw a box around some words I've put on my picture?

A That's one of the neat things the Shape Tools can do for you. You'll learn how to use them in Hour 13.

Quiz

1. How do you zoom in for a closer look at the page?

   a. Place the magnifying glass on the part of the picture you want to see, and click.

   b. Press Option/Alt and click the Zoom Tool.

   c. Press Shift and type `zoom`.

   d. Press Shift and the plus key.

2. How do you draw a line at precisely 45 degrees?

    a. Draw a square and then make a diagonal line from one corner to the opposite one.

    b. Press the 4 and 5 keys while you draw the line.

    c. Press Shift as you drag the line.

3. How do you zoom out to see the whole page?

    a. Press the Shift and minus keys.

    b. Type `zoomout`.

    c. Press Option/Alt and click the Zoom Tool.

Quiz Answers

1. a. Click again to magnify more.

2. c. The shift key constrains a line to horizontal or vertical, or 45 degrees. (Of course, answer a. would work, too.)

3. c. You'll see the symbol inside the icon change to a minus.

Exercises

1. Open a new page and try some of these tools. Click the Paintbrush and draw some squiggles and lines. Click an Eraser and erase part of them. Try dragging the Smudge tool across one of the lines. Select a piece of line with one of the Selection tools and move it to another part of the page. Explore. You're not going to break anything.

2. If you have an Internet connection, click the Adobe logo at the top of the toolbar. Visit Adobe Online and see what's there.

HOUR 2

Opening and Saving

Before you can do anything exciting with Photoshop 6, you need to learn how to open and view files. Photoshop can open a wide variety of file formats, so you can work on pictures from many different sources. If you have a scanner or a digital camera, you can bring in pictures that you've taken. You can also use photos from CD-ROM collections or images that you have downloaded from some online or Internet source. This hour will also cover methods of saving your work because, if you don't save, all the changes you make will be lost.

Working with Files

Photoshop can open and save images in many different file formats. *Formats* are ways of saving the information in a file so it can be used by other applications, printed, or placed on a Web page for use on the Internet.

In the Windows world, file formats are defined by three letter extensions to filenames, such as .doc for a word processing document, or .bmp for a bitmapped graphic.

Macintosh users are lucky because they don't need to deal with file format extensions. Macintosh files have what is called a resource fork and a data fork. The *data fork* contains the file's data, and the *resource fork* contains the file's information—whether it is a graphic file, a word processing document, or even a sound. Don't let this worry you, Windows users. Filenames are kind of a nuisance, but they aren't that difficult. Because you can toggle off the extension codes in Windows, you actually might not see extensions to known file types. Rest assured, they are there.

The most common file format in Photoshop is .psd, which is the native Photoshop file format (Photoshop document). The drawback to .psd is that, because it is native to Photoshop, other applications might have trouble opening this format. To move files between applications, to print, or to publish on the World Wide Web, you must save your files in a compatible format.

The following are some common formats with brief definitions of their uses. Note that Photoshop can handle many other graphics formats as well.

- *Bitmap (*.bmp*)*—This is a standard graphics file format for Windows.
- *GIF (*.gif*)*—GIF stands for *Graphical Interchange Format*. It is one of the three common graphics formats you can use for Web publishing. Because it is a compressed format, it takes less time to send by modem.
- *JPEG (*.jpg*)*—JPEG stands for *Joint Photographic Experts Group*. JPEG is another popular format for Web publishing.
- *PDF (*.pdf*)*—Adobe's Acrobat *Portable Document Format*, a system for creating documents that can be read cross-platform.
- *PNG (*.png*)*—Stands for *Portable Network Graphic*. It's a newer and arguably better format for Web graphics, combining GIFs' good compression with the JPEG's unlimited color palette. However, older browsers don't support it. (We'll discuss these formats and their use in Web publishing in the Hour 24, "Photoshop for the Web.")
- *TIFF (*.tif*)*—TIFF stands for *Tagged-Image File Format*. These files can be saved for use on either Macintoshes or Windows machines. This is also often the preferred format for desktop publishing applications, such as PageMaker and QuarkXPress.
- *EPS (*.eps*)*—*Encapsulated PostScrip*t is another format often used for desktop publishing. It uses the PostScript page description language, and can be used by both Macintoshes and PCs.
- *PICT (*.pct*)*—This is mainly a Macintosh format. It, too, is widely used in desktop publishing.
- *Raw (*.RAW*)*—This format saves image information in the most flexible format for transferring files between applications and computer platforms.

These file formats, and some less common ones such as Targa and Scitex CT, are available in the Save dialog boxes—File→Save, and File→Save As. Just look for the drop-down menu. Figure 2.1 shows the Save dialog box with the formats available. In Photoshop 6, the Save a copy function has been included as a check box within the Save dialog box.

If you work on a Macintosh and need to share files with non-Macintosh users, go to the Preferences, Saving Files dialog boxes. Click the check boxes to add an extension and to keep it in lowercase (as required by DOS users).

FIGURE 2.1

Photoshop 6 can save your work in any of these formats.

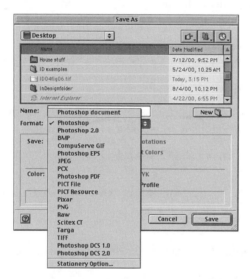

Opening Files

Opening a file in Photoshop is as easy as opening it in any other application. You can open as many images as you want or as many as your RAM can hold. If a file is of the proper type (a file format that Photoshop recognizes), all you have to do is double-click it with your mouse to not only open it, but to launch Photoshop as well—provided that Photoshop is associated with the file type in Windows or listed as the file creator in the Macintosh File Exchange control panel. If Photoshop is already open, you can either double-click a file or use the File→Open command. You can also drag and drop a compatible file onto the Photoshop 6 icon to open the file.

A technical note for Windows users: Double-clicking an image file will only open Photoshop if the extension (.bmp, for instance) is associated with Photoshop. Sometimes, installing new applications will change the extension

mapping to other programs. GIFs and JPGs are notoriously remapped to
Microsoft Internet Explorer, whereas BMP usually is grabbed by Paint. If dou-
ble-clicking doesn't work for you, check your extensions. Macintosh people:
You don't have to worry about this.

When you open the dialog box, Photoshop displays all the files in formats it can open.
Figure 2.2 shows the Photoshop Open dialog box. As you can see, if you click Preview,
Photoshop can display thumbnails of any image that has one. To create previews, go to
Preferences→Saving Files, and select Always Save Image Previews.

 A *thumbnail* or *thumbnail sketch* is an artist's term for a small version of a
picture, so called because they are often no bigger than a thumbnail.

To Do: Open a File

As you've seen, Photoshop supports most graphics formats. You must have some graphics files somewhere on your hard drive, so let's practice finding one and opening it.

1. Choose File→Open or press Command+O (Mac) or Control+O (Windows) to open
   the Open dialog box.

2. Use the dialog box to locate the file on which you want to work.

3. Select it and double-click, or click Open.

FIGURE 2.2

*Any file that's shown
can be opened in
Photoshop.*

▲

Importing a File

The Import command (File, Import) lets you open files that have been saved in formats
that use plug-in import modules. Typically, these include files saved with the TWAIN
interface, such as scanner programs and files, as well as Scitex files, PICT resources
(Macintosh), and files imported directly from any digital camera that has a Photoshop
plug-in import filter.

Importing from Digital Cameras

Most digital cameras can import pictures directly into Photoshop. The plug-in filter comes with the camera. Drop it into the plug-ins folder. (Remember that you need to quit the application before you install plug-ins. If you install while Photoshop is running, it can't see the new plug-in until you quit and restart it.) To import a picture, you simply plug the camera cable into the computer's modem (Mac) or Com1 port (Windows) or a USB port, if you have one. Then choose File→Import and whatever camera you are importing from. Figure 2.3 shows the Epson import window. Pictures in the camera are displayed as if they were slides on a sorting table. You can view a larger image and find out more about it by selecting a picture and clicking Get Info.

FIGURE 2.3

This is Epson's plug-in. Other cameras use a similar system.

Importing Files with the TWAIN Interface

The TWAIN Acquire and TWAIN Select commands found under the File→Import sub-menu don't actually import images. Instead, they enable you to open the appropriate scanner software to be used from within Photoshop and to use it to import the scanned images. Photoshop supports TWAIN, TWAIN32, and TWAIN_32 standards for scanning. Consult the scanner manual for more information.

Importing PICT Resources

This command opens dialog boxes just like the regular Open box, but they enable Macintosh users to open a specialized kind of PICT file.

PICT resources are images saved within the document's resource fork, often used as icons for the document, or as splash screens for a program. When you attempt to open a PICT resource for editing, you first open the document, and then Photoshop scans its resource fork for PICT resources. Any it finds are displayed in a window like the one in Figure 2.4. Open the resource and edit it from this dialog box.

FIGURE **2.4**
You won't find these in the Windows version of Photoshop.

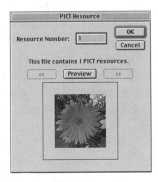

Saving Your Work

There's one very important thing to know about saving your work: Do it often! Computers are prone to unexpected shutdowns and errors. Saving takes only a couple of seconds, and it can make the difference between having to do your work all over again or just reopening it if the computer shuts down.

The first time you save a picture, you'll see the Save As dialog box, as shown in Figure 2.5. It's been changed from previous versions. Give the file a name and select an appropriate format to save it in from the pull-down menu. After this, choose File→Save or just press Command+S (Mac) or Control+S (Windows) to save the file.

FIGURE **2.5.**
Saving a file in Photoshop.

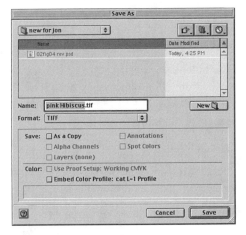

For Macintosh users only: If you have to work cross-platform, that is, on both a Macintosh and PC, you should always choose to include file extensions with your files. This option is found in the Preferences dialog box. Also, be sure to check Use Lowercase, to be sure your file is Windows/DOS compatible.

2

In addition to the familiar Save and Save As commands, Photoshop has more Save commands, such as Save a Copy. This option is now found in the Save dialog box. Save a Copy, like Save As, lets you save the file with a new name and in a new location. The difference is that after you use Save As, you're working in the new file.

If you use Save a Copy, you save a copy of the file as it is at that moment, but you'll still be working on the original file, not the copy. Save a Copy is especially useful for making a backup copy before you try a drastic change, such as reducing color depth or increasing JPEG lossiness, or for saving the file in a different format. Suppose you create a logo for your business and want to use it in print and on the Web. You'd save it as a TIFF or EPS file to print from, and you'd save a copy as a JPEG or PNG file for your Web page. The word copy is automatically added to the filename.

The final Save option is Save for Web. When you click this command, you see the same Save for Web dialog box that you see in Adobe ImageReady. It contains the settings you need to optimize the image for Web use, including letting you see and select the amount of JPEG compression to apply, so you can get the smallest file that won't compromise the image quality too much. We'll discuss this in detail in Hour 24.

Reducing File Size

As you start to work with different Photoshop files, you'll notice that your hard drive is starting to fill up. Photoshop files can get very large, very quickly. You can make your files smaller in several ways:

- Reduce the resolution or the physical size of the image.
- Reduce the number of colors in the image palette.
- Use a format that compresses the file.
- Use a compression utility after the file is saved.
- Merge layers in .psd files.
- Delete any Alpha channels that are no longer needed.

Reducing the resolution is not a good idea if you're going to print the image. If the picture is only going to be viewed on your computer screen or on the Web, reduce the resolution to 72 dpi. Be aware, though, that resampling reduces image quality. You can change the resolution in the Image, Image size dialog box. Don't make it less than 72 dpi.

Reducing the number of colors means reducing the bit depth. This can make your colors look blotchy onscreen and in print. If you are working in grayscale (no color in the picture), reduce the bit depth to 8 bits by choosing Grayscale in the Image Mode submenu. This gives you 256 shades of gray, which is more than a printer can print. Using a compressed format means choosing a file format, such as TIFF with LZW compression, which automatically shrinks the file down as small as possible when it saves. It does this by a means called *lossless compression*, so there's no image degradation or blotchy color. LZW compression (named for its inventors, Lempel, Ziv, and Welch) is also used by GIF, TIFF, and PostScript formats.

There are also formats, such as JPEG, that use "lossy" compression. This means, as you might guess from the name, that some of the data that makes up the image is lost in the compression process. Instead of 20 shades of blue in the sky in a TIFF file, the same image in a JPEG file might have only five shades of blue. And, yes, you *can* see the difference. Unfortunately, compression is necessary when you are putting images on the Web, in a multimedia presentation, or in another situation where upload time or storage space is limited. JPEG saves files in the least possible amount of disk space. One point to remember is that if you save a JPEG image a second time as a JPEG, it gets compressed again and loses more information. If you work on a JPEG file a lot, you can end up with a totally unreadable picture. If you're going to work on a picture, save it as a Photoshop file. Don't make it a JPEG until you're done with it and ready to post it on your Web page. If you have to change the image, trash the JPEG file and go back to the Photoshop version.

When you have files you want to save for future reference, you can save them in the normal way as .psd's (Photoshop documents) or in whatever format you prefer to work in, and then compress the files with a utility such as StuffIt (Mac) or PKZip or WinZip (Windows). All of these file compression utilities use lossless compression algorithms and shrink your image files by anywhere from 20% to 50%. That said, compressing .jpg or .gif files is relatively useless, since they're already compressed. You won't gain more than a few percent of additional compression.

Figure 2.6 is a typical digital photograph that I saved in a number of different file types. (The original is about 6 inches wide, and saved at 72 dpi.) Table 2.1 shows the more common file types and the sizes of the files that this picture required. The version shown is a high quality JPEG.

FIGURE 2.6

If storage space isn't a problem, don't compress the picture.

TABLE 2.1   File Format/File Size Comparisons for Figure 2.6

Format	File Size
.bmp	564K
.eps	1.5MB
.gif	188K
.jpg (high quality)	141K
.jpg (low quality)	94K
.pdf	141K
.pct	564K
.png (interlaced)	517K
.psd	564K
.tif	470K

Choosing a Format

With so many possible formats, how can you decide which one to use? It's really not so difficult. As long as you are working on a picture, keep saving it as a Photoshop document (.psd). This makes sense, especially after you learn to work in layers, because Photoshop's native format can save the layers, whereas other formats require that you merge the layers into one. After you have flattened the layers, you can't split them apart again. So, bottom line, as long as you think you'll want to go back to a picture and modify it more, save a copy as a .psd.

When you finish working on the picture and are ready to place it into another document for printing, save a copy as an .eps file if it's going to a PostScript-compatible printer. If you aren't sure how it will be printed, save it as a .tif, because .tif is compatible with most printers and page-layout programs. If you're going to place your picture onto a Web page, choose .gif if the picture is line art, has large areas of solid color or uses a limited color palette. Choose .jpeg or .png if the picture is a photograph or continuous tone art (lots of colors). If you want to import the picture into some other graphics program for additional work, choose .PICT if you are working on a Macintosh or .bmp if you're working in Windows. These two are the most generally compatible graphic formats.

Undoing and Redoing

Starting with Photoshop 5, Adobe's software engineers finally responded to user demands and introduced the History palette and History Brush Tool. The History palette keeps a listing of every tool you've used and every change you've made, up to a pre-determined number you can set in the History Options menu. You can also take "snap-shots" of the work in progress and use these as saved stages to which you can revert. Figure 2.7 shows the History palette for a picture that's had a lot of changes made to it.

FIGURE 2.7.

The History palette and its pop-out menu.

You can click any previous step to revert to it if you don't like what you've done. It's more useful in some ways than multiple undos, because the History palette lets you undo and redo selectively. More importantly, it lets you save your work as you do it and still go back and undo. In previous editions of Photoshop, and in some other programs, after you save your work, Undo isn't available. We'll discuss the uses of the History palette and the History Brush (which lets you undo as much or as little of a change as you want) in greater detail in Hour 7, "Paintbrushes and Art Tools."

Of course, you can always use Command+Z (Mac) or Control+Z (Windows) to toggle Undo and Redo in a single step. For multiple Undos, use Command+Option+Z for Mac and Control+Alt+Z for Windows.

Summary

Photoshop can work with many different kinds of graphics files from many sources. Those that it doesn't open directly, either by double-clicking or by using the File, Open dialog box, can be imported through plug-in filters. If you have a digital camera or scanner, it might have a Photoshop plug-in that enables you to open the image from within Photoshop. Check your owner's manual.

Logically enough, Photoshop can also save documents in all the formats it can open. Different formats have different purposes and different file sizes. Some are specifically intended for Web use, others for printing. Choose a format based on the intended use of the image.

The History palette saves a step-by-step list of everything you do to your picture. You can travel backward or forward through the History list and easily undo or redo your changes, even if you have already saved the document.

Q&A

Q Which kinds of files compress better as GIF than as JPEG or PNG?

A Because GIF uses a limited palette, any picture that has only a few colors will give you a smaller file as a GIF than in the other formats. Such graphic items as titles in flat colors, logos, posterized photos, or line art will make very small GIFs. Full-color photos will not.

Q When should I use Save a Copy?

A Use Save a Copy when you want to make a copy of the picture you are working on and then continue to work on the original instead of the copy. Suppose I have a picture called "Roses," which I have worked on and saved. If I save a copy as "Roses copy," and then keep working, I will still be working on the original "Roses" but will also have a copy of the picture in a closed file as it was before I did the additional work.

Q What file formats should I use for images I'll be putting in my Web page?

A You should try to stick with .psd files when creating your images. This enables you to use all the powerful Photoshop 6 editing features, such as layers. When you've finished your image, save it as a .gif, .jpg, or .png for use on the Web.

Q How does color depth affect image file size?

A Simply put, the more colors that are in your image, the larger the file size, because it takes more bits to encode more colors.

Quiz

1. .bmp is

    a. A PC format that stands for bitmap.

    b. A Macintosh format that stands for bump.

    c. A UNIX code for better management program.

2. PICTs are (is)

    a. Another name for pixels

    b. The Macintosh graphics format

    c. The little images used as icons on the desktop

3. `.tif` stands for

    a. Tiled Image Format

    b. Tagged-Image Format

    c. Typical Information Font

4. To use a scanner image,

    a. Use File→Open Scanner.

    b. With Photoshop open, turn on the scanner.

    c. Use File→Import→TWAIN (or your scanner plug-in).

Quiz Answers

1. a. Bitmaps are a pixel-by-pixel analysis of the picture. They're not necessarily large files.

2. a. The DOS extension for a PICT is `.pct`.

3. b. When you save a TIFF, you must choose whether to save it for Macintosh or PC.

4. c. Be sure the scanner software is installed. Its plug-in goes in the Photoshop Plug-ins folder.

Exercises

1. Open one of your own digital photos or art files and save it in different formats. See how the format affects the file size.

2. Macintosh users, here's one just for you. You can replace that silly "Welcome to Macintosh" message that pops up when you start your computer with a more interesting picture and/or message. Macintoshes use a type of file called a PICT resource to create "splash screens" that you see when you start the Macintosh or when you start an application. Because Photoshop can save in the PICT resource format, you can make any Photoshop picture into a Startup Screen. Follow these steps:

    1. Start with any image you like. (If it's not as big as your screen, that's okay. It appears with a gray border.)

    2. Open the File, Save As dialog box.

3. Choose PICT Resource from the format pop-up menu and click Save.

4. The PICT Resource dialog box opens.

5. Name the file **StartupScreen**. (You must type it exactly that way with both Ss capitalized and no space between the words.)

6. Choose None from Compression options. Choose a bit depth: 16 bits if your monitor displays thousands of colors, 32 bits if it is a high-resolution monitor and displays millions of colors.

7. Click OK to save the file.

8. Drag the file to your System folder and restart. The picture appears when you start the computer. (If you want to revert back to the Welcome to Macintosh screen, remove your new screen from the system folder, rename the old one, and replace it in the system folder.)

If you plan to go back to your original splash screen after you've completed this excercise, open your System folder and remove the existing StartupScreen. File it somewhere else, or change its name to something different and leave it in the folder if you prefer.

2

HOUR 3

Selection Modes

Now you're making progress. You've learned how to bring images in and out of Photoshop. The next step is learning to work with images and edit them. To do this, you have to select a part of the picture on which you want to work. Selections are just what they seem to be—portions of the image that you have selected.

The Selection Tools

There are several ways to select a piece of a picture. You can use any of the Selection tools: Marquee Tools, Lasso Tools, or the Magic Wand. You have different kinds of Selection tools because you sometimes need to make selections in a particular way, such as punching a shape out of an image or selecting all of the sky. Photoshop's Selection tools give you the power to select the whole picture or a single pixel. Just to refresh your memory, Figure 3.1 shows the Selection tools. (The rollout menus have been shifted so you can see what's on them.) In Photoshop 6, the tools are spelled out by name, rather than relying on the icons for identity.

FIGURE 3.1

*The Selection tools
are at the top of the
toolbox.*

Rectangle and Oval Marquees

The Marquee Tools, both Rectangular and Oval, are found in the upper-left corner of the toolbox. To select the Rectangular Marquee, just click it or press the letter M on your keyboard. To select the Elliptical Marquee (also known as the Oval Marquee), click and hold the Rectangular Marquee in the toolbox. When the rollout menu appears, select the Elliptical Marquee.

Assuming that the Rectangular Marquee is the currently selected tool, you can also press Shift+M to switch back and forth between the two. The Oval Marquee tool works the same way as the Rectangular Marquee Tool. The icon will change accordingly on the Tool Options bar.

To experiment with its many uses, first create a new file (go back to Hour 1, "The Basics," if you can't remember how). Again, give yourself some room to work. Set the dimensions at six inches square.

1. Click the Marquee Tool in the toolbox.

   As you move the tool over the canvas, the cursor appears as a crosshair.

2. While the cursor is over the canvas, click and hold the mouse button, and then drag out a marquee.

   Experiment with dragging out an elliptical marquee. Try to get a sense for how marquees appear. Try dragging from different directions.

If you press and hold the Shift key *after* you've made your first Selection and *before* you click again, you can make additional selections. Take care to continue holding the Shift key while making additional selections. (You'll see a plus sign beneath the crosshair.) Where the selected areas overlap, they'll merge to form one larger selected shape. In Figure 3.2, I've selected several areas with the Rectangle Marquee and the Elliptical Marquee to make a larger shape.

To draw a perfectly square box or round circle, select Constrained Aspect Ratio from the Style pop-up menu on the Tool Options bar, or press the Shift key as you drag the shape. Use Fixed Size to make multiple selections that are the same size.

To deselect an area inside another area (making what graphic artists call a "knock out"), press Option (Mac) or Alt (Windows) as you drag the inner shape. (You'll see a minus sign beneath the crosshair.) For instance, if you have a circle selected and drag another smaller circle inside it while pressing Option (Mac) or Alt (Windows), the selected shape is a donut.

FIGURE 3.2

You can also combine square and round selections.

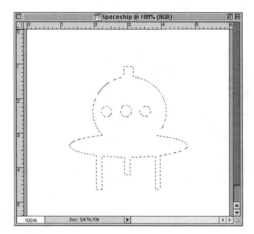

The thin, horizontal (Single Row) and vertical (Single Column) marquees select a single row of pixels, either horizontally or vertically. They are often useful for cleaning up the edges of an object.

When you are dealing with selections, it is important to remember that, for good or bad, only the area within the confines of the marquee can be edited. It is the only active area of the canvas. Thus, after a selection is made, you can perform whatever action you want, but before you move on, the selection must be turned off, or *deselected*, by clicking outside the selected area with one of the Marquee Tools or by pressing Command+D (Mac) or Control+D (Windows). Until you do so, you can only edit within the selection's boundaries. On the other hand, this restriction on editing can be extremely helpful if you need to draw a complex filled shape. Assemble the shape from multiple selections, as I have in Figure 3.2. Then you can pour paint into it, apply a gradient to it, or use the Paintbrush with no fear of coloring outside the lines.

If you copy or paste something onto your canvas, and then try to select a different part of the picture, you might find that the Marquee Tool doesn't work. You might also get a message saying "Could not complete your request because the selected area is empty." This is Photoshop's way of reminding you that you have added another layer to your picture by pasting into it, and the part you're trying to copy isn't on that layer. Look at the Layers palette, and click the layer on which you want to work. Clicking its icon will make it the active layer. You will learn all about working with layers in Hour 11, "Layers."

Lasso

As useful as the Marquee Tools and their modifier keys are, there will come times when you have to select irregular shapes. Perhaps you might need to select a single flower from a bunch or, as in Figure 3.3, a fish that you want to turn into a school of fish.

FIGURE 3.3

Selecting an object with the Lasso.

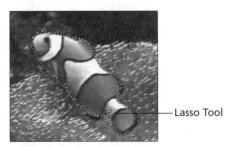

——Lasso Tool

Using the primary Lasso Tool to select an object in this way requires a steady hand and good hand-eye coordination, as well as a clean mouse and mousepad or trackball. As with the Marquee Tools, you can add to your lassoed selection by holding the Shift key and selecting additional parts of the object.

I've found that when I am trying to make a very careful selection with the Lasso Tool, and when I am using Photoshop in general, it helps to slow my mouse down. You can adjust the speed of mouse reaction time in the Mouse section of your machine's Control Panels. Start by setting the slider just a little higher than the slowest setting. Experiment to see what works best for you.

To Do: Create a Selection with the Lasso Tool

To make a selection with the Lasso Tool, follow these steps:

1. Select the Lasso Tool from the toolbox or press L.

2. Click and carefully drag the Lasso Tool around the piece of the image you want to select. You see a solid line as you drag. Be careful not to release the mouse. If you do, you won't be able to drag the selection any further. (Releasing the button automatically closes the selection).

3. When you're close to completely enclosing the selection, you can release the mouse button. The two ends of the selection marquee that you have drawn around the shape automatically join together, completing the marquee.

The Polygonal Lasso Tool

The Polygonal Lasso Tool behaves in much the same way as the regular Lasso Tool. The difference is, as its name implies, it makes irregular *geometric* selections. It's actually easier to use when you need to make detailed selections, because it can be controlled more easily. Instead of simply dragging a marquee line, as you do with the regular Lasso, you click the Polygonal Lasso to place points, and Photoshop inserts a straight-line marquee between the points. You can place as many points as you need, as close together or far apart as necessary. Figure 3.4 shows the tool in use.

FIGURE 3.4

The Polygonal Lasso Tool.

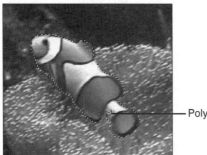

——— Polygonal Lasso Tool

3

To Do: Create a Selection with the Polygonal Lasso Tool

To use the Polygonal Lasso Tool, follow these steps:

1. Click the Lasso Tool and hold until you see the rollout menu.

2. Select the Polygonal Tool. (You can also do this by skipping step 1 and simply pressing Shift+L until you've selected the tool.)

3. Click once in the canvas. Now move your mouse. Notice that a line follows your Polygonal Lasso wherever you move it.

4. Click again. This draws the first line and sets another point from which you can drag. Place another line and click again.

    Now with two lines set, you have an option. You can either continue to select the image, or you can double-click. This automatically finishes the selection for you.

    When the cursor nears your starting point, notice that a small circle becomes appended to the cursor. This signals that, if you click, the selection will be completed.

5. Click to complete your selection.

Many of Photoshop's tools, including the Selection tools, have additional options for their use. These are found on the Tool Options bar. Whenever you select a new tool, be sure to look at its options.

The Magnetic Lasso

The Magnetic Lasso is one of my most-used tools. As you drag it around any shape with a reasonably well-defined edge, it snaps to the edge. Select it and use it just as we did the Polygonal Lasso. Because it finds edges by looking for differences in contrast, the Magnetic Lasso is most effective on irregular objects that stand out from the background. You can use the Tool Options bar to set the parameters. Detection width refers to how close to the edge you must be to have the Lasso recognize it (see Figure 3.5). Edge contrast determines how different the pixels must be in value for the Lasso to recognize them. Frequency determines how often the Lasso sets its anchor points. (*Anchor points* are the points indicated by boxes on a line. Drag them to adjust the line.)

FIGURE 3.5

Set the edge according to the contrast between the intended selection and what surrounds it.

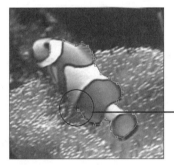

Magnetic Lasso Tool

Magic Wand

The software designers at Adobe Systems must not have been able to come up with a more descriptive name for this fantastic tool, choosing instead to let it, perhaps, speak for itself—the Magic Wand. Maybe it's better that way.

The Magic Wand is a different kind of Selection tool. So far we've looked at tools that select pixels based on their placement in the bitmap (the picture). The Magic Wand selects pixels somewhat differently; it selects them based on color values. This enables you to cut foreground objects, such as the fish out of the background. You might need to combine several selections by holding the Shift key, as we have in Figure 3.6, to select all of the object.

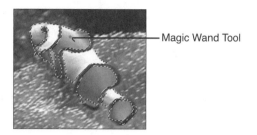

FIGURE 3.6

Selections being made with the Magic Wand.

—— Magic Wand Tool

As with the previously described tools, the Magic Wand can make and merge selections if you press the Shift key as you click the areas to select.

NEW TERM The Magic Wand selects adjacent pixels based on color similarities. Its tolerance can be set in the Tool Options bar. *Tolerance*, in this instance, refers to the Magic Wand's sensitivity to color differences.

The rule is easy to remember: The lower the Tolerance setting, the less tolerance the Magic Wand has for color differences. Thus, for example, if you set the Tolerance higher (it ranges from 0 to 255), it selects all variations of the color that you initially select.

Photoshop 6 has another option for the Magic Wand, enabling you to select only contiguous, or adjacent, pixels. If, for example, you have a red flower that varies in color from one side to the other, and your Tolerance setting is high, you'll select as much of the flower as fits the tolerance. If you check Contiguous in the Options palette, you'll select only the parts of the flower that are within the tolerance *and* have pixels that touch each other. In Figure 3.7, I've set the tolerance to 32, and clicked once on each screen. The screen on the left had Contiguous selected. The one on the right did not.

FIGURE 3.7

Selecting contiguous pixels can save you a lot of time.

The Magic Wand is best used for selecting objects that are primarily one color, such as the flower. It's ideal when you need to select the sky in a landscape. In a few minutes, you'll see exactly how to do this, but first, there are some other selection tricks to learn.

The Selection Menu

You might have noticed that, in addition to the Selection tools you have just learned about, there's also a Select menu, shown in Figure 3.8. Probably the most useful commands on the menu are the top four. Select All simply draws a selection marquee around the entire picture. Deselect removes the selection marquee from the image. Reselect replaces the marquee if you have accidentally deselected something. Inverse lets you select everything but one object by selecting the object and then inverting. For instance, if I had a photo of a lemon on a plate, I could select the lemon and then choose Inverse to select the plate. Inverting is extremely useful, and you'll soon discover that it's one of your favorite commands.

FIGURE 3.8

The Select menu and Modify sub-menu.

Feather

Feather lets you make selections with fuzzy, *feathered* edges rather than hard ones. It's very helpful when you want to select an object from one picture and paste it into another, because it adds a slight blur that helps the object to blend in. You can use the Feather Selection dialog box, shown in Figure 3.9, to determine how many pixel widths of feathering to apply. Experiment with feathering selections to find out what works best.

FIGURE 3.9

The Feather Selection dialog box.

To Do: Make a Feathered Selection

To make a feathered selection, follow these steps:

1. Choose an appropriate Selection tool and use it to select a piece of the picture or an object within the picture.

▼   2. Choose Select→Feather to open the dialog box.

      3. Enter an amount in the window. Start with 5 and increase or decrease until the
▲   selection looks right to you.

Modifying Selections

The Select→Modify submenu gives you some other options for working with your selections. Border changes the selected area so that, instead of the whole object, you have
only selected a border around it. You can set the width of the border in its dialog box.
Smooth is helpful when you have made a Lasso selection with a shaky hand. It smoothes
out bumps in the Marquee line by as many pixels as you specify. Expand and Contract
work, as their names suggest, to make your selection grow or shrink as necessary by as
many pixels as you designate in the dialog box.

Selecting Large Areas

It's often necessary to select a large part of the picture, like the sky, so that you can
darken its color or otherwise change it without changing the rest of the picture. Figure
3.10 shows a picture with a lot of sky and a very complicated object sticking up into it.
There are also branches, which have gaps where the sky shows through. Selecting the
sky in this case requires careful clicking with the Magic Wand.

You can download this picture from Macmillan's Web site mentioned in the Introduction.

Figure 3.10

*Selecting just the sky
will be difficult.*

To select the sky in this picture, follow these steps:

      1. Choose the Magic Wand Tool and double-click to open its Options palette.

      2. Set the Tolerance in the Tool Options bar to 45, as shown in Figure 3.11. This
          enables you to select only similar shades of blue. Be sure that Contiguous is not
          selected so that you can pick up the blue patches between the branches.

FIGURE 3.11

You can set the Tolerance anywhere from 0 to 255.

3. Click the Magic Wand on a typical piece of blue (see Figure 3.12).

FIGURE 3.12

You might need to make several selections to include all of the sky.

4. Hold down the Shift key and select additional pieces of sky until you have gotten it all.

5. Choose Select→Feather and set the feather amount to about one pixel, just enough to even out the selection. Figure 3.13 shows the result.

6. Now you can proceed to change the color of the sky, remove it, or do whatever else you intended.

FIGURE 3.13

The entire sky is selected.

Find a picture with a lot of sky and practice this yourself. It's not difficult. Remember, if you select more sky (or whatever) than you intended, Undo will deselect the last portion selected, leaving the rest of the selection active.

Cutting and Copying

If you have cut or copied and pasted in any other application, you can do it in Photoshop. The commands are identical and so are the results. You'll find the Cut, Copy, and Paste commands on the Edit menu.

Cutting, copying, and pasting enable you to "borrow" from one picture to add to another. In the examples that follow, I'll take a duck from one picture and add it to another. In Figure 3.14, I've selected the duck, and set the feather amount to three pixels. Next, I'll use the Copy command (Edit→Copy), Command+C (Mac), or Control+C (Windows) to copy the bird to the clipboard.

FIGURE 3.14

Before you can copy the duck, you have to select it.

Now I'll open the new picture and paste the duck in (see Figure 3.15). To improve the composition, I'll flip him so he faces the other way. Then, just for fun, I'll paint in a shadow behind the new duck. Figure 3.16 shows the final result. You'll learn how to add shadows in Hour 18, "Special Effects and Useful Tricks."

FIGURE 3.15

The new picture, with the added bird.

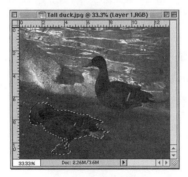

FIGURE 3.16
The picture is more
interesting with the
second duck facing
right.

Cropping

NEW TERM   *Cropping* is the artists' term for trimming away unwanted parts of a picture. You
could think of it as a specialized kind of selection, which is probably why the
people who created Photoshop put the Crop Tool in the same section as the Selection
Marquees (see Figure 3.17). In Photoshop 6, the Adobe engineers have made significant
improvements in the Crop Tool. Instead of just dragging a line around the area to be
cropped, you now see the image with the part you have cropped away dimmed out. This,
of course, makes it much easier to see exactly what you're doing. Of course, you can
also crop by making a selection with the Rectangular Marquee and then using the menu
command Image→Crop to trim the picture.

FIGURE 3.17
The Crop Tool.

To Do: Crop a Picture

To crop a picture, follow these steps:

1. Select the Crop Tool from the toolbox or press C on the keyboard. (It looks like two pieces of L-shaped mat board overlapped, the same tool artists use to help compose paintings.)

2. Drag it across the picture, holding the mouse button down.

3. Use the handles on the cropping window to fine-tune the selection. The area outside the window will be dimmed, so you can see what you're removing.

4. After you have the cropping window placed where you want it, double-click inside it to delete the area outside the window.

NEW TO VERSION 6 Photoshop 6 has added another new feature to the Crop Tool. You can now use it to correct perspective. Click the Perspective check box on the Tool Options bar. Drag the Crop Tool over an image that needs perspective adjustment, like the leaning tower in Figure 3.18. After you've drawn the cropping box, select one of the corners of the box and drag it until the side of the window is parallel to the side of the building. Repeat with the other side. Click Accept to apply the changes or simply double-click inside the cropping window.

FIGURE 3.18
Use Perspective cropping to straighten warped buildings.

Open any picture and practice cropping it. Remember, if you crop too much of the picture, you can undo. If it's too late to undo because you have already done something else, just go back to the History palette and click the uncropped picture. You can also choose File→Revert to go back to the last saved version of your picture. As long as you don't close the file, you can keep cropping and using the History palette to undo as much as you want.

Summary

Some of the most powerful tools in Photoshop are the Selection tools. They enable you to edit selectively as well as create interesting effects with the Transformation tools.

Try to develop a feel for when you can use selections. They can save you a great deal of time when you need to fill a space with color or an image, when you need to manipulate just a piece of an image, when you want to selectively brighten or adjust part of an image, or when you need to extract a piece of an image from a larger work.

We will refer to selections throughout the remainder of the book, so if you need to, dog-ear a page. See you next hour.

Q&A

Q Can I combine selections made with different Selection tools?

A Yes. Make a selection with one of the tools, switch tools, and then press the Shift key before you add to your selection. As long as you hold down the Shift key (making a tiny plus sign visible next to the tool), you can add to your selection as many times as you want.

Q How can I deselect *part* of a selection?

A The easiest way to do this is to press Option (Mac) or Alt (Windows) key with the Selection tool active. You will see a small minus symbol next to the Selection tool. Select the part of the selection to deselect, and it is removed from the selection and added back to the picture.

Q Can I use the marquee to draw a shape and then fill it?

A Yes, and that's exactly how to do it. With the selection active, use the Paint Bucket to pour a color into the selected shape(s).

Quiz

1. To change from the Rectangular to the Elliptical Marquee,

    a. Go back to the toolbox and select the other one.

    b. Press Shift+M.

    c. Either a or b.

2. To select a single row or column of pixels,

    a. Hold down Control+C and the Return key, while double-clicking.

    b. Press Return as you drag the mouse.

    c. Use the Single Row or Single Column marquees.

3. How do you make the Magic Wand more sensitive?

    a. Insult it.

    b. Set the Tolerance to a lower number.

    c. Set the Tolerance to a higher number.

Quiz Answers

1. c. Easy, huh?

2. c. (Answer a. isn't even possible unless you have three hands.)

3. b. A lower Tolerance setting means that the Magic Wand will select only the most similar pixels.

Exercises

Most pictures can be improved by careful cropping. Try this experiment. Cut two L-shaped pieces from a sheet of white paper or cardboard, as shown in Figure 3.19.

FIGURE 3.19

How to make a cropping frame.

Use these pieces as a cropping frame and look at your snapshots or pictures in a magazine to see how different cropping affects the picture. Try finding long, narrow compositions, square ones, and rectangles.

HOUR 4

Transformations

It's extremely rare, if not impossible, that your pictures will always be the right size and shape for your purposes. You might need to make an object bigger or smaller as you copy it from one picture to another. You might need to straighten a tilted horizon, or even stand the Leaning Tower of Pisa upright. Perhaps you simply need to make someone face left instead of right or turn an object upside down. You can do all this and more with just a few mouse clicks or simple commands. Ready? Let's start by looking at making the whole picture bigger or smaller.

Resizing

Photoshop makes it easy to change the size of the picture or of anything in it. You have two options: resizing the image or resizing the canvas. Resizing the image makes the picture bigger or smaller. Resizing the canvas makes the picture *area* bigger, while leaving the image floating within it. You'd do this if you need more space around an object without shrinking the actual image.

Resizing an Image

To resize an image, open the Image, Image Size dialog box, shown in Figure 4.1. You can see the pixel dimensions in pixels (logically) or percentages. You can also see the image print size (set in Output Size section of screen) in inches, centimeters, points, picas, or columns; percentages can also be found using the pop-up menus.

When you first open the Image Size dialog box, if you set the width and height pixel dimensions to Percent, you'll see the default setting of 100%. The easiest way to enlarge or reduce the image is to make sure that Constrain Proportions is checked at the bottom of the dialog box, and then simply enter new percentages in one of the fields and click OK. As if by magic, the other numbers will change to give you the correct percentage of enlargement or reduction. For now, ignore Resample Image. Leave it set to Bicubic. You'll get into what this means when you need to know it in Hour 23, "Printing."

FIGURE 4.1

The Image Size dialog box.

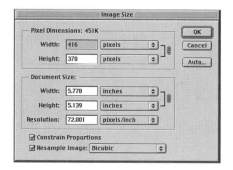

As you make changes in the Image Size dialog box, Photoshop will automatically update the file size at the top of the window.

Resizing a Canvas

Resizing the canvas to a larger size gives you extra work space around the image; it does not change the size of the image. Because resizing uses the current background color to fill in the added space, be sure it's a color you want. I always resize with white as the background color. Resizing the canvas to a smaller size is another way of cropping the picture by decreasing the canvas area. It's not recommended because you could accidentally lose part of the picture and not be able to recover it.

To resize the canvas, open the Image, Canvas Size dialog box and specify the height and width you want the canvas to be (see Figure 4.2). You can specify any of the measurement systems you prefer on the pop-up menu, as you saw in the Image Size dialog box earlier. Photoshop calculates and displays the new file size as soon as you enter the numbers.

FIGURE 4.2

The Canvas Size dialog box.

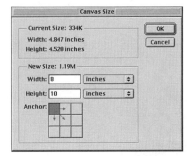

Use the anchor to determine where the image will be placed within the canvas. Click in the middle to center the image on the enlarged canvas, or in any of the other boxes to place it relative to the increased canvas area. Figure 4.3 shows the result of anchoring an image in the upper-left corner of the canvas. The image size hasn't actually changed, but we've made the canvas bigger and then reduced the whole page so you can see that the logo is now in the left corner.

FIGURE 4.3

Before view of canvas on the left; after view on the right.

Resizing a Selection

You can also resize a selected object. To do so, first select the object or a piece of an image to be resized. Use whichever Selection tool is most convenient. With the Selection Marquee active, choose Edit→Transform→Scale. This places a window that looks like the cropping window around your selected object (see Figure 4.4). Drag any of the corner "handles" on the box to change the size of the image while holding down the Shift key to maintain its proportions. If you drag the side handles of the box, you'll stretch the selection's height or width accordingly.

FIGURE 4.4
Resizing a selection.

Rotating

There are many reasons why you might want or need to rotate an image. If you have a scanned picture or a digital camera image that should be vertical but opens as a horizontally oriented picture, rotating it 90 degrees corrects the problem. This is a common occurrence when you use a scanner, because it's usually quicker to scan with the picture horizontal, regardless of its normal orientation (see Figure 4.5).

FIGURE 4.5
*A scanned image (left)
rotated 90 degrees
counterclockwise
(right).*

If you have used an older edition of Photoshop, you might be accustomed to looking for the Transform commands on the Layer menu. Since Photoshop 5, they've been moved to the Edit menu.

Rotate 180 Degrees and 90 Degrees Clockwise or Counterclockwise

To rotate the entire image, use the Image→Rotate Canvas submenu shown in Figure 4.6. Choose 90 degrees clockwise (CW) or counterclockwise (CCW) to straighten up a sideways image, or 180 degrees if you somehow brought in a picture upside down.

FIGURE 4.6

The Rotate Canvas submenu.

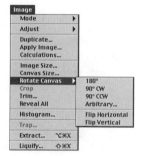

4

Rotate by Degrees

To rotate the canvas by something other than a right angle, choose Image→Rotate Canvas→Arbitrary to open a dialog box like the one shown in Figure 4.7. Enter the number of degrees to rotate. If you're not sure, guess. You can always undo or reopen the box and rotate more, or even change the direction if needed. Click the radio button to indicate the rotational direction: clockwise (°CW) or counterclockwise (°CCW). Then click OK to perform the rotation.

FIGURE 4.7

You can even rotate by fractions of a degree.

To Do: Straightening the Horizon

Using the Arbitrary Rotation dialog box is an easy way to fix up a picture that needs to be straightened. The picture in Figure 4.8 was shot just as I was about to fall into the Grand Canyon. Fortunately, fixing tilted horizons is an easy problem for Photoshop.

FIGURE 4.8

Oops, the horizon's not supposed to slant uphill.

You can tell just by looking at the picture that it needs to rotate counterclockwise several degrees. To straighten the horizon, follow these steps:

1. Open the Image, Rotate Canvas, Arbitrary dialog box. Enter the number of degrees by which you think the horizon is "off."

2. Click the CW (Clockwise) radio button to lower the right side or the CCW (counterclockwise) radio button to lower the left side of the horizon line. In Figure 4.9, we've rotated the canvas by four degrees counterclockwise. (The setting on the tool bar is –4.) Now the horizon is level, but the edges of the picture are no longer horizontal. Cropping will square up the corners again and improve the composition at the same time.

FIGURE 4.9

You can see the background color filling in the corners of the canvas.

3. Select the Crop Tool from the toolbox or press C. Drag the Crop Tool across the picture to position the cropping window. Use the handles to fine-tune your cropping. Figure 4.10 shows the cropping window in position.

FIGURE 4.10

Drag the cropping box until you get rid of the listing corners of the image.

4. If the horizon isn't completely straight, click the dashed line of the cropping window. When you see a double-pointed bent arrow, you can drag the cropping window at an angle until the horizon looks right.

5. Double-click inside the cropping window when the picture looks the way you want it. Figure 4.11 shows the corrected horizon.

> If you don't want to guess the proper angle for a rotation, use the Measure Tool (grouped with the Eyedropper Tool in the Toolbox). Make the Info palette visible, and then click at one point on the horizon (or another edge to be straightened). Drag along that soon-to-be-level line and read the angle in the upper-right corner of the Info palette. Don't worry about your image, either. As soon as you change tools, the measure line goes away.

FIGURE **4.11**

The horizon is level, and the composition's better, too.

Rotate a Selection

Rotating a selection, as opposed to turning the whole canvas, is done in the same manner as resizing one. First, make the selection. Then use Edit→Transform→Rotate to place a bounding box around your selection. Drag on any of the corner handles to rotate the selection around its center point. You can see the center point as the target-shaped object in the middle of the selection in Figure 4.12. If you need to rotate the selection off-center, drag the center point to where you want it and then rotate the selection.

Figure 4.12
Drag any corner point to rotate the selection.

Free Transform

You can use Edit→Free Transform to make any of the changes described. Drag the handles to rotate, skew, scale, or distort as much as you want. You can also access the numeric transformations in the Tool Options bar.

Flipping

Flipping sounds like something you'd do with a pancake, rather than a picture, but the general effect is the same. When you flip the pancake, you reverse it so the other side cooks. When you flip the image, you reverse it so you see a mirror image. You can flip horizontally or vertically. Figure 4.13 shows both.

Figure 4.13
The top pair of words has been flipped horizontally, and the bottom pair has been flipped vertically.

PANCAKEƎꓘAƆИAꟼ
PANCAKES
ꟼAИƆAꓘƎꙄ

Flipping is different from rotating because it changes the up/down or left/right orientation of the image. Of course, sometimes you might need to do both to get the image or selected object oriented the way you want it. For comparison purposes, Figure 4.14 shows the effects of rotation. To make this composition, I typed the word Rotate and copied it, rotating each copy.

> You can flip almost any object without anyone knowing, as long as there's nothing in it that would give the viewer a clue. You can't flip a picture that has type in it, obviously. You also need to be careful about flipping pictures of people who might be wearing shirts with a pocket on one side, a wristwatch, wedding ring, single earring, or other telltale item. Also, watch out for wording on signs in the background. In many cases, it won't matter, but you might find it helpful to edit out the jewelry, shirt pocket, and so on. (You'll learn how to do this in Hour 8, "Digital Painting.")

4

FIGURE **4.14**

You can rotate an image by dragging the selection or by choosing to rotate 90 or 180 degrees, or by entering the desired rotation amount in the Options bar.

Selection Transformations

Resizing and reorientation, as you've seen, can be applied either to the whole canvas, or to any selected object. The transformation methods that follow can only be applied to selections, not to the whole image (unless you start by selecting the entire image).

Skewing Selections

Skew, according to my trusty *Webster's*, means "…to place at an angle." When you skew an object in Photoshop, you can do more than just slant it. You can twist, stretch, and distort it as if the object were on a sheet of rubber instead of a computer screen. The Skew command, found under Edit→Transform→Skew, enables you to twist your selection in all possible directions. Just click the handles and drag the selection. Click the toolbox to apply the setting, or double-click inside the selection, or press Enter/Return.

Skewing is related to the Perspective crop function and can be used to serve the same purpose: restoring warped perspectives. The big difference is that, because it's used on a selection instead of the whole canvas, you can straighten individual objects. Figure 4.15 shows a photo of some gateposts. Because I shot it with a wide angle lens, the closer post appears to be slanting. In Figure 4.15, I've selected it with the Polygonal Lasso.

Now I can apply the Skew function (Edit→Transform→Skew) to the selected post to straighten it. Figure 4.16 shows this step.

Now, all I have to do is fill in the space where the post moved away from the mailbox, and I'm done. Because my selection is still active, I can slide it to the right a little, revealing the landscape behind the skewed area. A brush full of paint fills in any remaining gaps, and the result can be seen in Figure 4.17.

FIGURE 4.15

Selections can be made with any of the Selection tools, not just the rectangle.

FIGURE 4.16

It usually doesn't take much to straighten a tilting line.

FIGURE 4.17

Now the gatepost doesn't look like it's about to fall over.

Distorting Selections

All the transformation tools operate very similarly. They possess subtle differences in how they can move the selection. The Distort command (Edit→Transform→Distort) moves the selection something like the Scale command and Skew command do, but, instead of changing the size of the image, Distort crushes or stretches the image. Figure 4.18 shows a rear view of one of those fashion model dolls, and the way she'd probably look if she were a real person.

Select an object from one of your pictures and practice with skewing and distorting it. Remember that these commands are only available to you when the marquee is blinking, indicating that there's an active selection.

Changing the Perspective of a Selection

The Perspective command is one of the most useful functions in the Photoshop arsenal. When you want to create an image that appears to diminish in the distance, the Perspective tool can't be beat. Its movement is completely intuitive. When you drag a corner handle, the opposite corner becomes a mirror image—when you click an anchor and drag the mouse away from the selection, the mirror image moves away. When you click and drag the anchor in, it, too, follows suit.

The difference between Perspective and Distortion is that when you apply Distortion, you can do it to only one corner of the selection. Perspective automatically adjusts both corners when you drag one.

In Figure 4.19, I'm applying perspective to a different shot of the gatepost. In this case, I want to make it look as though the post and the lion are about ten feet tall instead of five.

FIGURE **4.19**

Apply the Perspective command to a selection to apply false perspective.

FIGURE **4.19**

Apply the Perspective command to a selection to apply false perspective.

Before   After

4

Liquify

Not all transformations have to be useful. The folks at Adobe have added something that's more of a wonderful toy than a tool. It's called Liquify, and it does exactly that to an image. You can swirl the image, make it bulge or shrink, and generally have fun with it. This tool is found at the bottom of the Image menu. Pick a photo, or just draw a squiggle on a blank canvas and play with it yourself.

Summary

Transformations are an important function in Photoshop, especially when you're combining elements from different pictures. It's often necessary to shrink or enlarge an object or the entire image. Use the Image size and Canvas size dialog boxes to adjust the size of the image or work area, respectively. Photoshop also lets you transform selected objects by stretching, distorting, or applying perspective to them. You can do any of these by simply applying a menu command to place a box around the object and then dragging the sides or corners of the box. Spend some time practicing the transformations. They'll be very useful later on.

Q&A

Q **How do you know when to skew, when to distort, and when to use perspective? They all seem to do similar things.**

A When you know that a transformation is needed but you aren't sure what kind, use Edit→Free Transform. You can also access it by pressing Command+T (Mac) or Control+T (Windows). This command places a similar box around the object to be transformed, but it lets you rotate, distort, and drag the object in any direction, or do whatever seems necessary.

Q **I saw type that seemed to have been set standing on a mirror. The letters were reflected backwards. How can I do that?**

A Set the type, make a copy of it, and flip it vertically. Slide the reflection into place under the original type, select it, and apply perspective until it looks right.

Q **What happens if I make a number of transformations and then change my mind about them later?**

A Using Photoshop's History menu, you can go back and undo some or all these operations. Just go back to the state before the transformations. If you're unsure about what you're doing, it's always a good policy to work on a copy of the original picture. That way, you've always got an unspoiled version if something unexpected happens.

Q **How can I tell when I've straightened the horizon enough?**

A The horizon should be level, so dragging a guide from the ruler at the top of the picture will give you something to judge it against. Remember, you can use fractions of a degree by typing their decimal equivalents. Half a degree is 0.5, and so on.

Quiz

1. I want the effect of a mirror to the right of an object. How can I achieve it?

   a. Copy the object to be reflected, flip horizontally, and paste it into place. (The two images sides will touch.) Then select the reflection and distort it, if needed for perspective.

   b. Select Edit→Mirror and then the object.

   c. You can't.

2. How can I put more whitespace around an object?

   a. Paint the background white.

    b. Use the Canvas Size dialog box to make the canvas bigger.

    c. Shrink the object by selecting it and applying Edit→Transform→Scale.

3 What items should you avoid flipping?

    a. Anything containing type

    b. Guys wearing one earring

    c. Signs that say "This side up"

    d. Any of the above

Quiz Answers

1. a. Edit→ Mirror doesn't exist (yet…).

2. b. or c. Either will work.

3. d. Don't flip anything that's obviously directional or that has clues suggesting direction, such as a watch, ring, or pocket.

Exercises

Create a new canvas. Paint a squiggle on it and select the squiggle. Practice flipping, skewing, distorting, and rotating it. Use all the tools discussed in this hour to find the ones you like best.

4

HOUR 5

Color Modes and Color Models

Color is all around us, a blessing few of us take time to think about or recognize. It is as common as the air we breathe, but when you become aware of its presence, you become aware of the minute variations that exist in every color. Notice the shades of green on the tree outside your window. Notice how those greens differ from the green of the grass. Watch the play of light and shadow. It becomes fascinating.

In this hour, we are going to investigate the different properties of color—both in Photoshop and in life. Some of the information at the beginning might seem a little esoteric, but, in the long run, it's useful to know. After all, the more you know about color and how Photoshop addresses it, the better off you'll be. But don't worry, I'll try to be as brief and painless as possible.

Before we begin, it must be said that the best way of learning this stuff is to have Photoshop up and running on your machine. You can glean a certain amount of information from merely reading, but the real learning won't start until you start working in Photoshop. This is for two reasons:

- As we all know, you remember something better when you do it yourself.
- Photoshop's treatment of color makes it very intuitive. Keep the Color palette open at all times (Window→Show Color) and keep an eye on the sliders. Notice how they change from mode to mode—the differences and similarities.

The first thing to know is that Photoshop addresses color in terms of modes and models. *Models* are methods of defining color. *Modes* are methods of working with color based on the models.

Color models describe the different ways that color can be represented on paper and on the computer screen. The color models are as follows:

- RGB (Red, Green, Blue)
- CMYK (Cyan, Magenta, Yellow, Black)
- HSB (Hue, Saturation, and Brightness)
- CIE Lab

We will examine these models for displaying and describing color, and then we will turn our attention to the Photoshop modes, which are the ways Photoshop provides for you to work with color.

Color Models

Figure 5.1 shows the Photoshop Color Picker. You can reach it by clicking either of the large blocks of color at the bottom of the toolbar. It has a graduated block of color, which you can click to select a particular shade, and windows that display the numbers for any chosen color in each of the four color models. In addition, Photoshop gives you a Color palette, which is shown in Figure 5.2. Open it, if it's not already open, by choosing Window→Show Color. It has a strip along the bottom that covers the full color spectrum, plus black and white. Clicking anywhere on it sets the Color Picker to that range of colors.

| If your Color Picker doesn't look like this one, open Edit→Preferences→General and set the Color Picker to Photoshop.

RGB Model

The RGB model, which computer monitors and TV screens use for display, assigns *values* on a scale of 0 to 255 for each of the three RGB primaries. As an example, pure Green (as you can see in the previous figure) has Red and Blue values of 0, and a Green value of 255. Pure white places the values of all three RGB primaries at 255. Pure Black places the values of the RGB primaries at 0.

FIGURE 5.1

The Photoshop Color Picker.

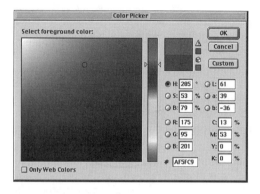

FIGURE 5.2

The Photoshop Color palette has adjustable sliders as well as a clickable strip representing the full color spectrum. Right now, it's showing pure green.

| NEW TERM | *Value,* in this usage, means the relative strength of the color. Because the RGB model mixes colors of light to achieve white light, the full strength is 255. When you combine all three primaries at a value of 128 (half of 255), you get medium gray. |

5

CMYK Model

The CMYK model, used for printing, defines colors according to their percentages of cyan, magenta, yellow, and black. These are the four colors of printing inks, both in your home inkjet printer and in the fancy, high-resolution color laser printers and printing presses that service bureaus and commercial printers use. A six-color inkjet printer, like the Epson 750, adds light cyan and light magenta.

Back a thousand years ago when I went to grade school, every child was given a box of crayons at the start of the school year. Your grade level determined the size of the crayon box. Kindergarten and first grade got flat boxes with eight big, thick crayons per box: the primaries, the secondaries, and brown and black. That was how we learned colors, even back then. The primaries were yellow, red, and blue. The secondaries were what you got when you mixed any two primaries: orange, from yellow and red; green, from yellow and blue; and purple, from red and blue. Brown was the mix of all three primaries, and black was…well, black was black.

That's how we knew them, until high school. By then, we'd outgrown crayons, of course. We filed into our physics class, and threw the previous nine years of learning out the window. The primary colors, according to the physics teacher, were red, green, and blue. And if you mixed them, you got, not brown or even the mysterious black, but…white!

Those of us still taking art classes listened to the physics lecture skeptically and went down to the art room to try mixing red, green, and blue paint. We got a sort of muddy brown, not the promised white. We asked the art teacher about this and were sent upstairs to the drama department for a demonstration. The stage lights had filters in red, green, and blue. When all the lights were on, the result was, sure enough, white light. Why? When you're dealing with light, the drama teacher explained, colors are additive. They total to white. When you're dealing with paint, the colors subtract from each other, giving that muddy brown mess. Aha! We were enlightened.

When you bought your computer system, you had to deal with this issue, whether or not you knew it at the time. Your monitor uses light to produce color. That's why it's called an RGB (Red, Green, Blue) monitor. Your printer uses ink to produce color. Not red ink, green ink, and blue ink, but a set of colors called Cyan, Magenta, and Yellow, along with our old standby Black. This color system is known by its initials, CMYK. Why K for black? For a long time, K was a mystery term, but an astute reader of an earlier version of this book explained that, "K stands for Keyline, which is a thin black line printed around colors to keep them separate." Makes sense to me…

HSB Model

When artists talk about color, they generally define it by using a set of parameters called HSB. Photoshop also includes this color model. H stands for *Hue*, which is the basic color from the color wheel, for example, red, blue, or yellow. It's expressed in degrees (0–360°), which correspond to the positions on the color wheel of the various colors. S is *Saturation*, or the strength of the color, and it's a percentage of the color minus the amount of gray in it. Pure color pigment with no gray in it is said to be 100% saturated. Neutral gray, with no color, is 0% saturated. Saturated colors are found at the edge of the color wheel, and saturation decreases as you approach the center of the wheel. If you look at the Apple Color picker in Figure 5.3, it's a little easier to understand this. *Brightness*, the relative tone or lightness of the color, is also measured as a percentage, from 0% (black) to 100% (white). Brightness is equivalent to the value used by the RGB model.

FIGURE 5.3

The Apple Color Picker uses a standard color wheel.

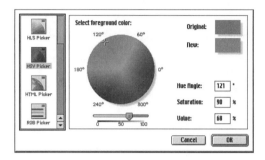

CIE Lab Model

The most encompassing of these color models is CIE Lab. It defines a color gamut (a range of colors) that is broader than any of the other models. Because of its broad color gamut, Photoshop uses the CIE Lab model to convert from one color model to another. Lab color is defined as Luminance, plus two components (a and b), which go, respectively, from green to red and from blue to yellow. Lab color is designed to be device-independent, meaning that colors defined in this model appear and print the same, regardless of whether you are seeing them on paper or on the video screen. However, this is probably not a model you will use frequently. Let's focus our attention now on the more commonly used models, and what you need to know to get up and running.

I suggest that you do your color work in RGB, regardless of whether your final image will be printed or viewed onscreen as, for instance, a picture on the World Wide Web. The reason for this is simple. Even if you specify CMYK as the color model, your monitor can only display as RGB. It doesn't have cyan, magenta, or yellow pixels, except as combinations of RGB light. Rather than make it do the conversion every time you change a piece of the image, wait and do it when you're ready to print. Actually, you needn't convert to CMYK for color printing, unless you're sending the image to a commercial print shop or fine arts Iris printer. Home/office inkjets are designed to work best with RGB input.

The Modes and Models of Color

First, forget about CIE Lab color. It's there. Photoshop uses it in the background, but you needn't concern yourself with it. The other three models, HSB, RGB, and CMYK, will have much greater impact on your work in Photoshop. The difference between the modes and the models is simple. The *models* are methods of defining color. *Modes* are methods of working with color based on the models. HSB is the only model without a directly corresponding mode. CMYK and RGB have corresponding modes in Photoshop. There are also modes for black-and-white, grayscale, and limited color work.

The Photoshop modes available under Image→Modes are as follows:

- Bitmap
- Grayscale
- Duotone
- Indexed Color
- RGB Color
- CMYK Color
- Lab Color
- Multichannel

There are only four of these color modes that you'll use often: Grayscale, RGB, CMYK, and Indexed Color. Let's take a closer look at them.

Bitmap and Grayscale

We'll start out here with the most basic of the color modes available within Photoshop—Bitmap and Grayscale.

The Grayscale mode offers 256 shades of gray that range from white to black, whereas the Bitmap mode uses only two color values to display images—black and white (see Figures 5.4 and 5.5 for examples).

FIGURE 5.4

A photo rendered in the Grayscale mode.

FIGURE 5.5
*The same image in the
Bitmap mode.*

Notice the vast difference in quality. The Grayscale image has a smooth transition between values, especially in the spotted fur, whereas the Bitmap image does not. There are, however, a number of ways to convert to Bitmap mode, which we'll discuss later in this hour.

Whenever a picture is printed in black-and-white or grayscale—for instance, as part of a newsletter or brochure—it makes sense for you to work on it in Grayscale mode. Doing the conversion yourself, rather than sending a color photo to the printer, gives you the opportunity to make sure that the picture will print properly. You can tell by looking at it whether the darks need to be lightened or the light grays intensified to bring out more detail.

To convert a color photo to Grayscale, simply choose Image→Mode→Grayscale. You'll be asked for permission to discard the color information. Click OK to confirm, and the picture is converted to grays.

RGB

RGB is the color mode for working on pictures that will be viewed on a computer screen. If you are preparing pictures in Photoshop that will eventually become part of a desktop presentation, a video, or a Web page, stick with RGB for the best color rendition. If your work is only going on the Web, I still recommend doing the color adjustments in RGB and then converting the picture to Indexed Color when you save it in its final form. Also, if you work in Indexed Color, you can't use Photoshop's filters or layers. That's too much of a limitation!

Indexed Color

Indexed Color, when it can work for you, is a wonderful thing. Because of cross-platform compatibility issues, Web designers are currently limited to the 216 colors shared by Macintoshes and PCs. Indexed Color is a palette or, rather, a collection of

5

palettes—256 to be exact. With this mode, you know exactly what you are getting, and if you don't like any of the palettes Photoshop supplies, you can build your own.

Indexed Color is perfect for the World Wide Web. The Indexed Color mode includes a specific Web palette. Indexed Color doesn't really limit you to 216 colors though. Dithering takes place in Indexed Color images. From RGB mode, choose Image→Mode→Indexed Color to take a look at the Indexed Color dialog box (see Figure 5.6).

NEW TERM   *Dithering* means that certain colors are combined, that is, adjacent pixels are interspersed, visually blending onscreen to create a new color although they retain their original color— or the closest index equivalent—when viewed at a large magnification.

FIGURE 5.6

The Indexed Color dialog box.

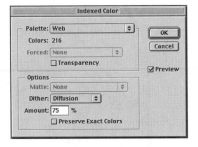

You are given a number of palette choices when you work with Indexed Color. (Several have changed from Photoshop 5.5) They are as follows:

- *Exact*—This option takes the colors that are in the RGB version of the image for its palette. This only works if there are less than 256 colors in the original image.
- *System (Mac OS)*—This option uses the Macintosh System.
- *System (Windows)*—This option uses the Windows System palette.
- *Web*—This palette uses the colors most often used by Web browsers. If you are planning to publish your work on the World Wide Web, this is the "safe" palette. Otherwise, you might have problems with incompatible colors dropping out when an image is viewed with a Web browser.
- *Uniform*—The Uniform option bases the colors in the palette on a strict sampling of colors across the color spectrum.
- *Perceptual*—This option creates a custom palette by giving priority to colors for which the human eye has greater sensitivity.
- *Selective*—The Selective option creates a color table similar to the Perceptual color table, but favoring broad areas of color and the preservation of Web colors.

- *Adaptive*—This is your best bet for most work in Indexed Color. During conversion, this option samples the most frequently used colors from the original. Adaptive usually provides you with the closest match to the original image.

- *Custom*—If none of the other options suit you, you can always build your own palette. See the Photoshop manual for instructions.

- *Previous*—This option simply remembers and reverts to whatever option you chose last time you did a conversion to Indexed Color.

CMYK

As you saw earlier, CMYK mode should be used only when your image is printed commercially. By converting to CMYK before you start to print (and being aware of gamut warnings), you can make sure your nice yellow banana or flower doesn't end up a muddy brown, or your bright blue sky doesn't print as purple.

NEW TERM *Gamut* refers to the range of colors that the combination of CMYK inks can print. Some colors are *out of gamut*, and can't be printed accurately. Very bright colors, particularly oranges and greens, are often out of gamut, and would trigger the gamut warning.

Converting Between Modes

All you have to do to convert, at least mechanically (this is not taking image degradation or changes into account), is to select Image→Mode and then choose your poison.

Although Photoshop uses the model (Lab) with the broadest gamut of color to change color modes (as if all the other modes are circles that will fit within Lab Color), this is no guarantee that your colors are going to turn out the same in another mode as they did in the original mode.

The rule of thumb is this, and I can't stress it enough: Do your work in RGB, even if you are going to output your images to print. Convert a copy of your image to CMYK immediately before you send it to the commercial print shop. To see whether all your colors are within the CMYK gamut, use the menu command View→Gamut Warning. If you are going to publish your images on the Web, use Indexed Color. (Use RGB and then convert.) Knowing this will save you many hours of wondering why the Web page that looks great on the office Macintosh looks funky on the Windows machine you use at home, or why the yellow in your printed piece looks brownish.

But what if the color mode you want happens to not be available in the Image→Mode menu? Nothing to worry about. It is true that sometimes the mode you want will not be available, but you can always get to it by first converting to Lab Color and then to the color you want. For example, when you have created or imported an image that is in

5

Indexed Color, the CMYK option is grayed out or not available. You actually have two choices here: Convert to Lab or RGB, and then take the image over into CMYK—but beware. Make sure that the color you get is the color you want. You might need to make additional color adjustments in CMYK mode to get the picture to print the way it looks onscreen.

To Do: Getting Started with Color

Just for fun, why don't we dive in with some hands-on before we go any further? Working through this exercise will give you a better idea of the concepts and ideas that we have been talking about, because the pictures in the book are in black-and-white. Let's look at a colorful image and examine how the modes affect the way the color appears.

1. First, find a colorful picture and open it. (You can download the photo in Figure 5.7 from Macmillan's Web site. To get to the Web site, point your Web browser to `http://www.mcp.com/sams/detail_sams.cfm?item=0672319551`. When the main book page has loaded, click the `Downloads` link to get to the files. If your picture doesn't have the letters RGB in parentheses after the title, choose Image→Mode→RGB Color. This is your starting point. If your monitor is correctly adjusted, you should see very good color.

FIGURE 5.7
Country garden.

2. Select Image→Mode→Grayscale. A dialog box appears, asking whether you want to discard the image's color information. Click OK. Photoshop then proceeds to examine your image and assigns all the colors to 256 shades of gray that range between white and black, inclusive.

   Notice in the status bar at the bottom of the picture how the size of your file diminishes. This is because color is difficult for a machine to reproduce. The amount of information or data in a color image is much greater than that required to display a Grayscale image

▼

▼ 3. Before we move on, we need to return the image to its original RGB state. Select File→Revert. When Photoshop asks whether you want to return to the last saved version of your file, click OK.

This time, we're going to change our RGB image to CMYK. This process becomes enormously important for anyone who will be taking his or her images to a commercial printer. RGB can display a number of colors that CMYK, by the nature of its four inks, cannot reproduce. The inks, for instance, can only approximate neon colors.

Before we make the mode change, let's take a closer look at some of the colors in our RGB image to see whether they can be reproduced in CMYK (see Figure 5.8).

A. Click the Eyedropper Tool in the toolbox.

B. Next, open the Colors palette by selecting Window, Show Colors.

C. Use the Eyedropper to select (click) a color in the image. Try clicking a very bright one.

Triangular Out of Gamut Warning Symbol

FIGURE 5.8

The triangle symbol means gamut warning.

D. Look in the Color palette. Is there an Out of Gamut Warning there? This little triangle indicates that the selected color cannot be reproduced precisely by the process colors of CMYK.

E. To get an idea how far out of gamut your colors are, select View→Gamut Warning. This gives you an indication of the colors that will be lost or modified during the translation of RGB mode to CMYK. Figure 5.9 shows what the gamut warning looks like for this picture. Out of gamut areas are shown ▼ as black patches.

5

egin
...

To change the color used in the display of the Gamut Warning, select File→Preferences→Transparency & Gamut. Click the color swatch at the bottom of the dialog box and choose a color that contrasts with the colors in the picture.

FIGURE 5.9
The black patches are out of gamut.

F. Click the warning triangle to select the nearest color that can be achieved with CMYK colors. You can quickly adjust a picture like this one that has many out of gamut colors by activating the Gamut Warning. You can then use the color adjustment tools you'll learn about in the next hour to bring the picture into a printable range.

4. To change the mode from RGB to CMYK, select Image→Mode→CMYK.

5. After you've seen and perhaps printed the picture in CMYK mode, feel free to experiment with the other modes, too.

If you have a color printer, you might want to print your picture and compare it to what you see onscreen. Does it look OK? If so, you're in luck. Your monitor is accurately calibrated. If not, you need to calibrate your monitor so that the images onscreen accurately display the colors as they print. We will discuss calibration in a Note in Hour 23, "Printing." If your monitor seems to need calibration, you can jump ahead to the Note.

The human eye is extremely sensitive to even the slightest variation in color. Think for a moment about something familiar—a can of Coca-Cola. I'll bet that if you were shown two swatches of red you could, without much hesitation, select the Coke's red and differentiate it from, say, the red used on the cover of *Time* magazine. If you saw cans of Coke displayed with a slightly off-color red, you'd probably think they were either outdated or perhaps counterfeit. Most people are very much aware of even slight color changes. That is why color becomes so important in the branding of products through advertising.

Summary

Color is fun to play with, but it's also rather complicated to understand. The world in general, and Photoshop in particular, uses color models as a way of describing colors. The four color models are HSB, RGB, CMYK, and CIE Lab Color. There are also color modes, which enable you to work with color. RGB is the most useful color mode, because it's the one the monitor displays. CMYK mode is used for printing, as is Grayscale.

In this hour, we discussed the color modes and the specific color models in Photoshop. We also looked at a few of the more salient issues regarding converting between modes.

In the next hour, you will delve deeper into the world of color by learning how to make tonal adjustments and general adjustments.

Q&A

Q What are those funny letters and numbers at the bottom of the Color Picker?

A Those describe Web colors. The alphanumerics define the selected color in HTML.

Q Is there ever a time when I would want to work in Lab Color?

A Well, I've been using Photoshop since version 2, and I haven't yet found a need for it. Without knowing who you are and how you use Photoshop, I can't say you'll *never* need it, but it's unlikely.

Q What are Web-safe colors, and why are there fewer than 256 of them?

A Macintoshes and PCs both can use a limited palette of 256 colors. However, the two palettes aren't quite the same. Only 216 of the 256 colors are identical. These are the "Web-safe" colors, meaning that no matter what kind of computer you use to surf the Web, if these colors are used, you'll see the page as its author intended.

Q If I want to print my pictures, *and* put them on the Web, should I be working in CMYK or RGB?

A I'd do my work in RGB mode, and then save a copy in CMYK and check the gamut before printing it. Your video monitor can't show you true CMYK colors, no matter how many times you calibrate it. It doesn't display color that way.

5

Quiz

1. RGB, used by your monitor, stands for

    a. Raster (white), Gray, Black

    b. Red, Green, Blue

    c. Initials of Apple's next CEO, Roy G. Biv

2. How many colors can a Web page display correctly?

    a. Millions

    b. 256

    c. 216

3. Which color mode should you use for printed pages?

    a. CMYK

    b. HSB

    c. PANTONE

Quiz Answers

1. b.

2. c., but only because that's all Macintoshes and PCs can agree on.

3. a. if they are intended for four-color process printing. Home/office inkjet printers handle RGB conversions very well.

Exercises

Using the Photoshop Color Picker, select a nice bright red. See how it's represented in the different color models. Click at the upper-right corner of the color square. Saturation and Brightness should be 100%, regardless of which color you have selected. Red will read 0 in the Hue window. Enter **60** in the Hue window. The color square will change to yellow. Knowing that Red is 0 and Yellow is 60, can you predict what number pure Blue will be? Look at some other colors and see how they affect the settings. Try to see the relationship of the colors on a theoretical color wheel to the colors you see in the spectrum.

HOUR 6

Adjusting Color

Are you one of those people who likes to play with the color adjustments on the television set? If you are, you're going to be absolutely astounded with Photoshop's color adjustment capabilities. If you haven't a clue as to what we mean by adjusting color, that's okay, too. By the end of this hour, you'll be able to turn red roses blue, change a sky from midday to sunset and back again, bring out the detail in shadows, and manage every imaginable aspect of color manipulation.

Photoshop includes a full set of tools for making color adjustments. You can find them all on the Image→Adjust submenu (see Figure 6.1). Some of these terms, such as Brightness/Contrast, might be familiar to you; others might not. Don't worry. You'll learn about them all in this hour.

FIGURE 6.1

The Adjust submenu gives you all the tools you'll need.

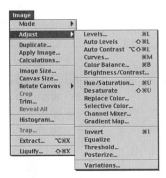

Before you start to adjust color, you need to evaluate what kind of color you have in the picture and how you'll eventually use the image. You learned about color models and color modes last hour, so you know that RGB color is the kind that is displayed on computer screens and CMYK color is the kind that is printed. If you're going to be adjusting the color in a picture, it makes sense to adjust it according to the way it will be displayed. If your picture is going on a Web page, you should work in RGB mode. If it's going to be printed on a four-color process commercial press, work in RGB to start with, but make your final adjustments (if any are needed) after you convert to CMYK mode. If you're printing on a home/office inkjet printer, stick with RGB. These printers are designed to make the conversion internally. If it's going to end up in grayscale, forget about trying to make the sky a perfect blue. Change the mode to Grayscale and make the contrast perfect instead. Just keep these few rules in mind and you won't go wrong. Table 6.1 will help you keep these options sorted out.

TABLE 6.1   Color Adjustment Matrix

Adjust Color In	If Output Is
RGB	Computer screen or inkjet
RGB first, then CMYK	Process Color print
Grayscale	Black and-white print

Adjusting by Eye with Variations

The most obvious way to make a color adjustment is to compare before and after views of an image. In Photoshop, the tool for doing this is called Variations. It's the last item on the Image→Adjust submenu. Variations combines several image adjustment tools into one easy-to-use system that shows you thumbnail images that are variations on the original image. You simply click the one that looks best to you. You can choose variations of hue and brightness and then see the result (which Photoshop calls Current Pick) compared to the original.

> If Variations doesn't appear on the Adjust submenu, it's because the
> Variations plug-in might not have been installed. Consult the Photoshop
> manual for information about using plug-in modules.

Figure 6.2 shows the Variations dialog box. When you first open it, the Current Pick is the same as the original image, because you haven't yet made changes. You can set the slider to the left (Fine) or right (Coarse) to determine how much effect each variation applies to the original image. Moving it one tick mark in either direction doubles or halves the previously selected amount. The finest setting makes changes that are so slight as to be almost undetectable. The coarsest setting should be used only if you're going for special effects and want to turn the entire picture to a single color. The default (middle) setting is the most practical for "normal" adjustments.

FIGURE 6.2

The seven thumbnails at lower-left adjust hue, whereas the righthand set of three adjusts brightness.

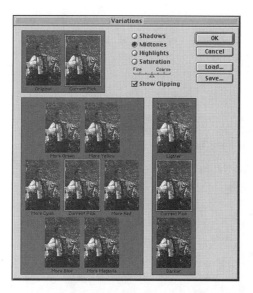

Adjusting Shadows, Midtones, Highlights, and Saturation

When you use Variations to adjust a color image, you also have the option of individually adjusting shadows, midtones, highlights, or overall color saturation. *Shadows*, *midtones*, and *highlights* are Photoshop's terms for the darks, middle tones, and light tones, respectively, in the picture (or what would be black, gray, and white in grayscale). Overall saturation adjusts all of them at once.

6

When you select shadows, midtones, or highlights, you adjust the hue and brightness of only that part of the picture. The advantage here is that you can adjust the midtones one way and the highlights or shadows another way, if you choose. Each setting is independent of the others, and you can, for example, set the midtones to be more blue, thus brightening the sky, yet still set the shadows to be more yellow, offsetting the blueness that they possess inherently.

NEW TERM *Clipping* is a term that describes what happens when a highlight or shadow value is adjusted so much it becomes pure white or pure black. Selecting Show Clipping displays a neon-colored preview of areas in the image that will be clipped by the adjustment. Clipping doesn't occur when you adjust midtones.

Remember, as you learned in Hour 5, "Color Modes and Color Models," Hue refers to the color of an object or selection. *Brightness* is a measurement of how much white or black is added to the color.

Selecting Saturation changes the strength of the color in the image; the setting choice is simply for less or more color strength. In Figure 6.3, I'm adjusting the saturation of this photo. Remember that you can apply the same correction more than once. If, for instance, less saturation still leaves more color in the image than you want, apply saturation again to get even less.

FIGURE 6.3

Less saturation gives you a lighter image. More saturation gives you a darker one. (Don't confuse saturation with brightness. Saturation changes the amount of color. Brightness adds light.)

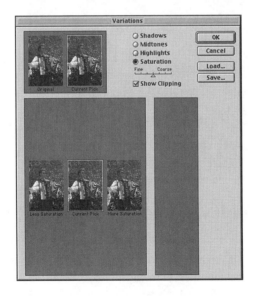

To Do: Adjust an Image Using the Variations Command

Learning to work with the Variations dialog box is an excellent way to understand how colors work.

1. Open any color image. Choose Image→Adjust→Variations.

2. Set the radio buttons according to what you want to adjust: Shadows, Midtones, Highlights, or Saturation.

3. Use the Fine/Coarse slider to determine how much adjustment to apply.

4. Create the desired variations by clicking the appropriate thumbnails. The following are some tips for getting the effect you want:

   • To add color, click the appropriate color thumbnail.

   • To reduce a color, click its opposite on the color wheel. To reduce magenta, for example, click green.

   • To adjust the brightness, click the thumbnail for a lighter or darker image.

   • If you're not sure exactly what you need to do, simply click the image that looks most "right" to you.

   • If you think you might have overdone your corrections and want to go back to the original image, press Option (Mac) or Alt (Windows) to change the Cancel button to Reset. This restores the settings to zero and reverts to the image saved prior to changes. (Note: This works with all adjustment windows.)

5. Click OK when done or Cancel to undo all your adjustments.

Saving and Loading Corrections

There's one other set of buttons that appears in this window, and in the other adjustment windows as well. These are the Load and Save buttons. They can save you a lot of time and effort if you have a whole series of pictures that need the same kind of corrections. Perhaps you used your digital camera to shoot several outdoor pictures with the same lousy light conditions. Maybe your scanner tends to make everything a little more yellow than reality. After you determine the settings that correct one picture perfectly, you can save those settings and then load them each time you want to apply them to another picture.

Click the Save button, and you'll see a typical dialog box that asks you to give your settings a name. You might call them "foggy day fix" or "scanner correction." Then, when you need to apply them to another picture, use the Load button to locate and open the appropriate setting file, and your corrections will be made.

6

Making Other Adjustments

As you've seen, Variations is the quick way to adjust color, but sometimes it doesn't give you enough control. Other times you just want to experiment. Maybe you have a picture that's mediocre, but if you play with the colors in it and beef up the contrast, you can make something out of it. These are the times when you'll want to work with individual adjustment settings.

There's a menu item under the Image menu called Histogram. It doesn't actually *do* anything, but if you learn how to use it, you can save yourself lots of time.

If you ever took a course in statistics, you already know that a histogram is a kind of graph. In Photoshop, it's a graph of the image reduced to grayscale, with lines to indicate the number of pixels at each step in the gray scale from 0 to 255.

You might wonder why this is important. The main reason is that you can tell by looking at the histogram whether there's enough detail in the image, so that you can apply corrections successfully. If you have an apparently bad photo or a bad scan, studying the histogram will tell you whether it's worth working on or whether you should throw away the image and start over. If all the lines are bunched up at one end of the graph, you probably can't save the picture by adjusting it. If, on the other hand, you have a reasonably well-spread-out histogram, there's a wide enough range of values to suggest that the picture can be saved.

The Histogram command has another use, which is to give you a sense of the tonal range of the image. This is sometimes referred to as the *key type*. An image is said to be either low key, average key, or high key, depending on whether it has a preponderance of dark, middle, or light tones, respectively. A picture that is all middle gray would have only one line in its histogram, and it would fall right in the middle.

All you really need to know is that, when you look at the histogram, you should see a fairly even distribution across the graph, if the image is intended to be an average key picture. If the picture is high key, most of the lines in the histogram are concentrated on the right side with a few on the left. If it is low key, most of the values will be to the left with a few to the right.

Adjusting with the Levels Dialog Box

Adjusting levels is a method of changing the brightness of an image. As you can see in Figure 6.4, the Levels window comes complete with a histogram, along with some controls that you can use to adjust the values.

FIGURE 6.4

*Be sure to click the
Preview box so that
you can see the effect
of your changes.*

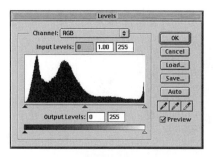

Setting the black point (the point at the left of the histogram that represents absolutely saturated black) to match the concentration of darkest levels in the image, and setting the white point (at the right, indicating completely unsaturated white) to match the concentration of the lightest levels in the image, forces the rest of the levels to reassign themselves more equitably. You can download the picture I've used in these examples at Macmillan's Web site discussed in the Introduction. The image is called Accordion.jpg.

To Do: Adjust Brightness Using Levels

▲ To Do ▼

When the colors are right, but the photo seems dull, adjusting the brightness helps.

1. Choose Image→Adjust→Levels, or press Command+L (Mac) or Control+L (Windows).

2. Click the Preview box so that you can see your changes in the image window. Just for fun, you can watch the Navigator and Layers palette change, too.

In a color image, you can adjust the composite RGB or CMYK color image, or individual colors, by using the Channels pop-up menu. For now, stay with the composite. (You'll learn more about channels later in this hour.)

3. Create the desired level adjustments by moving the three sliders below the histogram to the left or right. The following are some tips for getting the effect you want:

   • To set the black point in the image, move the slider at the left side of the Input Levels histogram to the point at which the dark lines begin to cluster.

   • Set the white point by moving the right Input Levels slider to the point where the light pixels begin to rise.

   • Adjust the midrange by watching the picture while you move the Input Levels middle slider left or right. Figure 6.5 shows the settings for this picture.

6

FIGURE 6.5

Adjusting the darks helps bring out shadow detail.

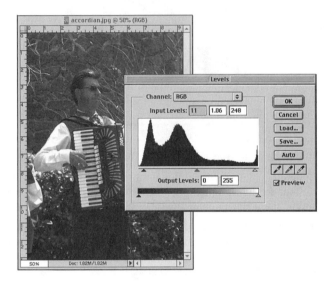

4. To adjust the contrast in the image, use the sliders on the Output Levels bar. The black slider controls the dark tones; moving it toward the center darkens the image. The white slider controls the light tones; moving it toward the center lightens the image.

5. Click OK when you're done.

You can also use the Eyedroppers to adjust the levels. Click the white Eyedropper (on the right) and click the lightest part of your image. Then click the dark-tipped Eyedropper (on the left) to select it and click the darkest point on the image. If you have an area in the image that seems to be right in the middle, click it with the midrange Eyedropper (in the middle).

> If you click Auto in the Levels window or choose Auto Levels from the Image→Adjust menu, Photoshop adjusts the levels based on its evaluation of the tonal range. However, this is usually not satisfactory. Try it, but be prepared to undo.

Adjusting with the Curves Dialog Box

Adjusting curves is much like adjusting levels, though a bit more subtle. You can use the Curves window instead of the Levels window to adjust the brightness. The big difference is that, instead of adjusting at only three points (black, middle, and white), you can adjust at any point (see Figure 6.6).

FIGURE 6.6

On this kind of graph, the zero point is in the middle.

When you open the Curves window, you won't see a curve. You won't see the histogram either. Instead, you see a different kind of a graph, one with a grid and a diagonal line. The horizontal axis of the grid represents the original values (input levels) of the image or selection, whereas the vertical axis represents the new values (output levels). When you first open the box, the graph appears as a diagonal line because no new values have been mapped. All pixels have identical input and output values. As always, be sure to check the Preview box, so you can see the effects of your changes.

As with the Levels window, you can click Auto or use the Eyedroppers to adjust the values. Because the Curves method gives you so much more control, you might as well take full advantage of it. Hold down the mouse button and drag the cursor over the piece of the image that needs adjusting. You'll see a circle on the graph at the point representing the pixel where the cursor is. If there are points on the curve that you don't want to change, click them (in Windows, Control+click) to lock them down. For instance, if you want to adjust the midtones while leaving the darks and lights relatively untouched, click points on the curve to mark the points at which you want to stop making changes, and then drag the middle of the curve until the image looks right to you. Dragging up lightens tones, whereas dragging down darkens them. Figure 6.7 shows what this actually looks like. To get rid of a point that you have placed, drag it off the grid.

6

FIGURE 6.7
*You can add up to 16
points on the curve.*

 To see the curves displayed with a finer grid, press and hold Option (Mac) or Alt (Windows) and click the grid.

Adjusting with the Balance Dialog Box

To really understand color balance, you have to look at the color wheel. In case you don't remember the order of the color wheel, there's a reference in Figure 6.8.

FIGURE 6.8
*It's impossible to
reproduce this color
wheel in gray. Use
your imagination.*

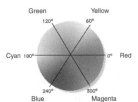

Every color on the wheel has an opposite. If you follow the line from one color through the center of the wheel, you reach its opposite. Cyan is opposite to red; green is opposite to magenta; and yellow is opposite to blue. When you use the Color Balance window to adjust colors in a picture, you're adding more of the color opposite to the one you want to reduce. Increasing the cyan reduces red. Increasing red reduces cyan, and so on, around the wheel.

Figure 6.9 shows the Color Balance window. Color Balance is intended to be used for general color correction rather than correcting specific parts of an image, although you can use it that way by selecting only the part to correct. It's especially helpful if you have a scanned image that is off-color, such as an old, yellowed photograph. It's very simple to apply the Color Balance tools to remove the yellow without altering the rest of the picture.

FIGURE 6.9

Move the sliders in the direction of the color you want to add.

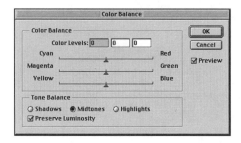

In addition to Color Balance, you can use the sliders to adjust tone balance. As with the Variations window described earlier, you can concentrate your efforts on adjusting shadows, midtones, or highlights by clicking the appropriate button.

To Do: Apply Color Balance

Color Balance can rescue pictures that have faded, and it can turn red roses blue. It's fun to play with.

1. Select the image or portion of the image to correct. Open the Color Balance window by choosing Image→Adjust→Color Balance or pressing Command+B (Mac) or Control+B (Windows).

2. Choose Shadows, Midtones, or Highlights. Generally it's advisable to start with midtones, if you are correcting the whole picture, because they comprise 90% of it.

3. Check Preserve Luminosity so that you don't change the brightness of the image as you shift colors. If maintaining the brightness isn't important, don't check the check box. Be sure to select Preview so that you can see how your changes affect the image.

4. Move the sliders to adjust the colors. The numbers in the boxes change to indicate how much of a change you are making. They range from 0 to +100 (toward red, green, and blue) and from 0 to –100 (toward cyan, magenta, and yellow).

5. Adjust the shadows and the highlights; repeat the corrections until the image looks right to you. (My settings for the Accordion photo were +36, +19, and –10. That means that I added Red and Green and removed some Blue.)

6. Click OK to apply the changes.

If Color Balance doesn't seem to do what you want, undo it.

Adjusting with the Hue/Saturation Dialog Box

The Hue/Saturation window is a very powerful tool with a slightly misleading name. Sure, it lets you adjust the hue (colors in the image) and the saturation (the intensity of the colors), but it also gives you control over the lightness.

First, look at the controls in the Hue/Saturation window (see Figure 6.10). The first pop-up Edit menu lets you select either a single color to adjust or the Master setting, which adjusts all the colors in the image or selection at once. For now, work with the Master setting. Check Preview so you can see the effects of your changes in the picture on which you're working.

FIGURE 6.10

Small adjustments to Brightness and Saturation are usually all that's needed.

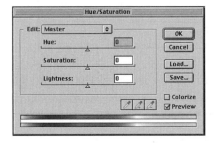

There are three sliders: Hue, Saturation, and Lightness. The Hue slider moves around the color wheel. With Master selected, you can move all the way from red (in the middle of the slider), left—through purple to blue or blue-green—or right through orange to yellow and to green.

The Saturation slider takes you from 0%, in the center, to 100% saturated (pure color, with no gray) on the right, or 100% unsaturated (no color) on the left.

The Lightness slider lets you increase or decrease the brightness of the image, from zero in the center, to +100 on the right, or –100 on the left.

As you move these sliders, watch the two spectrum strips at the bottom of the window, as well as the image itself. The upper strip represents the current status of the image, and the lower one changes according to the slider(s) you move. If you move the Hue slider to +60, for example, you can see that the reds in the picture turn quite yellow and the blues turn purple. In effect, what you are doing is skewing the color spectrum by that amount. If you move the Saturation slider to the left, you'll see the lower spectrum strip become less saturated. If you move the Lightness slider, you'll see its effects reflected in the lower spectrum strip as well.

Lightness is technically the same as brightness. The Hue, Saturation, Brightness (HSB) color model uses these terms to define a color, as opposed to the RGB and CMYK models that define it as percentages of the component primaries, which, of course, are red, green, and blue for RGB, and cyan, magenta, and yellow for the CMYK model.

Instead of selecting Master from the pop-up menu, if you select a color, the window changes slightly, as you can see in Figure 6.11. The Eyedroppers are now active, enabling you to select colors from the image, and adjustable "range" sliders are centered on the color you have chosen to adjust. You can move these back and forth to focus on as broad or narrow a range within that color as you want. This might not seem like a big deal, but it's really very powerful.

Suppose I want to change the musician's vest from red to green without changing his skin tones. I can set the sliders to include only the range of reds that need to be enhanced, and then make them more saturated and brighter without turning him seasick.

FIGURE 6.11

Click and drag to move the sliders. You can extend the range of colors to be affected by dragging the edges of the range selector between the two color bars.

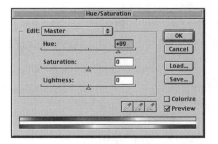

To Do: Adjust an Image Using the Hue/Saturation Window

This powerful tool is best applied in small doses.

1. Open the window by choosing it from the Image→Adjust menu or by pressing Command+U (Mac) or Control+U (Windows). Click Preview to see your changes as you make them.

2. Use Master (the default setting) to adjust all the colors, or use the pop-up menu to select the color you want to adjust.

3. Create the desired adjustments by moving the three sliders to the left or right. The following are some tips for getting the effect you want:

   • Drag the Hue slider left or right until the colors look the way you want. The numbers displayed in the Hue text box refer to the degree of rotation around the color wheel from the selected color's original location.

▼ To Do

6

▼

▼   • Drag the Saturation slider left to decrease the saturation of the colors and
             right to increase it.

           • Drag the Lightness slider to increase or decrease the lightness of the image.

▲   4. Click OK when done.

Adjusting with the Brightness/Contrast Dialog Box

If you need to make a simple adjustment to the tonal range of an image that scanned too
dark, the Brightness/Contrast window (Image, Adjust, Brightness/Contrast) provides an
easy way to adjust everything at once (see Figure 6.12). Instead of separately correcting
the dark, middle, and light values, it applies the same correction throughout the image.

Although the Brightness/Contrast window doesn't give you the same control that you
would have if you made the adjustments using Levels or Curves, or even the Variations
window, it's quick and easy. Sometimes it's all you need. Many images are improved by
just raising the brightness and contrast by a couple of points. As always, be sure to check
the Preview box so that you can see the effect your changes have on the image.

FIGURE 6.12

*Use the sliders to
adjust the brightness
and contrast.*

Dragging the sliders to the right of the middle-point increases brightness or contrast. Dragging them to the left decreases it. If you're not happy with the results you get with this
tool, undo your changes and use the Variations window, or Levels or Curves, to adjust the
brightness and contrast.

Auto Contrast is occasionally helpful. It automatically maps the darkest and lightest pixels in the image to black-and-white, causing highlights to appear lighter and shadows
darker. It might not be the best way to make the necessary adjustments, but, if you are in
a hurry, it can save you some time.

Adjustment Layers

An important point to remember about color correction is that you can apply it to the whole picture, selectively to a single area, or to all but a selected area. When you apply a correction to the whole picture, it might improve some parts and make others worse, so you really need to look carefully at the end result and decide whether the good outweighs the bad.

Fortunately, there's an easy way to apply a correction and then change your mind. One of the best features of Photoshop is the capability to work in layers. (You'll learn all about layers in Hour 11, "Layers".) You can think of layers as sheets of cellophane that you place over your image and paint or paste on. If you like what you do, you can merge the layers so that the additions become part of the image. If not, you can throw them away and try again. In addition to the layers that you paint on, Photoshop lets you apply *adjustment layers*. These work like normal layers except that instead of holding paint or pasted pictures, they hold the color adjustments that you make to the image.

> **NEW TO VERSION 6** In Photoshop 6, you'll apply adjustment layers differently from how they were applied in previous versions. They're now on a pop-up menu you reach by clicking a button at the bottom of the Layers palette. (Look for the button with the half-black, half-white circle.)

To open an adjustment layer:

1. Click the black-and-white circular icon at the bottom of the Layers palette (see Figure 6.13).

FIGURE 6.13

The New Adjustment Layer pop-up menu.

2. Select the particular kind of adjustment that you want to make from the pop-up menu. Click OK to open the appropriate adjustment dialog box.

Summary

In this hour, you looked at working with color. Variations make simple, "by eye" adjustments, letting you choose from differently enhanced thumbnails. Histograms and Curves apply adjustments more scientifically. You learned how to make the sky a perfect blue and the grass a greener green. Now you know that adjusting levels lets you set limits for dark, middle, and light tones in an image. You have learned about Color Balance and how to apply changes to hue and saturation. You have seen how to change the brightness and contrast of an image.

Color adjustment is one of Photoshop's most used features, and one that you'll rely on whenever you need to touch up a photo or a scanned image. Practice with it as much as you can, using your own favorite images.

Q&A

Q Levels and Curves seem to do more or less the same thing. How do you know which to use?

A If the picture seems to have the right color balance (not too red, green, and so on) but is too dark or light, use Levels. If the colors aren't right, adjust the Curves for individual colors and for the RGB (full spectrum) channel.

Q I have a sepia-tinted photo (brown tones) that I have scanned into the computer, but the scan came out yellow. Is there a way to get rid of the yellow cast without losing the sepia?

A The easy way is to convert it to grayscale, so you get rid of *all* the color. Then convert it back to RGB. Open the Image, Adjust, Curves dialog box. Instead of RGB on the Channels pop-up menu, select red and drag the curve up until you have added an appropriate amount of red. Then set the pop-up menu to green and drag the curve down until you have added enough of that color. Finally, set the pop-up menu to blue and drag down until you have removed the blue and achieved a reasonable sepia. Experiment until you get the color you want, and then click OK.

Q If the picture's going to be printed in black-and-white for a newsletter, do I really need to adjust the color balance and stuff?

A Always leave your options open. Adjust a *copy* of the picture in Grayscale mode, just to make sure the contrast is good for reproduction. For that, you don't need to think about color. But, keep a copy in color in case you want to put the same picture on a Web page or do something else with it later.

Quiz

1. A picture came out too green. What should you do?

    a. Open Variations and choose More Red.

    b. Open Variations and choose More Magenta.

    c. Say you took it in Ireland.

2. A picture was taken on a foggy day, and its colors look "washed out." Is there any way to fix it?

    a. Increase the Saturation.

    b. Lower the Lightness.

    c. Paint over the picture with brighter colors.

3. How can I lessen the amount of change in the Variations window?

    a. Hold Shift+Control+P while you click the thumbnail.

    b. Use the Coarse–Fine slider.

    c. You can't.

Quiz Answers

1. b. On the color wheel, magenta is opposite green, so adding more magenta removes excess green.

2. a. Weak colors lack saturation. Increasing saturation slightly brightens the picture, but don't overdo!

3. b. Moving the slider toward Fine lessens the amount of correction applied each time. (Trying to implement answer a. would probably sprain a finger.)

Exercises

Download some of the photos from our Web site. To get to the Web site point your Web browser to

`http://www.mcp.com/sams/detail_sams.cfm?item=0672319551`

After the main book page has loaded, click the `Downloads` link to get to the files.

Then see how much further you can go. Turn a cloudy day into a sunny one, and vice versa. Experiment. Try your hand at changing the colors by eye, and then see whether you can duplicate your efforts by using the histograms.

6

Hour 7

Paintbrushes and Art Tools

You are already a quarter of the way through, and now it's time to have some fun. Photoshop, as I'm sure you realize, is mainly an image editor. It was created for that purpose, and it accomplishes its purpose very elegantly. Yet there is more to Photoshop than just editing. You can also create artwork here from scratch, just as in any good graphics program. Photoshop's art tools include the following:

- Airbrush
- Rubber Stamp and Pattern Stamp
- Paintbrush
- History Brush and Art History Brush
- Eraser, Background Eraser, and Magic Eraser
- Blur, Sharpen, and Smudge
- Dodge, Burn, and Sponge
- Pencil

- Gradient

- Paint Bucket

- Eyedropper

Figure 7.1 shows the Painting tools. We'll look at the most important ones--the Brushes, Pencil, and Line tools, and the Eraser in this hour. We'll cover the others as we need them in the next couple of hours.

FIGURE 7.1

Tools for painting and drawing.

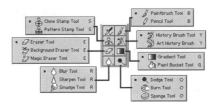

Each tool is highly configurable. You can adjust such settings as diameter, hardness, round-ness, angle, opacity, and so on. It's easy, too. You'll learn about this in the next few pages.

The Brushes Palette

Before discussing specific brushes, take a brief look at the Brushes palette, which drops down from the Tool Options bar after you select a tool that uses brush shapes. To open it, click on the downward-pointing arrow next to the window that shows the current brush shape. Although each tool has its own set of options, the Brushes palette (shown in Figure 7.2) works with all the art tools, from the Airbrush down to the Dodge Tool. (Only the pencil's brushes are different.) It gives you the ability to select any of Photo-shop's preset brush shapes or to create your own.

FIGURE 7.2

The Brushes palette, extended to show the texture brushes and brush options.

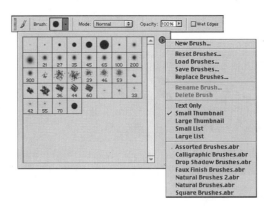

Just click to select one of the preset brush shapes. The size and shape you see in the box are the size and shape of the brush. The only exceptions are the brushes with numbers beneath, which indicate the diameter of the brush in pixels. A brush can be up to 999 pixels wide, which translates to almost 14 inches. Remember, clicking a shape doesn't select a tool. You have to do that in the toolbox or by typing a letter shortcut. The Brushes palette just influences the shape of the tool you select.

Photoshop comes with many different kinds of brushes. You can install the additional brush sets using the fly-out menu on the Brush palette.

Brush Options Dialog Box

Double-click a brush shape to open the Brush options dialog box (see Figure 7.3). Here you can select the diameter, hardness, spacing, angle, and roundness of the brushes.

The harder a brush is (closer to 100%), the more defined the edges of paint will be. A brush with a setting of around 20% has a much more diaphanous or translucent appearance.

FIGURE 7.3

The Brush Options dialog box lets you design custom brushes.

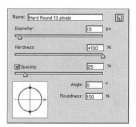

The next option is for Spacing. If left unselected, the speed of your mouse movements determines the spacing of discrete drops of paint. If you move more slowly, paint appears in a continuous line. If you move the mouse more quickly, circles of paint appear with spaces between them.

By selecting the Spacing check box, however, you are able to set a standard spacing of paint, no matter how fast you drag the mouse. Anything around 25% should give you a very smooth line of paint. As you increase the percentage (either by dragging the slider or entering a number into the box), the spaces increase (see Figure 7.4).

7

FIGURE 7.4

Spacing set at 25%, 50%, 100%, and 200%, respectively from top to bottom.

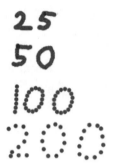

Finally, you also can set the Angle and Roundness of your brushes. Play around with this setting some. With a little experimenting, you can end up with a brush that behaves just as a real brush does--painting thicker and thinner depending on the angle of your stroke.

To make adjustments, you can enter values into the boxes provided, drag the sliders, or you can click and manipulate the graphic (on the lower-left of the options dialog box).

When you find a brush you are comfortable with, save it. Use the Brush Options dialog box to give it a name, and it will be available to you from then on. If you make up an assortment of brushes, you can save them as a group. There's a fly-out menu on the right side of the Brush palette. (Look for the right-pointing triangle.) Select Save Brushes to save a brush set.

FIGURE 7.5

The menu for the Brushes palette.

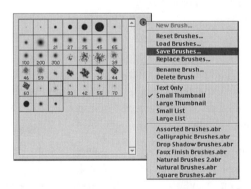

To open a set of your customized brushes, choose either Load Brushes to append brushes to the current set, or Replace Brushes to replace the current set. You'll find several sets of special brushes in Photoshop's Goodies folder.

Brush Options

In addition to the brush shape options, Photoshop also gives you some options for brush behavior. These are located on the Tool Options bar at the top of the screen (unless you've moved it).

Brush behavior options are set in the Tool Options bar, and they change according to the tool you're using at the time. Figure 7.5 also shows the options for the Paintbrush Tool.

Using the Opacity Slider

The first thing to notice in the Tool Options bar is the slider that sets the Opacity. Click and hold the right pointing arrow next to the Opacity field to enable the slider. A low setting applies a thin layer of paint--nearly transparent. The closer you come to 100%, the more concentrated the color is. Figure 7.6 contains some examples of different opacities.

FIGURE 7.6

I've applied white stripes over a background scene. The opacity percentages are listed below their stripes.

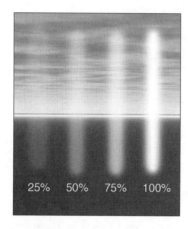

Using the Wet Edges Setting

Wet Edges creates a sort of water color effect when you paint. Figure 7.7 shows an example of the same brush and paint with Wet Edges on and off. Paint builds up at the edges of your brush, and, as long as you are holding the mouse down and painting, the paint stays "wet." In other words, you can paint over your previous strokes without building up additional layers of color. If, however, you release the mouse button and begin to paint again, you will be adding a new layer of paint, which creates an entirely new effect.

FIGURE 7.7

The Wet Edges effect darkens the edge of a stroke and makes the middle somewhat translucent.

Wet Edges On
Wet Edges Off

7

Setting Brush Dynamics

NEW TO VERSION 6 In previous editions of Photoshop, you could set a fade amount that simulated the effect of the brush gradually running out of paint. Photoshop 6 gives you much more control over the way a brush fades. The Brush Dynamics Window opens when you click the Brush icon at the far right of the Tool Options bar. You have three options for each of these settings: Off, On, and Stylus. Figure 7.8 shows the window and some sample strokes with the dynamics on.

FIGURE 7.8

These settings apply to any of the Painting tools.

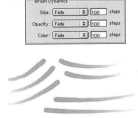

Setting Stylus Pressure

The Stylus options affect the way Photoshop responds to a pressure-sensitive digitizing tablet, such as the Wacom. If you don't have one of these devices, ignore it. If you do, when you use the tablet and stylus, you can set the way the stylus responds to your hand. Set the Brush Dynamics to Stylus, and then use the device control panel to select your settings. To most tablet users, it feels most natural and logical to let the pressure affect the brush size.

You'll also see a pop-up menu on the options bar with Normal as its default setting. This is the Blending Modes selector. Blending modes affect the way a layer of paint interacts with whatever is under it. You'll learn about them in the next hour. For now, just leave the Blending mode set to Normal.

Brushes

Now turn your attention to the Painting tools themselves. For the rest of this hour, you'll be working with the Airbrush, Paintbrushes, Eraser, and Pencil tools.

To Do: Working with the Painting Tools

To Do

Before you go any further, why not stop and try out some of these tools? Follow these steps:

1. Open a new page, making it big enough so that you have some elbow room. About six to eight inches square is fine.

▼ 2. On the right side of the screen, look for the Swatches palette. Click on the tab to bring it forward, if necessary. Click Swatches to open an electronic paintbox. For now, just click any color you like.

3. Press B to select the Paintbrush from the toolbox.

4. Click on the down pointing triangle next to the Brush icon to open the Brushes palette. Choose a brush.

5. Press and hold the mouse button as you move the brush over the canvas to paint.

▲ 6. Try the Airbrush and Eraser tools, too. Press J for Airbrush and E for Eraser. See what changing the options does for each tool.

The Airbrush

This tool, as its name suggests, sprays paint (or pixels) on the canvas. It's like an artist's airbrush that uses compressed air to spray paint through an adjustable nozzle. The Airbrush applies paint with diffused edges, and you can control how fast the paint is applied. You can adjust it to spray a constant stream or one that fades after a specified period. Experiment with different amounts of pressure and different brush sizes and shapes.

Remember that the longer you hold the Airbrush Tool in a single spot, the darker and more saturated a color becomes. Press J to activate the Airbrush or click it in the toolbox. (Why J? Think "jet" of paint.)

Figure 7.9 shows a drawing done with just the Airbrush. The spotty effect comes from using a Blending mode called Dissolve. (You'll learn about Blending modes in Hour 8, "Digital Painting.")

FIGURE 7.9
Varying the pressure and changing brush sizes gives the picture some variety.

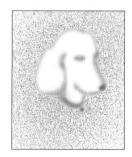

The Paintbrush

The Paintbrush Tool is the workhorse of all the painting tools in Photoshop. Press B to use the Brush, or select it in the toolbox. The Paintbrush behaves very much like the Airbrush, only paint is applied more evenly. That is to say, if you hold the mouse clicked in one area, paint does not continue to flow onto the canvas.

7

Although you can press Caps Lock to get a precision painting cursor, there is an even better option. Instead select Edit→ Preferences→Display & Cursors. In the dialog box that appears, look into the Painting Cursors section. An option is there that enables you to select from the following choices: Standard, Precise, and Brush Size. Choose Brush Size because this changes your painting cursor from a paintbrush or a crosshair to a circle that is the actual size of your brush.

If you need to paint a straight line, constrained either vertically or horizontally, hold down the Shift key as you drag the brush. To draw a straight line between two points, click once on the canvas to set the first point, and then Shift+click to mark the end point. A line draws itself between the two points. Figure 7.10 shows some work with the Photoshop Paintbrushes.

FIGURE 7.10

The pepper was painted with several different brushes.

The History Brush

The History Brush is a very useful tool when you're making changes in an image and aren't sure exactly how much change to make or where to make it. It enables you to selectively put back parts of the picture in which you've made a change, by selecting a brush size and painting out the new image with the old one. In Figure 7.11, I have applied the glass distortion filter to a photo, and then used the History Brush to undo the effect of the filter in one area of the photo.

FIGURE 7.11

Notice that only the area where I've applied the History Brush is clear.

To use the History Brush, click the box at the left side of the History palette next to the image or state you want to use as the source. In Figure 7.11, I clicked the original image because I wanted to put parts of it back into the altered version. Then, choose a brush shape, click on the History Brush, and start painting.

The Art History Brush shares a box on the Tool palette with the History Brush, and you can press Shift+Y to toggle between them. The Art History Brush Tool paints with a variety of stylized strokes, but--like the History Brush--it uses the source data from a specified history state or snapshot. Following the motto "Different strokes for different folks," it allows you to select from a menu of different kinds of strokes. Then you paint onto the image with the chosen stroke and change your image into something perhaps resembling an impressionistic watercolor, pointillist oil, or some other "artistic" style. Figure 7.12 shows the Art History Brush Styles menu on the Tool Options bar.

FIGURE 7.12

Curls imitate Van Gogh at his wildest; Dab does Monet; and Loose Medium resembles a Renoir. Experimenting with these is fun!

In Figure 7.13, I've applied the Art History Brush to a photo, and then gone back into it with the History Brush to put back some of the edges and detail.

FIGURE 7.13

Combining the Art History Brush and the History Brush lets you restore some of the original image after you've changed it.

7

To Do: Apply the Art History Brush

▼ To Do

Let's try the Art History Brush.

1. Open an image. On the History palette, click the left column of the state you want to use as the source for the Art History Brush Tool. You'll see a brush icon next to the thumbnail image.

2. Double-click the Art History Brush. The Art History Brush Tool is grouped with the History Brush Tool in the toolbox.

3. Set the Blending mode to normal (for now; you'll learn more about Blending modes later). Set the opacity to 75%. You can change it as you see the effect.

4. Choose an option from the Paint Style menu, located to the left of the Fidelity setting in the Tool Options bar. This choice controls the shape of the paint stroke.

5. Enter a value for Fidelity or drag the slider to control how much the paint color deviates from the color in the source. The lower the fidelity, the more the color will vary from the source.

6. For Area, enter a value to specify the area covered by the paint strokes. Larger sizes mean larger areas covered and more paint strokes.

7. Enter a Spacing value or drag the slider to limit the regions where paint strokes can be applied. A low tolerance lets you paint unlimited strokes anywhere in the image. A high tolerance limits paint strokes to areas that differ significantly from the color in the source.

▲ 8. Select a brush shape and start painting.

The Art History Brush is capable of some really nice effects, if you spend time learning to work with its settings. Like any complex tool, it takes practice to use correctly.

The Eraser

The next tool in the toolbox that we'll investigate is one that most of us, unfortunately, have to use far too often--the Eraser Tool. You'll quickly learn that the hotkey to select the eraser is E. One nice thing about the Eraser is that it, too, can be undone, so if you happen to rid the canvas of an essential element that you wanted to keep, just choose Edit→Undo to restore.

The Eraser Tool is unique in that it can replicate the characteristics of the other tools. It can erase with soft edges as if it were a paintbrush painting with bleach. It can erase a single line of pixels, as if it were a pencil, or it can erase some of the density of the image, as if it were an airbrush. Of course, it can also act as an ordinary block eraser, removing whatever's there. The Options bar lets you determine how the eraser will work; whether it will be a block or a brush; how much you want to erase; and even whether you want to erase to a step on the History palette or to the background. The Eraser's Options bar is shown in Figure 7.14.

FIGURE **7.14**

The Eraser and its options.

The Pressure slider controls how much is erased. This is useful for blending parts of images, and it also can create a nice watercolor effect.

The Fade option, found in the toolbar's Brush Dynamics menu, works just like the Fade option in the Airbrush Tool. After a certain number of steps, which you specify, the Eraser no longer erases. This is useful to create feathering around irregularly shaped images. Set the Opacity slider to around 75% and the Fade to about eight steps and then drag away from the image you want to feather.

Instead of erasing to the background, you can choose Erase to History. This command lets the Eraser work with the History palette, so you are actually erasing to an earlier version of the picture. Before you begin to erase or make any other drastic changes to your picture, you can take a snapshot of it by choosing New Snapshot from the History palette.

Experiment with this tool until you really understand what it's doing. It can save you lots of time when you're trying new techniques.

The other two erasers in the set are the Background Eraser and Magic Eraser. They share space in the toolbox with the regular Eraser. These erasers make it easier for you to erase sections of a layer to transparency. This can be helpful, for instance, if you need to delete the background area around a hard-edged object. The Background Eraser Tool lets you erase pixels on a layer to transparency as you drag. By specifying different Sampling and Tolerance options, you can control the range of the transparency and the sharpness of its boundaries. In Figure 7.15, I've set the background color to the color of the carpet in my photo and am using the background eraser to remove only the carpet.

FIGURE **7.15**

You have to be extra careful if the foreground object has colors similar to the background.

7

When you click in a layer with the Magic Eraser Tool, the tool automatically erases all similar pixels to transparency. You can choose to erase contiguous pixels only or all similar pixels on the current layer.

To Do: Use the Magic Eraser Tool

Now, let's try the Magic Eraser. Pick any image that has an area of fairly even color, like a sky.

1. Select the Magic Eraser. The toolbar will change to show its options.

2. Enter a Tolerance value. The tolerance defines the range of colors that can be erased. A low tolerance erases pixels within a range of color values very similar to the pixel you click. A high tolerance erases pixels within a broader range.

3. Specify the opacity to define how much is erased. An opacity of 100% erases pixels to complete transparency. Lower opacity erases pixels to partial transparency.

4. Set up the remaining options as needed:

    • Select Use All Layers if you want to sample the erased color using combined data from all visible layers.

    • Select Anti-aliased to smooth the edges of the area you erase.

    • Select Contiguous to erase only pixels of the same color contiguous to the one you click, or leave it unselected to erase all similar pixels in the image.

5. Click in the part of the layer you want to erase. All similar pixels within the specified tolerance range will be erased to transparency.

In Figure 7.16, you can see the results of using the Magic Eraser Tool. You might have to make several selections to erase all of the area you want to remove. You might also need to use the regular Eraser to clean up pixels it misses. But this tool is by far the fastest way to remove the background from an image. You'll use it a lot in Hour 20, "Compositing," when you work on composite images.

FIGURE 7.16

The Magic Eraser removes all pixels that are similar to the one you click.

The Pencil

The Pencil Tool, in large measure, works like the Paintbrush Tool, except that it can only create hard-edged lines--that is to say, lines that don't fade at the edges as paintbrush lines can. Click the Pencil Tool in the toolbox or press B to select it. (Press Shift+B if the Brush Tool is selected.) It shares space in the toolbox with the Paintbrush. Selecting it activates its options on the bar, as shown in Figure 7.17.

FIGURE 7.17

The Pencil Tool options.

You can set the diameter of your Pencil in the Brushes option palette, but remember, hardness is not an option. You can, however, set all the other options, just as we have with all the other tools up to now--I won't bore you with a recap.

The Pencil Tool does have one option, though, that you haven't seen in the tools we've looked at so far.

In the Tool Options bar, there is a check box for Auto Erase. When you turn on Auto Erase, any time you start to draw on a part of the canvas that already has a pencil line on it, your Pencil becomes an Eraser and will erase until you release the mouse button.

Summary

Photoshop's painting tools are easy and fun to use. In this hour, you took a look at the Airbrush, Paintbrush, History Brush, Pencil, and Eraser tools. Brush shapes apply to all the tools, not just to the Paintbrush. You can alter the brush shape or its behavior by using the controls on the Tool Options bar. You learned to activate the Airbrush, Paintbrush, Pencil, or Eraser by pressing a single keyboard letter. You learned about some of the tool options and how they affect the quality of the brush stroke.

Q&A

Q Can I make a custom brush that's not round?

A Sure. You can even make part of your image into a custom brush. Use the rectangular Marquee to select a portion of an image. (You can use the Pencil Tool to draw a particular brush shape if you want.) With the Marquee active, select Define Brushes from the Palette menu on the Brushes palette. The new brush appears on the Brushes palette. Double-click it to set its spacing option. Set Anti-aliased to make the brush blend with the background image. When you're done creating brushes, choose Save Brushes from the Brush Options palette menu to save your current brush set.

7

Q Real airbrushes can spray a very light mist of color. How can I duplicate this effect?

A On the Options menu, set the pressure very low. A large brush and a pressure of 10 or less will give you the effect you want.

Q How do I make my brush strokes look like a watercolor?

A Easy. Just click the Wet Edges check box. If you'd rather use "oil paint," leave the check box unchecked.

Quiz

1. Are there other brush sets? If so, where?

    a. No, but you can make your own.

    b. Photoshop comes with many sets of pre-made brushes. Check the fly-out menu on the Brush palette.

2. What happens if I hold the Airbrush in one spot?

    a. Nothing.

    b. You deposit more paint in that spot.

    c. The paint runs down the screen.

Quiz Answers

1. b. Actually, answer a. is only partly wrong. You can make your own brushes and brush sets, and you can use the ones Adobe provides.

2. b. Just like with a can of spray paint, if you hold the Airbrush in one spot, the paint piles up.

Exercises

Let's do some more practice with the Airbrush, Paintbrush, and Eraser. Follow along with these steps:

1. Start by opening a new page. Make it at least six inches square so that you have room to work.

2. Click the Paintbrush in the toolbox. Set your opacity to 100%, choose a medium size, hard-edged brush, and draw a star.

3. Click the check box to turn on Wet Edges and draw another star.

4. Choose a soft-edged brush and draw another star.

5. Now turn off Wet Edges and draw another star with the soft-edged brush. Your result should look something like Figure 7.18.

Okay, it's not great art, but you have four distinctly different brush looks.

Figure 7.18

Four kinds of brush strokes.

6. Scroll to the top of the History palette and click the blank page labeled New. This returns to your freshly opened page, minus stars. (It's a quick way to erase everything.)

7. Press J to activate the Airbrush. Set the pressure to 100%, and draw a star.

8. Set the pressure to 50%, by typing the number **5**, and draw another star. (You can change Paintbrush Opacity settings by typing a number, too.)

9. Change brushes. If you have been using a soft-edged brush with the Airbrush, try a hard one, or vice versa. Draw more stars with different brushes and pressure settings.

10. Press E to bring up the Eraser. Set the Eraser mode to Paintbrush and the Opacity to 50%. (Type a number **5**.) Try to erase one of your stars. Don't click the mouse more than once while you're erasing.

11. Change the Opacity to 100%, and erase another star.

12. Experiment with different settings until you are comfortable with these tools.

7

HOUR 8

Digital Painting

Now that you know a little bit about brushes and Painting tools, you need to know how to choose some colors with which to paint. Some of the nice things about digital paint are that it doesn't get under your fingernails, and you don't have to clean out your paintbrushes afterward.

In this hour, you're going to learn about choosing and applying color. There are several ways of choosing colors, and we'll also discuss Blending modes, which affect the way colors (and layers) interact with each other.

Foreground and Background Colors

At any given moment while working with Photoshop, you have two colors available. Only two? Don't worry—that's really kind of misleading. Perhaps it's better to say that you have two colors *active*, a foreground color and a background color. The *foreground color* is the one you use to paint, to fill or stroke a selection. It's the color that's currently on your brush or pencil. (You'll learn about filling and stroking later when we talk about paths.) The *background color* is the color Photoshop uses when you erase or delete a selected area on the background layer. You might think of it as the color of the canvas under your painting.

Selecting Colors

The fastest and easiest way to select color is to use the foreground or background swatch in the toolbox (see Figure 8.1). The color swatch to the upper-left is your foreground color, and the one to the lower-right is the background color. You can set either color by clicking its swatch.

NEW TERM *Swatches* are those two little squares of color at the bottom of the toolbox—not overpriced wristwatches.

FIGURE 8.1
*Click to select the fore-
ground or background
color.*

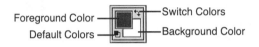

The small icon to the lower-left of the swatches, which looks like a miniature version of the swatches, resets to the default colors (black and white). The little curved arrow to the upper-right of the swatches toggles between background and foreground colors.

> Here are a couple of quick keyboard shortcuts for you. You can reset the default colors by pressing D. Press X to toggle between the background and foreground colors.

To change the color of either of these swatches, click the swatch. This opens the Color Picker that you selected in the Display and Cursors preferences dialog box. If you haven't made a choice, the Photoshop Color Picker is selected by default. Your other choice is either the Apple or Windows Color Picker, depending on which operating system you use. The examples in this hour use the Photoshop Color Picker.

The Color Picker

Photoshop's Color Picker lets you select a foreground or background color in any of several ways. Figure 8.2 shows the Color Picker window. You can click the color spectrum to select a color, or drag the triangle slider up or down if you'd rather. You can click the large swatch (the color field) to select a color, or you can enter numbers in any one of the color model boxes.

By default, the Color Picker opens in HSB model, which stands for Hue, Saturation, Brightness, with the Hue radio button active. This makes the color field show you all the possible saturation and brightness of the particular hue that's selected. If you click anywhere in the color field, you'll see the saturation and brightness numbers change, but the Hue setting remains the same.

Hue = Color, measured as location on the color wheel in degrees.

Saturation = Strength of the color measured as percentage from 0% (gray) to 100% (fully saturated color).

Brightness = Relative lightness of the color measured as a percentage from 0% (black) to 100% (white).

FIGURE 8.2

The Photoshop Color Picker.

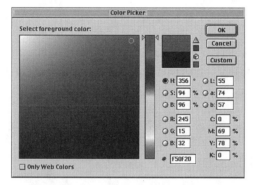

If you click the Saturation button, the color field changes to something like the one in Figure 8.3. It shows you all the possible hues at the designated saturation value. If you click anywhere in the color field, the other numbers change, but the saturation stays the same.

FIGURE 8.3

Saturation Color Picker.

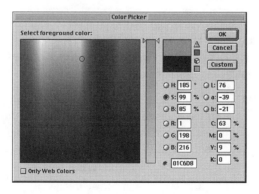

HSB mode is the one artists generally prefer because it's easy to understand. You're not stuck with it, though. Feel free to select RGB as a working model. This is the model that governs how your computer displays color. (It uses red, green, and blue, just like a projection television, for instance.)

It's a little bit more complicated to choose a color in the RGB mode. When you click the Red radio button, the color that you see in the color field is just as likely to be blue or green. Here's where the spectrum slider and the numbers start to make a difference.

Remember, in this model, colors are made from three components, red, green, and blue, in amounts from 0 to 255. Pure red has a value of 255 Red, 0 Green, and 0 Blue. If you set those numbers in the Color Picker, as I have in Figure 8.4, the pure red will be way down in the lower-left corner of the color field. Colors representing mixes of green and blue with red will fill the rest of the field. Because we're dealing with relatively small amounts of green and blue, the colors you'll actually see mixed with the red are yellow and magenta. The yellow comes from the addition of green, and the magenta from the addition of blue.

FIGURE 8.4

The selected color is mixed with percentages of the other two primaries.

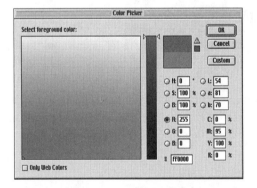

The best way to learn about this color mode is to work with it. Open up your Color Picker and click a color. Then watch the numbers as you click a different one. Explore the different radio button settings and their color fields.

Ever wondered about those little letters and numbers at the bottom of the window? You can see the HTML code for the Web-safe color closest to any color you select, right there at the bottom of the dialog box. Those codes are in hexadecimal format, ready to enter in your Web page HTML source, if you're one of those brave Web warriors who hand-codes HTML. If not, don't worry about it. When you place your Photoshop picture into your Web creation program, it'll all happen automatically.

The Color Palette

The Color palette has several advantages over the Color Picker when you're working in Photoshop. First of all, you can leave it open on the desktop, so you can change colors without having to go through all the fuss of clicking a swatch in the toolbox, finding the color, and okaying your choice. For those of us who are mathematically challenged, there are fewer numbers to contend with, and the ones you see, as in Figure 8.5, are logically related to the sliders. By default, it opens in whatever mode you used last, but you can set it to Grayscale, or whichever color model you prefer to work in, by using the pop-out menu as shown in Figure 8.5. You can even choose Web colors, as a variant of RGB.

FIGURE 8.5

The Color palette and its menu.

The menu also enables you to reset the color bar at the bottom of the Color Palette window, according to the color model with which you are working. If your work will be printed and you want to avoid using colors that are out of gamut (or can't be achieved with CMYK inks), you can set the color bar to the CMYK spectrum and know that any color you click will be printable. Similarly, if you click Make Ramp Web Safe, the only colors displayed on the color bar will be the 216 colors that all current Web browsers can display.

FIGURE 8.6

If you're using your pictures on the Web, use the Web Safe color ramp and Web color sliders, as shown here.

The Swatches Palette

Remember, I said at the beginning of the hour that Photoshop gives you several ways of choosing colors? Well, here's the easiest one of all. The Swatch palette (shown in Figure 8.7) works like a child's box of watercolors on your screen. You simply dip your "brush" in a color and paint with it. To choose a foreground color, simply click the one you want.

To choose a background color, press Option+click (Mac) or Alt+click (Windows) to
select the color you want to use.

FIGURE **8.7**

*The Swatches palette
and its pop-out menu.*

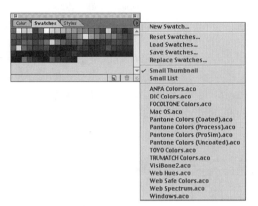

The Swatches palette, by default, opens with the current system palette. You can choose
colors from the Color Picker to add to the Swatches palette, or you can select a color
system, such as PANTONE, Focoltone, Trumatch, or Toyo, and have an additional 700 to
1000 or more *Process Color* (printing ink color) swatches appended to the palette. You
can also add custom color to it using the Eyedropper Tool described in the next section.

To Do: Add New Colors from the Color Picker onto Your Palette

Swatches are easy to work with, but Photoshop's choices won't always match yours.
Here's how to add your own colors to the swatch set.

1. Click the foreground color swatch in the toolbox.
2. Use the Color Picker to select the desired color and click OK.
3. Open the Swatches palette (Window→Show Swatches).
4. Using the tab in the lower-right corner of the Swatches palette, drag the window
   out so that it resembles the one in Figure 8.8.

FIGURE **8.8**

*Adding a new color to
the Swatches palette.*

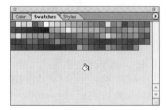

▼   5. Move your cursor into the space below the existing swatches. It changes into the
         Paint Bucket Tool.

       6. Click anywhere in the unused space, and the new color is added after the existing
          colors. You'll be asked to give the new color a name.

       7. If you press Shift, you can add the new color anywhere you like, replacing what-
▲   ever swatch you click.

If you use a lot of the same colors over and over, and they are not represented in any of
the palettes that ship with Photoshop, just elect to save a palette. Choose Save Swatches
from the Swatches palette menu. This saves you time and the headache of having to reselect all your favorite colors each time you open Photoshop. You can also use the
Swatches palette menu to open any of the 15 or so different swatch palettes that ship
with Photoshop. Color Swatches are saved in the Presets folder.

The Eyedropper Tool

You've seen the Eyedropper appear when you moved the pointer over a color swatch or
over the color bar in the Color Palette window. Its function, quite obviously and intu-
itively, is to pick up a bit of whatever color you touch it to, making that the active color.
What's neat about this tool is that is works in the same way on a picture—you can pick
up a bit of sky blue, grass green, or skin and not have to try to identify a match for it
with the Color Picker.

The Eyedropper Tool is extremely helpful, especially when you are retouching a picture
and need to duplicate the colors in it. Click it on any spot in the image and the color
underneath its tip becomes the new foreground color. Use Option+click (Mac) or
Alt+click (Windows) to select a background color instead. If you drag the Eyedropper
across an image, the swatch of color in the toolbox changes each time the Eyedropper
touches a new color.

Remember that the Eyedropper, like all the tools, is active only at its *hot
spot*, in this case, right at the tip. If you find it hard to work with the hot
spot, just go to Preferences→Display Cursors, and change the display to
Precise in the Other Cursors area.

Eyedropper Options, on the Tool Options bar shown in Figure 8.9, lets you select how
much of a sample to pick up with the Eyedropper. You can take a single pixel sample, or
average a 3×3– or 5×5–pixel color sample.

FIGURE 8.9

Set the Eyedropper
Options here.

You can convert any other Painting tool (except the Eraser) into an Eyedropper to change foreground colors on-the-fly by pressing Option (Mac) or Alt (Windows) while you're working.

To Do: Choose a Color and Save It as a Swatch

Here's another way to add to the Swatches palette. This time we'll borrow colors from a photo.

1. Click the Eyedropper Tool in the toolbox, or press I to select it.

2. Click the image at the spot where you want to capture the color. If you're saving a background color, Option+click (Mac) or Alt+click (Windows) the color you want.

3. Open the Swatches palette, if it's not already open. Put the Eyedropper on any empty (gray) space in the Swatch palette. It turns into a Paint Bucket.

4. Click once to put a swatch of the selected color into the palette.

5. Choose Save Swatches from the palette's pull-out menu.

6. Follow the usual procedure to name your Swatch file, and save it in Photoshop Presets.

To load a saved swatch file, use the Swatch palette's pull-out menu. Select Load Swatches. Locate the Swatch file you want to use in the Presets folder, as shown in Figure 8.10, and click OK.

FIGURE 8.10

The swatches are
identified with
swatch icons. For
Windows users, they
have an .aco *extension*
in addition to the icon.

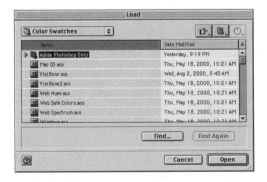

To Do: Using the Eyedropper and Paintbrush

Let's take a few minutes to do some practicing with the Brush and Eyedropper. Pick out a picture that has lots of color and open it in Photoshop. Then perform the following steps:

1. Before you begin, choose Save a Copy from the File menu and save a back-up copy of your picture, just in case you accidentally save a messed-up version.

2. Press B to activate the Paintbrush Tool. Open the Brush palette and choose a medium-sized brush shape.

3. Put the Paintbrush on an area of dark color in the picture, as I have in Figure 8.11. Press Option (Mac) or Alt (Windows). The Paintbrush turns into an Eyedropper and copies the dark color to the foreground.

FIGURE 8.11

Click to copy the color.

4. Paint on the picture with the color you've just picked up.

5. Open the Color palette (Window→Show Color) if it's not already open. Put your brush onto the Color bar at the bottom of the palette. It turns into an Eyedropper.

6. Choose another color and add something else to your picture. Use the same brush or switch to the Pencil (press Shift+B) or Airbrush (press J). Experiment with colors and brushes until you feel comfortable with them.

7. If you run out of space to paint, choose File→Revert to go back to the original version of the picture and start over.

As you get accustomed to using Photoshop, or any other graphics program for that matter, you'll begin to realize that drawing with a mouse isn't really the best way to draw. As for using the trackball and touchpad—well, they're even more difficult. They simply weren't designed for artwork.

The natural way to draw is to pick up a pencil or pen or brush and draw on something. People have been doing it for thousands of years, all the way back to cave painters at Lascaux, who used crude crayons made of animal fat and colored clays; the ancient Sumerians, who used a stylus and slab of wet clay; and the Egyptians, who wrote and drew with squid ink and feathers on papyrus.

Today, we have something much better—graphics tablets that work with Photoshop and programs like it. These consist of a flat drawing surface, tethered to the computer by a cable, and a stylus about the size and weight of a ballpoint pen. The drawing surface is sensitized to "read" the motion and pressure of the stylus and sends the input to the screen. A tablet like the Wacom Graphire 4x5 costs less than $100 and will save you a good deal of time and frustration. Try one at your friendly local computer store, and you'll be sold on it, too.

Blending Modes

In the real world, when you place a second brush full of paint over one that's already there, different things happen, depending on the color of the paint you're applying—how opaque it is, whether the first layer is wet or dry, and so on. In Photoshop, you can control all these factors by applying what's called *Blending modes*. You'll find them on a pop-up list in the Tool Options bar, as shown in Figure 8.12. Blending modes apply to all tools that can draw or paint, including the Pencil, Rubber Stamp, and Gradient tools, as well as the more obvious ones. As you can see, there are quite a few different ones. Take a quick look at the Blending modes and how they work.

FIGURE 8.12

This shows the Airbrush blending modes. Other tools have similar choices.

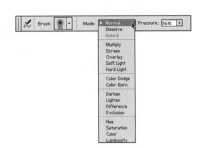

8

Suppose that you're working with only two colors. One is the *base* color, the one that's already in place. The second is the *blend* color, the one that you apply with each Blending mode enabled. You get a third color, a *result* that varies according to how you blend the first two.

Figures 8.13–8.30 display what happens when you choose each of the options. (The examples were painted with a firm brush in lime green on a hot pink background.)

FIGURE 8.13
Normal—*This is the default mode. The blend color replaces the base color.*

FIGURE 8.14
Dissolve—*A random number of pixels become the blend color. Gives a splattered or "dry brush" effect.*

FIGURE 8.15
Behind—*Works only on transparent parts of a layer. You appear to be painting on the back of a sheet of acetate laid over the picture. (Behind is not available if nothing is transparent, or if there's no layer other than the background.) In Figure 8.15, the triangles were drawn first, in Normal node, then the word added with the blending mode changed to Behind.*

FIGURE 8.16

Multiply—*Multiplies the base color by the blend color, giving you a darker result color. The effect is like drawing over the picture with a magic marker. Where the background is light, you see the original blend color.*

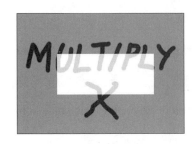

FIGURE 8.17

Screen—*Multiplies the base color by the inverse of the blend color, giving you a lighter result color. The effect is like painting with bleach. The hearts were drawn with the brush set to Wet Edges.*

FIGURE 8.18

Overlay—*Either multiplies or screens, depending on the base color. Preserves the highlights and shadows of the base color. If the two colors have similar brightness, the effect is subtle. In this example, I went over the drawing several times to build up some color.*

8

FIGURE 8.19
Soft Light—*Darkens or lightens depending on the blend color. The effect is said to be similar to shining a diffused spotlight on the image. With a light blend color, it has very little effect.*

FIGURE 8.20
Hard Light—*Multiplies or screens the colors, depending on the blend color. The effect is similar to shining a harsh spotlight on the image.*

FIGURE 8.21
Color Dodge—*Brightens the base color to match the value of the blend color.*

FIGURE 8.22
Color Burn—*Darkens the base color to match the value of the blend color. The zigzag was drawn using Wet Edges.*

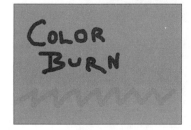

FIGURE 8.23

Darken—*Evaluates the color information in each channel and assigns either the base color or the blend color, whichever is darker, as the result color. Lighter pixels are replaced, but darker ones don't change.*

FIGURE 8.24

Lighten—*Evaluates the color information in each channel and assigns either the base color or the blend color, whichever is lighter, as the result color. Darker pixels are replaced, but lighter ones don't change. This is the exact opposite of Darken. The flower was drawn with Wet Edges.*

FIGURE 8.25

Difference—*Compares brightness values in the base and blend colors, and subtracts the lighter. Overlaps are interesting in this mode. They cancel the previous action.*

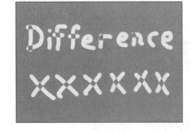

FIGURE 8.26

Exclusion—*Similar to the Difference mode, but has a softer effect.*

FIGURE 8.27

Hue—*Gives you a result combining the luminance and saturation of the base color and the hue of the blend color.*

FIGURE 8.28

Saturation—*Gives you a color with the luminance and hue of the base color and the saturation of the blend color. Unless you reduce the saturation of the blend color significantly, nothing shows.*

FIGURE 8.29

Color—*Combines the luminance of the base color with the hue and saturation of the blend color. Useful for coloring monochrome images because Color mode retains the gray levels.*

8

FIGURE **8.30**

Luminosity—*Gives a result color with the hue and saturation of the base color and the luminance of the blend color. Opposite effect to Color Blend mode.*

Summary

In this very full hour, we covered the different ways to choose and apply color to a picture in Photoshop. First, you learned the difference between the foreground color (the color that's on your brush or pencil) and the background color (the color of the canvas under the painting).

The Color Picker, Color palette, and Swatch palette all contain colors with which you can paint. The Color palette and Swatch palette are easier to use than the Color Picker because you can leave either one of them open on the desktop as you work. You learned to use the Eyedropper Tool with the Paintbrush to choose colors from the palette or from the picture itself.

Finally, we covered Blending modes, the way that two layers of paint or image interact with each other.

Q&A

Q The Color Picker has too many buttons and numbers in it! Which ones should I use if I want to change colors?

A If picking colors by numbers is difficult for you, as it is for me, use my solution. Forget the numbers and click directly on the color you like. Either click the color bar at the bottom of the Color palette, or click a swatch to open the color picker.

Q Is it better to use the Photoshop Color Picker instead of the Apple or Windows version?

A I think so. Even though the Macintosh color pickers give you lots of different ways to choose colors, I think the Photoshop version is easier to understand and to use. The same is true of the Windows color picker.

Q What happens when I have the Eyedropper set to sample a 5×5–pixel area, and there is more than one color there?

A Photoshop takes an average of all 25 pixels in the square and makes that the selected color.

Q **Under the Swatches listings, I've heard of PANTONE, but what are all the others?**

A Like PANTONE, they are sets of spot color inks. Printing systems can use many brands of inks. If you are sending work to a printshop, be sure to ask what spot color system they use.

Quiz

1. Blending involves

    a. Taking paint and mixing it in a bucket.

    b. Using home appliances.

    c. Being able to blend colors in different ways in Photoshop.

2. How many *active* colors do you have to work with in Photoshop?

    a. 16 million

    b. 256

    c. 2

3. How do I get black-and-white as my foreground and background colors?

    a. Select them from the Color Picker.

    b. Press D.

    c. Sample them from the image with the Eyedropper Tool.

Quiz Answers

1. c. Photoshop can blend colors much as you can on a canvas with real paint.

2. c. Remember, your foreground and background colors are the active colors, not the total number of colors available.

3. b. Actually, any of these will work, but b. is the easiest.

Exercises

To further explore this hour's topic of picking Color and Blending modes, fire up your Web browser and visit the Museum of Modern Art (www.moma.org). Navigate to the painting and sculpture section and look through the collection. Pay special attention to the use of color and blending effects. (Click the small images on the index page to see larger versions.)

Compare and contrast the use of color and blending in Van Gogh's *Starry Night* and Rousseau's *The Dream*. See whether you can duplicate Van Gogh's brush strokes. (Wet edges are part of the secret.)

HOUR 9

Moving Paint

Did you ever wonder why artists always have those paint soaked rags lying around, and why they always have paint on their hands, under their finger-nails, and all over their clothes? It's because you don't just paint with a brush; you sometimes paint with your finger, or with a piece of cloth, or with some other tool that will help you blend the paint or lighten or darken it just a little bit. In this hour, you will learn the tricks that painters and dark-room technicians have been using ever since their respective art forms were invented.

Smudges

Smudge is the artist's term for blending two or more colors. In Photoshop, there are, naturally, several ways of doing it. There are several ways of doing virtually anything in Photoshop. Be that as it may, the Smudge Tool is the most obvious and the quickest way to blend something into its background.

Using the Smudge Tool

The Smudge Tool looks like, and works like, a finger. It's in the same toolbox compartment with the Blur and Sharpen tools. The Smudge Tool picks up color from wherever you start to drag it and moves it in the direction in which you drag. Honestly, nothing could be much simpler. You do, however, have to use the Tool Options bar to set the pressure of your smudging finger. At 100% pressure, the finger simply wipes away the paint. At 50%, it smears it. At 25%, the smear is smaller. Figure 9.1 shows these different smear pressures. Photoshop considers the Smudge Tool to be a brush, so you can set the width of the "finger" by choosing an appropriate brush size from the Brush palette.

FIGURE 9.1

Smudges at different pressure settings.

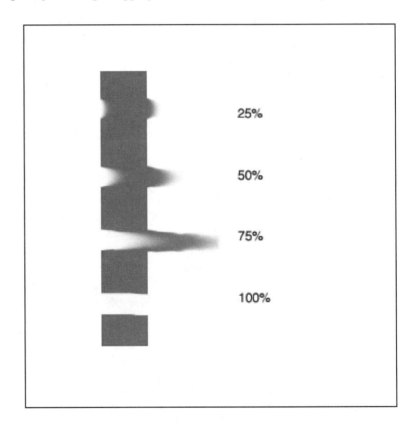

You can also use the Smudge Tool to mimic finger painting. This option starts each stroke with the foreground color. You'll find it quite handy if you need to blend some color into an existing picture, perhaps to hide something that's part of the original photo that you'd rather do without. Figure 9.2 shows an example of finger painting.

FIGURE 9.2

There were some lumps you'd expect to find in a barnyard, but not in a photo. I just smudged them out.

9

Setting Smudge Options

Pressure and finger painting options and blending modes are set in the Tool Options bar, shown in Figure 9.3. Click and hold the arrow next to the pressure setting to access the setting slider, and drag the slider to set the pressure. If you'd rather not access the slider, type a single digit to set it to a multiple of 10. For instance, type **4** to set to 40. (That trick works with all of Photoshop's sliders.) If you like that shortcut but want more precise control, simply type the digits of the measurement you desire in quick succession.

FIGURE 9.3

The Smudge Tool Options bar.

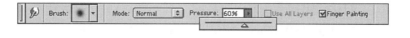

Check Finger Painting if you want to use the Smudge Tool to add some smudged color as you drag. Otherwise, leave the check box empty.

The Blending modes are on a pull-down menu. This tool doesn't give you all the Blending mode options you learned about in the previous hour, but you can choose-- aside from Normal--Darken, Lighten, Hue, Saturation, Color, or Luminosity. Of these, Darken and Lighten are obviously the most useful. The Darken and Lighten modes only affect pixels that are lighter or darker, respectively, than the beginning color. The Darken mode changes lighter pixels and the Lighten mode affects darker pixels.

If the Smudge Tool doesn't achieve the effect you intended, there's also a Smudge stick filter, which you'll learn about in Hour 15, "Filters to Make Your Picture Artistic." *Filters*, in case you haven't encountered the term before, are tools that apply special effects to your picture. Photoshop has 99 different filters.

Focus Tools

Now turn your attention to the Focus tools. These tools, Blur and Sharpen, are great for touching up an image, fixing tiny flaws, and bringing items into sharper contrast. They can't save a really bad photo, but they can do wonders for one that's just a little bit "off." Sharpen can bring up the contrast to create the illusion of sharper focus, while Blur is most useful to rid the background of unwanted clutter and to de-emphasize parts of the picture that you don't want viewers to notice. The focus tools can be seen in Figure 9.4.

FIGURE 9.4

The Focus tools, with Smudge thrown in for good measure.

The Blur Tool

The Blur Tool, simply put, creates blurs in images. By blurs, I mean a softening or evening out of pixel values. Select the Blur Tool from the toolbox. The Tool Options bar will show you the Blur Tool's options (see Figure 9.5). When you are working with the Blur Tool, you can temporarily select the Sharpen Tool (and vice versa) by pressing Option (Mac) or Alt (Windows). The Use All Layers option is only available if your image has more than one layer.

FIGURE 9.5

The Blur Tool Options bar.

Options for the Blur and Sharpen tools are much the same as those for the Smudge Tool described earlier. You have the same choices of Blending mode and the same Pressure settings.

Figure 9.6 shows a close look at the Blur Tool's effect. The picture had too much of the background in focus, detracting from the flowers. Working with the Blur Tool let me knock the bark mulch out of focus so that the viewer's attention goes where it belongs, to the narcissus. Figure 9.7 shows the picture before and after retouching.

FIGURE 9.6
The Blur Tool in use.

9

FIGURE 9.7
Before blurring (top) and after (bottom).

Make sure that as you blur you cover the entire area that you intend to blur. A missed spot stands out very conspicuously. Also don't forget that you can change the size of your Brush Tool by choosing a different brush from the Brush palette. For the Blur Tool, I recommend using a brush with a soft edge, but not for the Sharpen Tool. When sharpening, I prefer to use a small brush with hard edges, so I know exactly where I am. You'll also find it helpful to work on a magnified view of your picture, just so you have a little better control of the tool.

One of the things you'll begin to notice as you become more accustomed to working with Photoshop is the use of image manipulation techniques in advertising and even in magazine and news editorial photos. You'll begin to recognize--in magazines and other printed pieces--pictures that betray the work of a digital retoucher. You should also begin to examine them for technique and skill. Take note of the next automobile advertisement you see in a flashy, four-color magazine or brochure. Note the foreground. Check the highlights. Examine the reflections in the headlights. Do they look good? Too good? Almost all advertising images are retouched (mainly in Photoshop), and the people doing this are incredible professionals. Learn from them. Notice how the backgrounds fade, how the trees blur, or how the highlights appear. Not to foster any conspiracy, but evidences of Photoshop are all around you. Just keep your eyes open...

The Sharpen Tool

The Sharpen Tool is the exact opposite of the Blur Tool. Where the Blur Tool softens pixel values, the Sharpen Tool hardens them and brings them into greater relief by increasing the contrast between adjacent pixels. Because of their equal-but-opposite relationship, they share a space on the toolbox, with a pull-out that lets you choose either one, or the Smudge Tool. You can also activate the Blur and Sharpen tools by pressing R (for Retouching?). Press Shift+R to toggle between the two. Figure 9.8 shows the flowers again, with sharpening being applied to the edges of the petals. Compare it to the "before" picture shown in Figure 9.7.

Sharpening is best done in very small doses. If you go over a section too much or have the pressure set too high, you can end up burning the color out of an image, which will probably make it look worse than it did initially. See Figure 9.9 for an example of over-sharpening.

FIGURE 9.8

Applying the Sharpen Tool. Compare the area inside the circle to the same picture before sharpening.

Remember, too, that not even the magic of Photoshop can put back what wasn't there originally. Always work with the clearest, sharpest pictures you can manage. Rather than trying to salvage a bad scan, do it again. If your photo is fuzzy all over, instead of trying to sharpen it, set it aside until we start working with filters (see Hour 15).

FIGURE 9.9

Too much sharpening.

To Do: Using the Focus Tools

Let's take a quick break here and try out these tools. Open any convenient picture in Photoshop and follow these steps:

1. Click once on the Magnifying glass to zoom in on your picture. This gives you a magnification of 200%.

2. Select the Blur Tool. Choose a soft-edged brush shape from the Brush palette on the Tool Options bar.

3. Type **5** to set the pressure to 50% in the Tool Options bar.

4. Drag the Blur Tool across the picture. Notice the effect (see Figure 9.10).

FIGURE 9.10

Blurring the flower petals with the image (and tool) enlarged.

5. Switch to the Sharpen Tool by pressing Shift+R. Choose a hard-edged brush. Drag it over a different part of the picture. Try to drag it along the edge of an object and note the effect (see Figure 9.11).

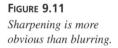

FIGURE 9.11

Sharpening is more obvious than blurring.

6. Try sharpening the area you previously blurred. Can you restore it to its previous appearance? (Probably not.)

7. Now, just for fun, switch to the Smudge Tool and see for yourself the difference between Blur and Smudge.

8. Practice with these tools at different pressure settings and with different brushes. Use Revert (File→Revert) or click on the snapshot at the top of the History palette to restore the picture if you run out of practice room.

The Toning Tools

Photoshop is primarily a digital darkroom program, so it makes sense that some of its most useful tools mimic the darkroom techniques that photographers use to lighten and darken portions of an image or to brighten colors. The Toning tools include the Dodge, Burn, and Sponge tools. Dodge and Burn are opposites, like Sharpen and Blur, but instead of affecting the contrast between adjacent pixels, they either lighten or darken the area to which the tool is applied. Sponging changes the color saturation of the area to which you apply it.

Dodge and Burn Tools

Dodging, in the photographer's darkroom, is accomplished by waving a Dodge Tool, usually a cardboard circle on a wire, between the projected image from the enlarger and the photographic paper. This blocks some of the light and makes the dodged area lighter when the print is developed. It's also called "holding back," because you effectively hold back the light from reaching the paper. Photoshop's Dodge Tool, shown in Figure 9.12, looks just like the darkroom version.

FIGURE 9.12

The Toning tools: Dodge, Burn, and Sponge.

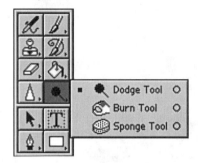

Burning has the opposite effect to dodging--instead of lightening a small area, it darkens the area. In the darkroom, burning in is accomplished either by using a piece of cardboard with a hole punched out (the opposite of the Dodge Tool) or by blocking the enlarger light with your hand, so the light only reaches the area on the print surface to be burned. Photoshop's Burn Tool icon is a hand shaped to pass a small beam of light.

Click the Dodge Tool and look at the drop-down menu in the Tool Options bar. As you can see, it gives you three choices:

- Shadows
- Midtones
- Highlights

These options indicate the types of pixels that the tool will affect. If you want to adjust the shadows, such as making them lighter and leaving the lighter pixels untouched, select Shadows. The default option for the Dodge Tool is Midtones. This is a good choice when you want to affect the midtone pixels, or when you are unsure of how to proceed. Select the Highlights when you want to lighten already light-colored areas, leaving the darker areas untouched. Figure 9.13 shows the effects of dodging and burning on an old, scanned Polaroid photo.

FIGURE 9.13

I lightened his face, darkened hers, and darkened the background some.

9

Sponging

Surprisingly enough, sponging is also a darkroom trick. When a picture in the developing tray isn't turning dark enough or looks to be underexposed or weak in color, the darkroom technician can often "save" it by sloshing some fresh, full-strength developing chemical on a sponge and rubbing it directly on the wet print in the tray. The combination of the slight warmth from the friction of the sponge and the infusion of fresh chemical can make the difference between a useless picture and an okay one. It's no substitute for a proper exposure, of course.

Photoshop's Sponge does much the same thing. On a color image, it increases (or reduces, versatile tool that it is) the color saturation in the area to which you apply it. On a grayscale image, it increases or decreases contrast by moving the grayscale level away from or toward middle gray. When you use the Sponge, you also need to adjust its setting in the Options palette to determine whether it intensifies color (saturates) or fades it (desaturates). Figures 9.14 and 9.15 show before and after views of a woodland scene with the Sponge applied. You can't truly appreciate this one in black-and-white. Check it out at our Web site. To get to the Web site point your Web browser to `http://www.mcp.com/sams/detail_sams.cfm?item=0672319551`. Once the main book page has loaded, click the `Downloads` link to get to the files.

FIGURE 9.14
Before using the Sponge, the colors are somewhat dull.

FIGURE 9.15
After using the Sponge, the colors are much brighter.

Have you ever wondered what's meant by "middle gray?" If you consider the grayscale as going from 0% (white) to 100% (black), middle gray is the tone that's exactly 50%. In practice, highlights are anywhere from 0 to about 20%–25%. Shadows are 70%–100%. So anything between a 25% gray and a 70% gray is considered a *midtone*.

These tools are great for fine-tuning images and creating shadows or highlights. Use them in small doses to enhance the appearance of your images.

For this sort of precision work, I strongly recommend that you change your cursors to Brush Size in the File, Preferences, Display & Cursors dialog box. This permits you to see exactly what you are doing, when using these precision tools. Enlarging the picture is also helpful.

Summary

Photoshop provides several different ways to move paint around once you have applied it. The Smudge Tool is useful for blending small areas of color. It has the same effect as dragging your finger through wet paint. Blur and Sharpen are two sides of the same coin, so to speak. One increases the contrast between adjacent pixels, whereas the other diminishes it. The Toning tools (Dodge, Burn, and Sponge) are the digital darkroom equivalents of real darkroom tools and procedures. They can darken or lighten an image, or change the color saturation by either adding more color or removing some. These tools are mostly used for retouching pictures that you have scanned or shot digitally, rather than for creating your own art.

Q&A

Q What's the difference between smudge and blur?

A The main difference is in the way you apply them. Smudging, because you're moving the pixels from point A to point B, tends to show the direction of the move. Blurring decreases the contrast between adjacent pixels, so they seem to blend together visually but with no hint of movement.

Q Can I saturate and desaturate on the same object? I want to make one side lighter and the other darker.

A Of course, you can, but the Sponge Tool might not be your best choice for darkening an object. Remember, it makes the color more or less saturated, which is not quite the same as darkening it. Try it and, if the effect isn't what you're looking for, try burning instead.

Q I understand the Sharpen Tool, but there also seem to be Sharpen filters. (Okay, I peeked ahead.) When do you use the tool and when do you use the filter?

A Use the tool when you have a small area that you want to sharpen. Use the filters when you have a soft focus image, or one that needs all-over sharpening. You'll learn how to work with the filters in Hour 14, "Filters That Improve Your Picture."

Q My scanned picture has a very dark shadow. Should I desaturate it or dodge it?

A Yes. Try both approaches and see which works best for you.

Quiz

1. What effect does 100% pressure have on the Smudge Tool?

    a. None.

    b. It turns the smudges black.

    c. Rather than smudging, it completely replaces color in the path of the stroke with the adjacent color. You can almost use it as an eraser, dragging background color over the object you're trying to smudge out.

2. If you sharpen a piece of the picture too much, what happens?

    a. It turns into a random collection of black and colored pixels.

    b. It turns white.

    c. It turns black.

3. What should I do if I oversaturate part of my picture?

    a. Use the History palette to backtrack to the step just before you used too much saturation.

    b. Set the sponge to desaturate and use it on the bright spots.

    c. Apply Filter→Fade Sponge Tool, and use the slider to back off the color.

Quiz Answers

1. c.
2. a. This effect is not recommended.
3. a. or b., but the first is usually the better method.

Exercises

Find a photo that's too light and too fuzzy. Apply the Sharpen Tool and the Dodge, Burn, and Saturate tools as needed until you've fixed it. Now do the same with a photo that's too dark. Which was easier to adjust?

9

HOUR 10

Advanced Painting Techniques

Digital paint is so much easier to work with than the real kind. It doesn't smell, it never spills on the table, and there are no messy brushes to wash out when you're done. It doesn't get all over you and you don't even have to wait for it to dry. In Photoshop, you can either paint a picture from scratch, starting with a blank page and using it as if it were any other graphics program, or you can take an existing image and convert it into a painting. In the course of this chapter, you'll explore both ways of working.

When we talk about "paint" in the digital realm, we're talking, of course, about image manipulation that mimics "real-life" painting techniques. Because we're imitating real life, you might think that you'd be limited in the number of painting techniques that you can use—but this isn't the case. You're not limited to just watercolor or oil paint, for instance. Under the broad category of painting, you can include colored pencil drawing, pastels, chalk, charcoal, and even neon tubing, as many of today's artists and art students are doing. Even though digital painting is the most spectacular part of

Photoshop, as well as the most fun, you'll be amazed at how easy it is. More important, mastering Photoshop's painting tools will take you a long way toward becoming a more proficient digital artist.

Quite honestly, Photoshop wasn't designed to be a graphics program. It lacks some of the tools that you'll find in Adobe Illustrator, CorelDRAW, or Fractal Painter (to name just a few of the very best programs). However, it can be used very effectively for many kinds of graphics. Because of its plug-in filters, which you'll learn about shortly, it can do some very remarkable things with graphics, most of which would be way beyond the capability of an ordinary painting or drawing program. Should Photoshop be your *only* graphics program? Probably not, if you need to do a lot of drawing. Although the new release has added some limited vector drawing tools, it's still not the perfect multi-use graphics program. But for painting and digital darkroom work and retouching, nothing can top it.

Simulating Different Media

One of the remarkable tricks Photoshop can do is to simulate the appearance of other media. The effect can be achieved through the use of a filter (we'll jump ahead a little in this hour and introduce you to some of Photoshop's "artistic" filters). It can also be achieved through the use of the Smudge and Blur tools, or by choosing custom Paintbrushes and carefully applying paint with a particular blend mode. You can either create a picture from scratch, or you can start with a photograph and make it look like a watercolor, an oil painting in any of a half-dozen different styles, or even a plaster bas relief. Whatever the method, the results will amaze you.

Watercolors

Artists who work in conventional media have a great deal of respect for those who choose watercolors. It's probably the most difficult medium of all to handle. You have to work "wet" to blend colors, but not so wet that the image turns to mud. Doing it digitally is much easier. We'll start with a filter technique that makes a photo appear to have been created as a watercolor painting.

Converting a Photograph to a Watercolor

Photoshop has a watercolor filter that converts a picture to a watercolor version of itself. You can find the filter in the Filter→Artistic submenu, as shown in Figure 10.1.

Figure 10.1

Watercolor is one of fifteen "artistic" filters.

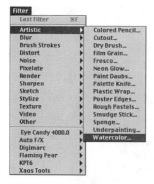

New Term *Filters*, in Photoshop terminology, are sets of instructions built in to the program (or "plugged-in" as added features) that apply specific effects to your pictures. For instance, one of Photoshop's filters converts your image to a pattern of dots. Another simulates flames shooting out of a selected object. Dozens of filters are available. Some come with the program, whereas others are sold by third-party vendors or distributed as shareware or freeware. In Hours 14–16, we'll talk more about what kinds of filters you can get and where.

The Watercolor filter works most effectively on pictures that have large, bold areas and not a lot of detail. Because it also tends to darken backgrounds and shadows, it's best to start with a picture that has a light background. The photo in the figures that follow is a digital photograph I took recently near Breaux Bridge, Louisiana.

When you select the Watercolor filter (or virtually any other Photoshop filter, for that matter), you open a dialog box like the one shown in Figure 10.2. It has a thumbnail view of your picture and a set of sliders that allow you to set the way in which the picture is converted. If you click and drag on the thumbnail image, you can slide it around to see the effect of your settings on different parts of the photo. Most Photoshop filters have dialog boxes and settings very much like this one. After you have tried even one, the rest will be just as easy.

Filters can take anywhere from a few seconds to a minute or more to apply. If you don't see the effects of the filter on the thumbnail view immediately, look for a flashing underline beneath the percentage number under the thumbnail window on your Macintosh, or a progress bar in the Status bar at the bottom of the window on your PC. It flashes to tell you that the computer is calculating the Filter effect. When the underline disappears, the filter is applied.

10

FIGURE 10.2
Use the + and – symbols to zoom in and out on the thumbnail.

Brush detail varies from 1 to 14, with 14 giving you the most detail, and 1 being a sort of Jackson Pollock splatter effect. Depending on the nature of the picture you are converting and your own preferences, you may want to start experimenting with settings around 9 to 12. Shadow intensity can be adjusted from 0 to 10, but, unless you are looking for special effects, leave it at 0. The Watercolor filter darkens shadows too much, even at the 0 setting. By the time you move it past 3 to 4, the picture's gone almost totally black. Texture settings vary from 1 to 3. These are actually quite subtle, and you may wonder if they have any effect at all. They do, but are more noticeable combined with less detailed brush settings. In Figure 10.3, I've gathered samples of different brush detail and texture settings so you can see the differences.

To Do: Converting a Photograph to a Watercolor

You might not want to convert all your photos into imitation watercolors, but some look really good with this treatment.

1. Find a picture that you think might look good as a watercolor, or download the one shown in this To Do from our Web site. It's called Snag.jpg. To get to the Web site point your Web browser to **http://www.mcp.com/sams/detail_sams.cfm?item= 0672319551**. Once the main book page has loaded, click the Downloads link to get to the files. Open it in Photoshop and make any color adjustments you think necessary.

▼

FIGURE 10.3

All three texture settings have been applied to each sample brush setting.

10

I think it could be lighter, so that's what I did. (If you've forgotten how, turn back to Hour 6, Figure 10.3 "Adjusting Color," to refresh your memory.) Remember not to let the colors get too dark before you start applying filters. Photoshop filters, in general, tend to add more black to the image.

2. Then, choose Watercolor from the Filter→Artistic submenu.

3. In the Watercolor filter window, shown in Figure 10.4, use the sliders to choose a combination of texture and brush detail that you like.

Set the shadow intensity to 0, unless you want a lot of black in the image.

FIGURE 10.4

I've set the brush detail to 14 and texture to 1.

▼

▼   4. Move the thumbnail image to check details by clicking and dragging the hand symbol that appears when you place your cursor in the thumbnail window.

▲   5. Click OK when you're done to apply the changes.

Watercolors from Scratch

Sometimes you either don't have a photo of what you want to paint, or you just want to do it yourself. Perhaps you want a different style of watercolor than what's possible with the filter. If you work patiently and with some forethought, you can produce watercolors that you'd almost swear were painted with a brush on paper. Let's open a new page in Photoshop and do some painting.

You learned about working with the Paintbrush Tool in Hour 7, "Paintbrushes and Art Tools." As you recall, using the Tool Options bar, you can switch from a large brush to a small one, or change the opacity, with just a click. I also like to open the Swatches window and use it as a paintbox to select colors, rather than going to the Color Picker each time. Please feel free to flip back if you need to refresh your memory about any of these things.

If you drag on the tabs at the top of the palettes, you can move them around so you can use the layers, history, colors, and swatches all at once, or whatever combination of palettes you need. Close the ones you aren't using to make more room. (Figure 10.5 was created with my usual painting setup.)

Transparency is one of the distinguishing features of "real" watercolor. To make a "synthetic" watercolor, you'll want to set the Brush opacity at no more than 75%. This means, because transparent is the opposite of opaque, that your paint will be 25% transparent, which is about right for watercolors. Try out the brush on a blank page, and you'll notice that, as you paint over a previous stroke, the color darkens. Click the Wet Edges check box for even more authentic brush strokes. This option adds extra color along the edges of a stroke, making it look as if the pigment gathered there, as it does when you paint with a very watery brush.

Watercolor artists painting on paper often start with an outline and then fill in the details. Figure 10.5 shows the beginnings of a watercolor painting of an apple. I've drawn the fruit and its stem and leaves, and now I'm working on filling in the leaves with a small brush. It's often easier to work in a magnified view when you're doing small details like this.

FIGURE 10.5

Use the brushes with soft edges.

Another useful trick for creating a watercolor is to use the Eraser as if it were a brush full of plain water to lighten a color that you have applied too darkly. Use it at a very low opacity to lighten a color slightly, and at a high opacity to clean up around the edges if your "paintbrush" got away from you. Don't forget that the Eraser always erases to the background color. If you have been changing colors as you paint, make sure to set the background color to what you want to see when you erase.

For this kind of task, a pressure-sensitive graphics tablet, though not an absolute must, is certainly helpful. Drawing with a stylus is far more natural than drawing with a mouse or trackball, and the pressure-sensitive function permits you to make brush strokes that trail off like the real ones, rather than having to rely on the less versatile Fade Steps option to create the effect.

Most real watercolors are painted on a heavily textured watercolor paper. If you would like yours to have the same grainy character, you can use the Texturizer (Filter→Texture→Texturizer) filter to add the watercolor paper texture to the picture after your painting is completed. Don't apply it until everything else is done, though, because any further changes you make will alter the texture. Figure 10.6 shows the Texturizer filter being applied.

The Canvas texture comes the closest to replicating watercolor paper, especially if you scale it down some. I like to set it at 70%, with a relief height of 10. Use the sliders to set relief and scaling. I find that applying the same texture a second time with the light coming from the opposite direction gives me the best imitation of textured paper. Of course, you can also print your images on real watercolor paper. Lighter weight papers run through an inkjet printer very nicely.

Figure 10.6

The direction of the light affects the shadows that make up the texture.

Oil Painting

Oil paint has a very different look from watercolor, and it's a look that Photoshop duplicates particularly well. The qualities that distinguish works in oil are the opacity of the paint, the textured canvas that adds a definite fabric grain to the image, and the thick, sometimes three-dimensional quality of the paint. To get the full effect in Photoshop, you may have to combine several different techniques. We'll start, as artists do, with underpainting.

Underpainting

When an artist starts an oil painting of a landscape or a seascape, she usually sketches out the subject with a few lines, often working with charcoal or a pencil to locate the horizon and major land masses. Then she dips a big brush in thinned out paint and begins the process of underpainting. This blocks in all of the solid areas; the sky, the ground, the ocean, and any obvious features like a large rock, a cliff, or whatever else may be included. Underpainting builds the foundation of the picture, establishing the colors and values of the different parts of the image. After that, all that's left is to fill in the details.

Photoshop's Underpainting filter looks at the image that you're applying it to and reduces it to the same sort of solid blocks of color. In Figure 10.7, I'm applying the filter to a photo of a lighthouse. If you want to download this photo and work along, it's called Portland Head Light, and it's at the Macmillan Web site discussed earlier in this chapter.

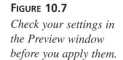

Check your settings in the Preview window before you apply them.

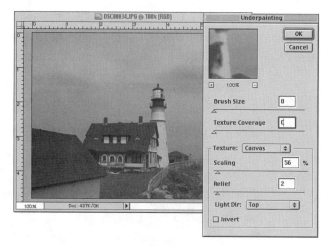

10

Underpainting gives you the basic elements of the picture, minus the details. Using the Underpainting filter requires making some settings decisions. The Texture settings are exactly the same as in the Texturize filter we used on the watercolor. Here, though, we want to bring out more of the texture, so we would use a higher relief number, and possibly a larger scale on the canvas. You can also paint on burlap, sandstone, or brick, or on textures that you import from elsewhere. The Brush size setting ranges from 0–40. Smaller brushes retain more of the texture and detail of the original image. Larger brushes give a somewhat spotty coverage and remove all the detail. Texture coverage also ranges on a scale from 0–40. Lower numbers here reveal less of the texture; higher numbers bring out more of it. In underpainting, the texture is revealed only where there's paint, not all over the canvas.

To Do: Turn a Scene into an Oil Painting

The character of an oil painting is quite different from that of a watercolor. Let's try to apply the oil paint technique to a photo.

1. As always, start by preparing the picture. Adjust the colors if necessary and crop as needed.

2. Open the Underpainting filter (Filter→Artistic→Underpainting).

3. Set the Brush size to 3 and the Texture coverage to 3. These settings will retain most of the detail in the picture.

4. Set the Texture to Canvas and Scaling to 65%. You want to keep the texture small so it doesn't interfere with the detail you will be adding to the picture later.

▼   5. Set the Relief to 8 and the Light direction to Top. This shows just enough texture
        to establish that your painting is on canvas rather than stone.

▲   6. Click OK to apply the filter. Figure 10.8 shows the result so far.

FIGURE 10.8

The scene with just the
underpainting applied.

Overpainting

The Underpainting filter leaves us with a somewhat indistinct picture, fine for some purposes but definitely unfinished. An artist would proceed to go back and overpaint the
areas that need to have detail, so that's what we'll do to complete this lighthouse scene.

Because oil paintbrushes tend to be rather stiff, choose a hard brush rather than a soft-
edged one. Be sure to turn off Wet Edges in the Options box, if it happens to be on.
You'll probably also want to change the Blending mode, though Normal will work fine
for some parts of the painting where you want to make actual strokes of paint. However,
Dissolve may be the most useful mode for working into our lighthouse. Use it, as shown
in Figure 10.9, to stipple colors into the underpainting. (Stippling means to paint with the
very end of a hard round brush, placing dots rather than strokes of paint. Dissolve does
this effect very well.) Vary the Brush size and Opacity to add more or less paint with
each stroke.

FIGURE 10.9

I've added flowers and brighter greens to the bushes to the right of the fence, and sharpened up the roof lines and the top of the lighthouse, by defining their outlines with the brush.

10

You can go on painting into this picture until it looks exactly like an oil painting, or you can use it as a basis to experiment with other filters and effects. In Figure 10.10, I've taken the lighthouse and applied the Texturizer filter (Filters→Texture→Texturizer) and used it to put the painting on canvas.

FIGURE 10.10

Putting a canvas texture under this image makes it much more like an oil painting.

Pencil and Colored Pencil

The Pencil Tool has been part of every graphics program since the very first ones. It's an extremely useful tool when you know how to use it properly. Several things about the pencil are different in Photoshop 6. The first is its location. It now shares a space in the toolbox with the Paintbrush Tool. You can use the Pencil Tool (or any of the brushes) in a sort of "connect the dots" mode. Click where you want a line to begin, and shift+click again where it should end. Photoshop draws the line for you. Keep shift+clicking and it adds more line segments. The Pencil can also serve as an eraser if you click the Auto-Erase function on the Tool Options bar. With Auto-Erase enabled, when you click the Pencil point on a colored pixel that is the same color as the current foreground color, you erase it to the background color. Use this feature to clean up edges or to erase in a straight line.

Pencils are great for retouching and drawing a single pixel-width line, but difficult to use for an actual drawing. (Yes, you can set the Pencil to any of the brush shapes, but if you do that, it's functionally a brush.) The Pencil is easier to use if you zoom in to 200% so you can see individual pixels. Opening the Control panel and setting the mouse acceleration to Slow will also help, but it's even better to use a graphics tablet instead of a mouse.

If you want to get the look of a pencil drawing, without all the effort, try the Colored Pencil filter (Filters→Artistic→Colored Pencil) or the Crosshatch filter (Filters→Brush Strokes→Crosshatch). The Colored Pencil filter, shown in Figure 10.11, gives you a light, somewhat more stylized drawing from your original image. It looks even better if you convert the drawing to grayscale after applying the filter. The Crosshatch filter, applied to the same image in Figure 10.12, retains much more of the color and detail, but still looks like a pen-and-ink drawing.

Chalks and Charcoal

Chalk and charcoal drawings date all the way back to prehistoric times. When the cave dwellers at Lascaux decided to decorate their walls, they used colored clays, chalk, and charcoal, with animal fat as a binder.

Artists today use almost the same medium, except that the chalks are now compressed so well they don't need tallow. Natural birch charcoal is still considered the best of its kind. Chalk drawings in the real world can be found on virtually any surface, from grained paper, to brick walls, to sidewalks. Chalk drawings in Photoshop let you take advantage of the capabilities of the Texture filters. Place your drawing on sandstone, burlap, or on a texture that you've imported from another source.

FIGURE 10.11
The Colored Pencil filter adds a light, airy feel.

10

FIGURE 10.12
Cross-hatching uses a different, more detailed drawing style.

Chalk and charcoal are linear materials, which is to say that they draw lines rather than large flat areas like paints. Choose your subjects with that in mind. You can, of course, apply shading as a pattern of lines or a crosshatch, and you can smudge to your heart's content. If you're drawing from scratch, start with a fairly simple line drawing and expand on it. If you're translating a photo or scanned image into a chalk or charcoal drawing, choose one that has strong line patterns and well-defined detail.

Chalk and Charcoal Filter

When you apply the Chalk and Charcoal filter, which is found on the Filters menu (Filters→Sketch→Chalk and Charcoal), you'll see that it reduces your picture to three colors, using a dark gray plus the foreground and background colors that you have set in the tool window. Chalk uses the background color and Charcoal becomes the foreground color. Areas that aren't colored appear in gray. You will probably want to do some experimenting to find the "right" colors. It's a little bit counterintuitive, because the foreground color is usually the lighter one, and this filter applies it to the darker areas of the image.

Figure 10.13 shows the Chalk and Charcoal dialog box, which controls how this filter works. In it you can set amounts for the chalk and charcoal areas. These sliders have a range from 0 to 20. Start somewhere in the middle and adjust until you get a combination that works for your picture. The stroke pressure varies from 0 to 5. Unless you want the picture to turn into areas of flat color, keep the setting at 1 or 2. Intensity builds up rather fast with this filter.

FIGURE 10.13

Move around in the preview window to see the filter's effects on different parts of the image.

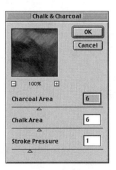

To Do: Convert a Photograph to a Chalk and Charcoal Drawing

The chalk and charcoal filter looks great with any reasonably high contrast subject. Try it on a portrait.

1. Open the image (Jay.jpg) and then the Chalk and Charcoal filter dialog box (Filters→Sketch→Chalk and Charcoal).

2. Set the Charcoal and Chalk areas to 10 or less. When you work with a filter for the first time, always start in the middle of the settings range and increase or decrease as necessary.

3. Set the pressure to 1 or 2. Move on to step 4 if you like the view in the Preview window, or experiment with other numbers.

4. Click OK to apply the filter. Figure 10.14 shows this filter applied to the same portrait as in the previous examples.

5. Study the result. Decide what areas need touching up.

6. Select the Eraser Tool and erase to bring up more of the background color.

7. Select the Paintbrush Tool to apply more of the foreground color.

8. Use the Eyedropper to select the gray tone, if you need to apply more of it. (The gray is an arbitrary color used by this filter and can't be adjusted.)

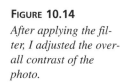 9. When you're satisfied with the drawing, save it.

FIGURE 10.14

After applying the filter, I adjusted the overall contrast of the photo.

The Smudge Tool works nicely with chalk and charcoal. Use it exactly as you would to soften a line or blend two colors using your finger or hand on paper. Photoshop's Blur and Sharpen tools can also be used to define edges or to soften a line without smudging it.

Photoshop 6 includes nearly 100 different filters! If you master one each week, within two years you'll know them all.

Charcoal

Use the Charcoal filter (Filters→Sketch→Charcoal) to convert an image to a good imitation of a charcoal drawing. Because charcoal doesn't come in colors, your charcoal drawings will be most successful if you set the foreground to black and the background to white, or to a pale color if you want the effect of drawing on colored paper. The Charcoal filter dialog box is shown in Figure 10.15. You can adjust the thickness of the line from 1 to 7 and the degree of detail from 0 to 5. The Light/Dark Balance setting ranges from 0 to 100 and controls the proportion of foreground to background color.

FIGURE 10.15

Experiment with these settings. Every image is different.

Figure 10.16 shows before and after versions of a portrait converted into charcoal and lightly retouched with the Paintbrush, Blur, and Sharpen tools. Using a graphics tablet instead of a mouse makes it easier to reproduce the filter's crosshatched lines.

Summary

Whew! This has been a very full and intense hour. Spend some time trying out these techniques before you move along further.

In this hour, you saw that digital painting is an area where Photoshop truly excels. You can work either "from scratch" or converting images you have uploaded as digital photos or scans or have created in some other compatible program. Once you have the image in Photoshop, the various filters and brushes enable you to turn your work into a good imitation of an oil painting, watercolor, or drawing. The "artistic" filter set includes filters that can do much of the work of conversion for you. For best results, though, you'll want

FIGURE 10.16

Retouching brought back the details that were lost in translation.

Before   After

to go in and touch up the picture after the filter has done its work. Choose tools and colors that are appropriate to the medium you're trying to imitate. Experiment, and if you find a technique or filter combination that works especially well, make notes on it. Yes, you can even write in this book! (Well, not if it's a library book…)

Q&A

Q How do you know which pictures will make good digital paintings?

A For digital watercolors, look for photos with large plain areas and not a lot of detail. In general, try lighter colored pictures, because the Watercolor filter tends to darken images. Though almost any picture makes a good oil painting, I like to use the technique to rescue otherwise bland landscapes. It helps if the subject has interesting contrasts (like ocean and rock) or if there's a good deal of color.

Q Can I use more than one filter on a picture?

A You can, and many times you may want to use a combination of several filters to achieve a particular effect.

Q In the watercolor discussion earlier in this chapter, you recommended waiting until the very end to apply the texture because any changes made before the final save would alter the texture's appearance. Shouldn't those same rules apply to oil paintings as well?

A Actually, no. Texture is an integral part of oil painting. Paint builds up and hides the canvas or is thinned to bring out the canvas texture. The canvas texture should be applied with the underpainting so that, as you go back and add more paint, you will naturally obscure some of the texture. This makes the picture look less digital and more "painted."

Q Why do some filters have ellipses after their names, whereas others don't?

A There are two kinds of native Photoshop filters. The ones with an ellipsis (…) open a dialog box with parameters to set before the filter is applied. The filters with no ellipsis are one-step filters. You have no control over the way the filter is applied. When you select a one-step filter from the menu, it's applied—period. You can apply it a second time to double the effect.

Quiz

1. The Watercolor filter works best on pictures with

    a. Large flat areas

    b. Lots of detail

    c. Dark backgrounds

2. Wet Edges makes a brush stroke that is

    a. Drippy

    b. Fuzzy along the edges

    c. Darker at the edges

3. Oil painting and watercolor look

    a. Very different

    b. Very similar

    c. A lot like colored pencil

4. Charcoal comes in many colors.

    a. True

    b. False

    c. True only in Photoshop

Quiz Answers

1. a. Detail tends to get lost in a watercolor, and the process darkens the image somewhat, so lighter ones come out better.

2. c. Try it and see.

3. a. In Photoshop, as in the fine arts world, oils emphasize texture, whereas watercolor is flat.

4. c. You want pink charcoal? Go for it.

Exercises

Find a picture with a good range of light and dark colors and moderate detail. Apply the filters discussed in this chapter to the picture, and be sure to experiment with different background and foreground colors, as well as with various settings for brush width, pressure, and so on.

10

HOUR 11

Layers

You're almost halfway through. You've already learned a great deal about Photoshop, but there is, as always, more to learn. From this point on, most of it's fun stuff, too. Right now, we are going to discuss one of the most important and useful features of Photoshop—layers.

At first, layers might seem confusing, but don't worry—they're not as bad as they sound. In fact, they are exactly what their name implies—layers within one image—and each layer can be adjusted and edited separately from the others. That's what makes this feature so cool.

If it helps, think of it this way. Consider a Bugs Bunny cartoon. Imagine Bugs walking through the woods. The artists at the Warner Bros. Studios created the backdrops and then drew Bugs on pieces of transparent cellophane, which they laid over the background. They often put his body on one layer and his arms and legs on another, and as they cycled through the several sets of arms and legs they made the animated Bugs appear to move through the woods or chase Elmer Fudd, who was on yet another layer or two of cellophane.

Photoshop has a capability similar to this animation technique, and you can create as many layers as you need, up to 999, in Photoshop 6. You can hide layers while you work on others. You can link layers together. In Hour 6,

"Adjusting Color," you learned how to use adjustment layers that enable you to make color and tonal corrections in your images. Now, you'll learn the rest of the story about layers.

Using the Layers Palette

Step one is to open a new page and then open the Layers palette. Just select Window→Show Layers. The Layers palette (see Figure 11.1) is where you control your layers' behavior—creating, adding, deleting, hiding, and showing. Think of the Layers palette as "command central" for working with layers. The small versions of your images on the left of the palette are called *thumbnails*. Each of these small rectangles displays a separate layer. For the moment, because you have not created any new layers, you should have only one blank thumbnail in the Layers palette. That's the background layer.

FIGURE **11.1**

The Layers palette.

Add Layer Mask

Create New Dynamic Fill Layer

Delete Current Layer

Add Layer Effects to Current Layer

Create New Set

Create New Layer

If the thumbnails are too small for your liking, select the Palette Options command from the palette's menu (the arrow in the upper-right corner) and check out Figure 11.2.

FIGURE **11.2**

Optional thumbnail sizes.

You can choose from three different sizes or no thumbnail image at all. Remember that every image on your screen consumes a certain amount of the RAM available to run Photoshop. So if you can get by with the smallest thumbnail, try to. The smaller the thumbnail, the less space the palette will take up on your desktop. This is an advantage as you begin to work with three, four, five, and more layers at a time.

To Do: Creating a New Layer

Now let's make some layers. First of all, let's put something on the background layer, just so we'll know where it is. Follow these steps:

1. Start a new page. Use the Oval Marquee to draw a large circle on the page. Fill the circle with a color. Type Command+D (Mac) or Control+D (Windows) to get rid of the marquee.

2. Look at the thumbnail called Background. (It's the only one on the palette.) It should look something like Figure 11.3.

FIGURE 11.3

The background layer is your blank canvas when you open a new document.

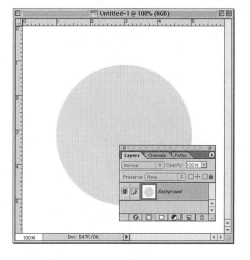

▲

11

3. Click the small page icon at the bottom of the Layer palette. You've just added a layer! Now your palette should look like Figure 11.4.

Let's pause here for a moment and take a close look at the new layer's thumbnail. Compared to the background layer, it has a double-line frame around it. The double frame indicates that this is the *active* layer. You will notice a box that contains a paintbrush. This also indicates the active layer—or the layer on which you can work. Paint all you want, but only the layer with the paintbrush receives the paint.

To change the active layer, click in the whitespace to the right of the layer's name on the layer to which you want to change. Figure 11.5 shows what the palette looks like after the active layer change has been made. (Note that the space to the right of the icon in the selected layer is now shaded.) If you try to click in the empty box where the paintbrush icon should appear, you end up with a chain icon, which indicates that the layers are linked. We'll look at this option in just a few pages, but for now, it is not what we want. (Click the chain to make it go away.)

FIGURE **11.4**
Adding a layer.

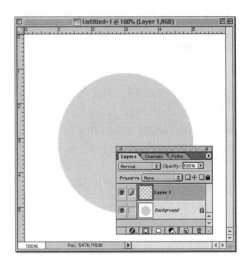

FIGURE **11.5**
We've changed the Active layer. I've also linked the background layer. Clicking the chain will make it go away.

To Do: Getting Started with Layers

Let's make some layers to see how they work. Download the following files from the Web site: Plate, Bread, Lettuce, Cheese, and Lunchmeat. To get to the Web site point your Web browser to http://www.mcp.com/sams/detail_sams.cfm?item=0672319551. Once the main book page has loaded, click the Downloads link to get to the files. Then follow the steps below.

1. Open the files called Plate and Bread. Bring the bread page to the front, if necessary, by clicking it. Copy the bread by pressing Command+A (Mac) or Control+A (Windows) to select the page, and then Command/Control+C to copy it. Bring the Plate page to the foreground. Press Command+Y (Mac) or Control+V (Windows) to paste the bread on the plate. Look at the Layer palette. You've added a new layer! Close the Bread file. (You don't want it to get stale, do you?)

2. Open the file called Lettuce. Notice that the background is a checkerboard, indicating that it's transparent. Align the two images so you can see both, as in Figure

11.6. Click on the lettuce and tomato with the Move Tool and drag it into the plate. Use the Move Tool to center it on the slice of bread. It's also on a new layer.

FIGURE 11.6

Drag the lettuce and tomato on the bread. It will appear as a new layer.

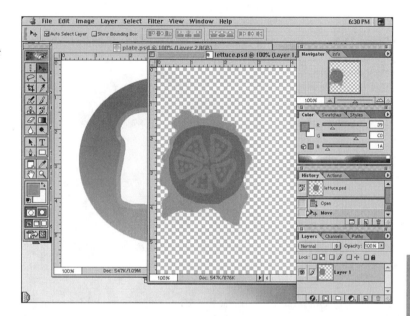

3. Now, let's add some mayo. Click the new layer icon on the Layers palette, as shown in Figure 11.7. Choose a medium brush and a nice, pale yellow mayonnaise color, and paint it on.

FIGURE 11.7

Adding a layer from the Layer palette.

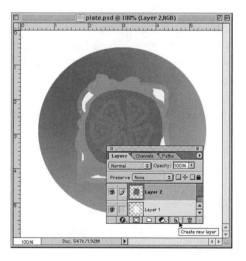

▼   4. Open the Cheese file, and drag the cheese onto the sandwich. Cheese should be slightly translucent, if it's sliced thin, so change the opacity on the Layers menu to 90%, as I have in Figure 11.8.

FIGURE 11.8

*Either use the slider to move the opacity, or click on the Opacity percentage window and type **9**.*

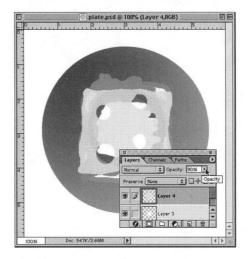

5. Open the Lunchmeat file. Click the lunchmeat layer on the Layers palette and drag it across to the sandwich. Open the Layer→Layer Properties dialog box and change the name of the layer to Meat. (There's no good reason why you should do this except to show you that you can name your layers.)

6. Add another layer, this time by using either the pull-out menu on the right to open New Layer, or choosing New from the Layers menu.

7. Paint a nice, thick squiggle of mustard on the lunchmeat. It doesn't quite look like mustard while it's flat, so let's give it some dimension with a Layer Style. Choose Bevel and Emboss from the Layer→Layer Style menu. Figure 11.9 shows the Emboss dialog box. Set the style to Inner Bevel, and the Technique to Smooth. Make the depth 100% and the size 5 pixels. Soften should be at 0. Ignore the Shading window for now. Figure 11.10 shows the completed sandwich.

▼

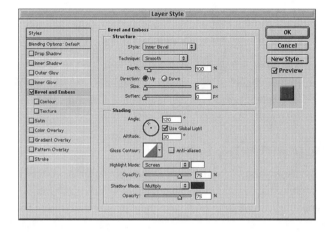

FIGURE 11.9

This box lets you do dozens of neat tricks. Play with it a lot!

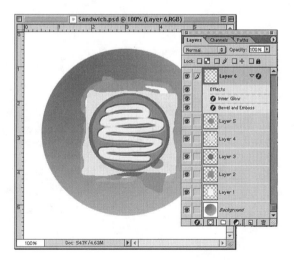

FIGURE 11.10

You could copy Layer one and put a second slice of bread on top, but then you couldn't admire the mustard.

11

You can move, add to, or erase anything on the active layer, but doing so doesn't affect layers above or below it. For instance, if you make Layer 2 the active layer, you can use the Move Tool to slide the bread around, but you can't move the plate or the cheese.

Reordering Layers

You also can change the order of the layers. You might want to do this if one is supposed to look as if it's on top of another, but wasn't created in that order. (New layers are always created above the current active layer.) To do so

1. Click to the right of the thumbnail of the active layer and hold. The active layer changes color.

2. While still holding the mouse button down, drag the layer up to the top of the stack. It then becomes the topmost layer.

If you want to move a layer up or down one level, select it and press Command+] (Mac) or Control+] (Windows) to raise it, and Command+[(Mac) or Control+[(Windows) to lower it. The left bracket lowers the layer's level, and the right bracket raises the layer's level. Remember, **l**eft to **l**ower, **r**ight to **r**aise.

Hiding/Showing Layers

Another great feature of layers is that when you want to concentrate on one part of your image, you can hide all the other layers. To the left of the thumbnails, you will notice small icons that resemble eyes. These indicate that a layer is visible. If you see the eye, you can see the layer. If you click the eye, however, the eye disappears, and the layer becomes hidden. In Figure 11.11, you can see that I've turned off the lettuce and tomato, but the bread, cheese, and meat are still visible.

FIGURE 11.11

To turn a layer visible again, click on the space where the eye should appear.

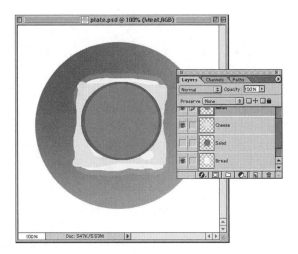

Let's try it. Click the eye icons next to Layers 1 and 2. They disappear, as will the corresponding layers in your image. Click again and the icons reappear--with the layers. While the layer is hidden, you can't paint on it or do anything with it, except drag it up or down (or use the commands detailed previously) to change its order.

Removing Layers

The simple way to remove a layer is to click to make it active and then click the small trash can icon at the bottom of the palette. You can also select Delete Layer from either the Layer menu or the Layer palette pull-out menu. When you do this, you'll see a warning box asking if it's really okay to delete the layer. If you press Option+click (Mac), you can skip the warning. (You can also skip the warning by dragging the layer to the palette's trash icon.) Undo brings back the layer, if you have done nothing else in the meantime. If you have, use the History palette to return to a previous state.

Working with Multiple Layers

You have seen how to create, move, and remove layers, but we still haven't really addressed the question of what they're good for. You will use layers in many different situations. Whenever you are combining two or more images (in Photoshop terms, *compositing*), the elements you paste over the background image are added on separate layers. You can use the Layer palette to control precisely how these elements are combined. You can control the opacity of objects you paste onto a layer or paint that you apply to it. (The layer itself is transparent, even if you set the paint on it to 100% opacity). You can also control the blending modes that affect how one layer appears on top of another, just as you could when painting over an image or background.

Opacity

The Opacity slider at the top of the Layers palette controls the opacity of the active layer. We used it briefly above to change the opacity of the cheese. Make the slider knob appear by clicking the triangle to the right of the percentage window. It can be adjusted from 5%–100% by dragging the slider. If you'd rather not access the slider, enter a value by typing **0** for 100%, **1** for 10%, **2** for 20%, and so on. If you desire more precise control, simply type the digits of the measurement you desire (**57**, for instance) in quick succession.

Let's practice some more with the Opacity slider. You should still have the sandwich open on your desktop. Make the cheese layer active and drag the Opacity slider (by clicking and holding down on the arrow key to make it appear) to about 50%. Can you still see the cheese? Drag the slider down to 10% and then to 0%. Then move it back to 100% again. Pretty cool, huh?

The background cannot be affected by the Opacity slider. It always remains at 100% opacity. There is, however, a way around this. There is a difference between the background of your image and what Photoshop sees as the *background* to your layers.

You can start a page with a transparent background by opening a new file from the File→New menu and selecting Transparent as the contents, as we have in Figure 11.12. When the canvas opens, you'll see a checkerboard pattern as a placeholder, indicating that there's nothing on the layer. If you look at the Layer palette, you'll notice that the blank page is called Layer 1 and not Background. That's to help you remember that you

11

can change the opacity. Anything you paint on that layer will have a transparent background. Anything you copy from another source and paste in will go on a new layer that can also be made transparent. (If you don't see the checkerboard pattern, open File→Preferences→Transparency & Gamut, and change the Grid Size from None to Small.)

The background layer can be changed into a regular layer simply by double-clicking and renaming it, or accepting the default "Layer 0". The layer can be renamed "background", but it will in fact act as a regular layer. Real background layers have the name italicized.

FIGURE 11.12

Making a transparent background.

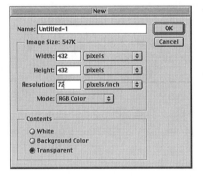

Now that we have a document with a transparent background, let's create another layer for the sandwich. I happen to like pumpernickel bread, so I'll make a slice of that, using a brush and some brown paint. And then, a second layer, with a toothpick to hold the sandwich together, like they do in the delicatessen. I can make the toothpick translucent plastic by reducing the opacity. As a final touch, I'll add a third layer with an olive. In Figure 11.13, you can see the top of the sandwich, by itself and set in place.

Layer Blending Modes

In Hour 8, "Digital Painting," you learned about Blending modes and how they affect the way paint goes on. The same set of modes is available to you for blending layers, and they produce the same general effects, but only on the layers beneath the one to which you have applied the Blending mode. (If you're not clear on what the effects are, refer back to Hour 8.) The layer in this case is the Blend color, and the image below is the base color. As with the painting tools, the Layer Blending modes are found on a pull-down menu on the Layer palette.

FIGURE 11.13

Each layer can have a different transparency. If you look closely, you can see the sandwich through the toothpick, but not through the olive.

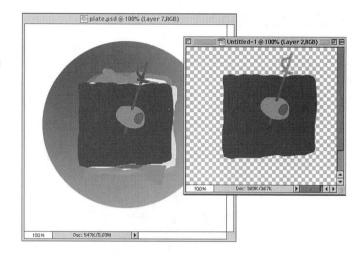

Just as a reminder, the Blending modes are

- Normal
- Dissolve
- Multiply
- Screen
- Overlay
- Soft Light
- Hard Light
- Color Dodge
- Color Burn
- Darken
- Lighten
- Difference
- Exclusion
- Hue
- Saturation
- Color
- Luminosity

You can apply blending modes directly from the Layers palette or by using Layer→ Layer Style→Blending Options. This opens a dialog box that gives you a great deal of control over the way blending happens. When you're ready to tackle the Advanced Blending controls, consult the user Manual or Help screens.

11

Linking Layers

If you click in the box on the Layers palette next to the eye icon, on any layer that's *not* the active layer, you'll place a piece of linked chain in the box. This indicates that the layer is linked to the active layer, meaning that if you move the contents of the active layer, the linked layers move with it. Figure 11.14 shows the Layers palette with sandwich layers linked to the bread.

FIGURE 11.14

Layers linked to the active layer move with it. In this case, the fillings move if you slide the bread off the plate.

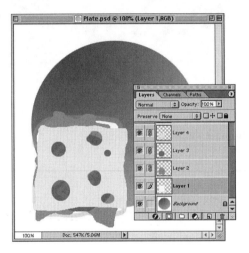

Layer Sets

Layer sets are a new feature in Photoshop 6. They help you organize and manage groups of layers. Once you define a set of layers, you can collapse them or reveal them as necessary, without actually flattening the image. Remember the sandwich we worked on earlier? We could have designated everything between the slices of bread as a set. If we'd needed to move them or change their size or color, we'd do so to the whole set rather than a layer at a time. Layer sets must be contiguous. You couldn't make a set of layers 1, 3, and 5 unless you remove layers 2 and 4 to somewhere else. To create a layer set, use the dialog box Layers→New→Layer Set. To make the set easier to locate, you can assign it a color. All the thumbnails in the set will show on the Layers palette with the assigned color as a background.

Merging Layers

The more layers you add to an image, and the more effects that you add to those layers, the larger your image file will become. If you have a large capacity hard drive and can back up to removable media, size isn't a problem.

It does, however, make a big difference if you want to use your files for anything else, such as publishing in print or on the Web. The only format in which you can save a multilayered image is the Photoshop native format, which is great for Photoshop, but bad for other uses. For the Web, you need to save images as either GIF, PNG, or JPEG. For print, you probably will need to save as TIFF. That's why you need to either merge layers or flatten the image when you're done working with it.

The differences between merging and flattening are

- Merging groups of layers without flattening the entire image conserves memory space but still allows you to work on the layers that you haven't yet finished. Merging Down merges a layer with the one directly below it. You also can merge just the visible layers choosing the appropriate Layer→Merge command.

- Flattening, on the other hand, compresses all visible layers down to one layer. Any layers that you have made invisible at the time of flattening are lost. To flatten an image, simply choose Layer→Flatten Image, but make sure that you are done. At this point, all the layers are reduced to one. Transparency is lost and the single layer you've created is a background layer.

You can use either the Layer menu or the Layer palette pull-out menu to merge or flatten layers, or the keyboard combination Command+E (Mac) or Control+E (Windows) to Merge Down. Figure 11.15 shows the Layer menu with the Flatten Image command highlighted.

11

FIGURE 11.15

This compacts all the layers to one.

Transferring Layered Images to ImageReady

If you're working on an image for use on a Web page, you'll probably want to do the initial work in Photoshop and then jump into ImageReady to save it for Web use. You can transfer layered images between Photoshop and ImageReady by simply clicking on the Jump to button at the bottom of the toolbox. All layers, layer masks, layer effects, and adjustment layers are preserved. (Adjustment layers can be applied and edited only in Photoshop, but can be viewed in ImageReady.)

You'll notice one important change when you move a file from Photoshop to ImageReady. In ImageReady, the background layer is locked.

Layer Effects

Photoshop and ImageReady both include layer effects, a number of automated effects that you can apply to layers, including drop shadows, glows, beveling, and embossing, as well as a color fill effect. You've already tried the Embossing effect on the mustard. ImageReady also includes pattern and gradient layer effects. Figure 11.16 shows the Photoshop Layer Effects submenu.

FIGURE 11.16

Most of these effects are best used with type or with a selected object.

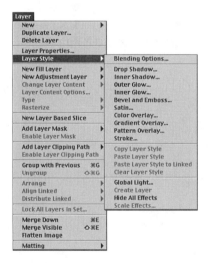

We'll apply these effects to type and to composited images in Hours 16, 18, and 20.

Summary

In this hour, you learned the mechanics of working with layers. You saw how to use the Layer palette and how to create, delete, and move layers. Layers are an important part of the Photoshop interface, and knowing how to apply them will help you a great deal, especially when you work with type and composite images later.

Q&A

Q How can I convert a background to a layer?

A The easy way is to rename it. If you double-click the background layer in the Layer palette, you open up its dialog box. By default, it appears as Layer 0. If you click OK, it is renamed and won't be a background layer.

Q Can I add a background layer to a page that doesn't have one?

A Yes. Use Layer→New→Background to add a background layer.

Q Can I have more than one background layer?

A Sorry, only one per document.

Q How many layer sets can I have?

A As many as you have layers.

Q When I went to change the size of the thumbnails by opening Palette Options, I also pressed the Option/Alt key by mistake. Something strange happened. What was that about?

A Congratulations! You discovered one of Photoshop's hidden Easter Eggs! Easter Eggs are little goodies put in by the programmers to add some extra fun for us users. You discovered Merlin! If you open the About Adobe Photoshop screen and wait for a bit, you'll see another one. After a while, the credits will begin to roll. You can speed them up by pressing Option (Mac) or Alt (Windows). Watch for the last credit. It's a good one. Macintosh users: Click over the word Adobe and wait after the credits scroll. There are some cute quotes. (Sorry, PC folks. It's a Macintosh thing.)

Quiz

1. How many layers can you have?

    a. 10.

    b. 100.

    c. 999.

    d. It depends on how much RAM you have.

2. The active layer is

   a. The layer on top

   b. The layer that's highlighted on the Layers palette

   c. The layer with an eye icon

3. To hide a layer

   a. Drag it to the trashcan.

   b. Press H.

   c. Click the eye icon to close it.

Quiz Answers

1. c. (at least theoretically). d. is probably also true.

2. b. If it's not highlighted, you can't do anything to it. The eye simply means it's visible.

3. c. Think of it as playing peekaboo. If the eye can see you, you can see the layer.

Exercises

Let's do some more experimenting with layers. First, click the background color swatch and choose a medium-light color for a background. Then open a new document. Be sure to click the button to use the background color. Choose a contrasting foreground color, make a new layer, and use a medium brush to write the number 1. Add layers, with a number on each, until you have about 10. Then, starting with the first one, apply different blending modes. Try changing the transparency of a layer. Move the number 5 to the upper-left corner of the screen. Merge layers 2 and 3. Play around until you understand how the layers are working.

Hour **12**

Using Masks

Masks can be your best friends when you're working on a complicated picture. They can also be a darned nuisance, simply because there are several different kinds of masks that you can apply to your image, and they do somewhat different things. So you not only have to create a mask, you have to know ahead of time what you want the mask to do for you, and then you have to apply the right kind of mask.

So, what exactly *is* a mask? In a sense, any selection that you make is a mask, because it permits you to do something that affects only the selected area, effectively masking anything that's not selected. *Masks* can let you change one part of a picture, without changing all of it.

You can select a single flower from a picture of a garden, for instance, and change its color, without changing everything else. You can also delete the selection, which permanently masks it. Masks can cover the part of the picture you don't want to change, much like masking tape covers the woodwork you don't want to paint when you're painting the walls.

The confusion about masks comes from there being so many different types. You can have Layer masks, Mask channels, Transparency masks, Clipping paths, and Clipping groups; and there's also Quick Mask. All can be used to isolate an area that you want to protect while you make changes to the rest of the picture. Masks are well worth learning because they can save you a lot of time and effort.

Applying Masks

Masks can hide either a selected object or the background, and can be opaque or semi-transparent. (If the mask is totally transparent, it isn't masking anything. Masks—and channels, which you'll learn about later—are actually grayscale images of your picture. An opaque mask is black, a 50% transparent mask is 50% gray, and so on.

In Figure 12.1, I have a nice photo of a deer against a terrible background. There are several ways to rescue this picture. One is to mask the deer, and then blur the background and adjust the color so it doesn't look so bad. I can select the background or—if it's easier—select the deer and invert the selection. In this example, I have used the lasso to trace around the edges of the animal.

FIGURE **12.1**

I've done my best to select the deer, so I can work on the background without disturbing him.

This is the most basic kind of masking. It's not always perfect, though. In Figure 12.2, you can see that the Lasso Tool didn't really give us a very accurate mask. The edges aren't very smooth, and there's a lot of background included that shouldn't be there. What's needed is a way to edit the mask.

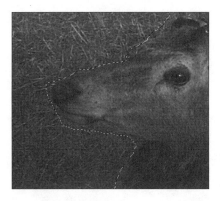

FIGURE 12.2

Up close, you can see that the selection isn't very accurate.

Using Quick Mask

Photoshop provides a very quick and easy way to make a temporary mask that can, in fact, be edited. It's called Quick Mask, and one of its advantages is that you can see both the image and the mask at the same time. You can start with a selected area and use the Paintbrush Tool to add to it or take away from it, or you can create the mask entirely in Quick Mask mode. Let's apply a Quick Mask to an image.

To Do: Create a Quick Mask

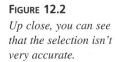

Quick Masks are a great time saver, as you'll soon see. Follow along as we try them.

1. Find a photo with an subject that stands out against the background. Using whatever Selection tool seems appropriate, select the part of the image you want to change—in this case, the background. It's okay if your selection isn't perfect. (Don't forget that you can select the object, and then invert the selection, if that's the easiest way.)

2. Click the Quick Mask button at the bottom of the toolbox (see Figure 12.3).

   You see a color overlay indicating the mask on the protected area, which is to say, the area *not* selected. (By default, the mask is 50% opaque red, imitating a piece of the rubylith film that artists use to mask photos for retouching. If you have a red object or red background that you are masking, you can change the color by double-clicking the Quick Mask icon and using the Quick Mask options dialog box to select a contrasting color.)

12

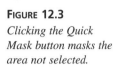

FIGURE 12.3

Clicking the Quick Mask button masks the area not selected.

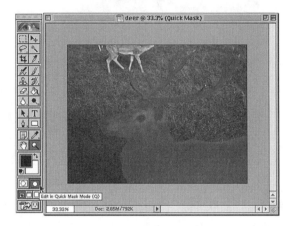

3. If the mask needs editing, as this one does, click the Paintbrush, or press B to activate it and select an appropriate Paintbrush size from the Brush palette.

   Because masks are essentially grayscale images, painting with black adds to the mask. Painting with white (or erasing) takes it away. Painting with gray gives you a semi-transparent mask. You will notice that the foreground and background colors change to black and white when you enter Quick Mask mode. (If, for some reason, they didn't, press D for Default.) Figure 12.4 shows the edited mask.

FIGURE 12.4

The mask, touched up and ready to use.

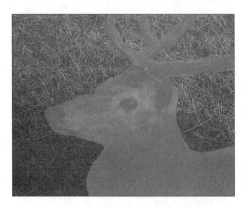

4. When the mask is edited to your satisfaction, click the Standard Mode button in the toolbox (to the left of the Quick Mask button) to return to your original image. The unprotected area (in this case, the background) is surrounded by a Selection marquee (see Figure 12.5). Now we can apply any change we want to make to this area without affecting the area that we masked.

FIGURE 12.5
Here I applied the Blur
filter to blur the back-
ground details.

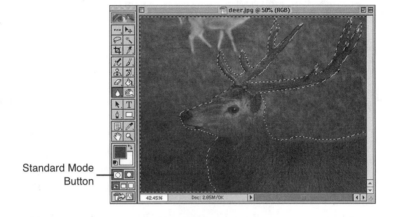

Standard Mode
Button

 5. When you are done making changes, press Command+D (Mac) or Control+D
(Windows) to deselect the area and get rid of the mask.

If you think you might need the same mask again, you can save it by going to the
Channels palette and clicking the Mask icon at the bottom of the palette. (It looks like
the Quick Mask icon with the colors inverted.) This saves your mask as an Alpha channel. You can come back and reapply it as needed.

> If you need a straight edge on your mask, use the Line tool to draw a single
> pixel line. It appears in the Mask color as long as you are in Quick Mask
> mode when you draw it.

12

Layer Masks

Layer masks enable you to hide and reveal parts of layers, as well as to apply special
effects, such as filters, in a controlled and precise manner. Layer masks, like Quick
Masks, can be edited. One advantage of applying effects to a Layer mask is that, if you
don't like the result, you have only to discard the mask, and your image is left
untouched. If you like what you see, apply the mask to make the changes.

Layer masks are raster (bitmap) images. They are altered with Brush tools. There's also a
kind of mask called a *vector mask*, or *layer clipping path*. Instead of painting the mask
on the screen, you draw its boundaries with the Path tools. You'll learn more about those
in the next hour.

You can't place a Layer mask on the background layer. If the image is on the background layer, you can double-click it in the Layers palette and rename it. This removes the associated properties of a background layer.

To make a Layer mask, first select an area of the image to mask and click the New Layer icon at the bottom of the Layer palette to make a new layer. Then click the Layer Mask icon (the second leftmost icon at the bottom of the Layers window) to make the new layer into a mask. When you do, you see a Layer mask thumbnail next to the image thumbnail. Figure 12.6 shows an example. Black indicates the portions of the layer that are covered and white shows the parts that are revealed. If the mask is made to be semi-transparent, the partially masked areas would be shown in gray.

FIGURE 12.6

Layer 1 masks everything but the sky and Layer 2 masks everything but the foreground rocks.

Notice the links between the two thumbnails, indicating that the mask is linked to the layer. After you create the mask, you can edit it simply by making the layer with the mask the active layer and clicking the mask icon. The foreground and background colors revert to the defaults, and you can apply black to add to the mask or white to remove parts of it.

To see the actual size and shape of the mask as you're working, *before you create the mask*, select the part of the image to be masked, and then go to the Layer menu. Select Layer→Add Layer Mask, and choose either Hide Selection or Reveal Selection, depending on whether you're masking the area around the selected piece of image or the image itself. Figure 12.7 shows the menu for this. This will show you the mask on the Layers palette without the image behind it. It's easier to see if you switch the palette view to a large icon. To see both the mask and the image at the same time, open the Channels palette and scroll to your mask. Click the eye icon to open the channel and make the mask visible over the image.

FIGURE **12.7**

The Layer menu.

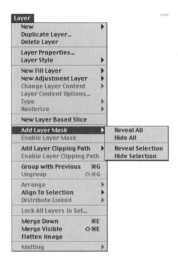

Hide Selection hides the area that you have selected, so you can work on the rest of the image. With this mask, you can protect part of the picture while you work on the rest. Reveal Selection obviously does just the opposite of the first command, Hide Selection. This command hides everything on a layer *except* that area within the Marquee selection. The other commands, Hide All and Reveal All, work a little differently. These, as the names suggest, are based on the entire layer.

Looking back to Figure 12.6, you can see both the Layer masks for the sky and the middle ground. The black section of the Layer mask is the actual mask. To apply one of these masks, turn off the other, by clicking the eye icon to hide the layer. In Figure 12.8, I've masked the foreground and then scribbled across the entire picture. The scribbles are only visible on the unmasked sky area.

FIGURE **12.8**

Black is masked; white can be edited.

12

Each layer can have only one Layer mask. If you need to do additional masking, activate the layer and apply Quick Mask.

To Do: Adding a Mask to a Layer

The business of making masks can seem very confusing, so let's take the process step-by-step.

1. Open the Layers palette, if it's not already active.
2. Select the layer to which you want to add a mask. Make sure there are no other masks already applied to that layer.
3. To hide the entire layer, choose Layer→Add Layer Mask→Hide All.
4. To make a mask that hides or reveals a selected area, first make the selection on the active layer.
5. Choose Layer→Add Layer Mask→Hide Selection *or* select Layer→Add Layer Mask→Reveal Selection, whichever is appropriate for your needs. Once you have made the mask, you can edit it as necessary with the Painting and Selection tools.

Take some time now to open a picture and practice applying masks. Try Quick Mask first, and then make a selection and turn it into a Layer mask. If you practice these skills while they're fresh in your mind, you'll remember them later when you need to do a quick color change or preserve an object while changing its background.

Editing Layer Masks

If you click the Layer Mask thumbnail in the Layers palette to make it active, you will see the mask icon appear in the small square to the left of the layer thumbnail. This indicates that the mask is active. Option+click (Mac) or Alt+click (Windows) on the thumbnail of the mask to place the mask on the work area. Select a Painting tool and paint the mask with black to add to it. Paint with white to subtract from the mask, or paint with gray to make the layer partially visible, and the mask thumbnail displays your changes. Figure 12.9 shows a mask being edited. I switched the view to the larger thumbnail to make it a little easier to see what I was doing. Just as a reminder, you can do this in the Layer palette options dialog box, which is reached from the Layers Palette pull-out menu.

FIGURE **12.9**

I've painted white over part of the black mask to add some symbols and lettering.

To edit the layer instead, either click its thumbnail or go to the Layer menu and select Disable Layer Mask, or Shift+click it in the Layers palette. This option puts a large X through the mask thumbnail so you know it's inactive (see Figure 12.10).

FIGURE **12.10**

The mask is temporarily disabled.

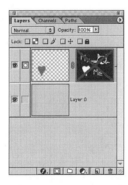

Using Layer→Disable Layer Mask allows you to get rid of the effects of the Layer mask temporarily. When you want it back, just choose Layers→ Enable Layer Mask, and you are back in business.

Removing the Layer Mask

There are two ways for you to get rid of the Layer mask when you are done with it or you want to start over. The first way, possibly the easiest, is simply to drag the Layer Mask icon found in the Layers palette onto the small trash can icon at the bottom of the window. You also can get rid of a layer by selecting Layer→Remove Layer Mask, and either Discard or Apply (see Figure 12.11). If you drag the mask to the trash, you are

12

presented with the dialog box, shown in Figure 12.12, in which you are also prompted to apply the effects of the mask or discard the mask without applying it.

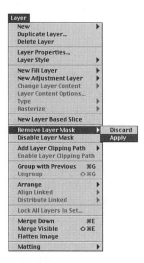

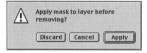

Even though a detailed explanation of channels and how to use them is somewhat beyond the scope of this book, a few words about channels may prove helpful to you at this point. Photoshop creates Color Information channels when you open a new image. An RGB document starts with four channels—one for each color and the composite that merges them. These are akin to the color separations used in four-color process printing. You can also create additional channels, called *alpha channels* in Photoshop parlance, which hold information about the masks you create for the image.

Channel thumbnails can be viewed in the Channels palette, which shares a window with the Layers palette. Click the Channels tab to open it. The composite is listed first, and then the Color channels, and finally the masks or alpha channels show up at the bottom of the list. If you have made several Layer masks, you may need to use the scrollbars or resize the palette to see them all.

As with the Layers thumbnails, you can increase the size of the Channels thumbnails to see them more easily. You can also click the eye icons in the Channel palette to hide or show single channels in the image window. This is the function of the Channel palette you will use most.

It's often helpful to arrange the Channel palette so that you view the Mask and the Color Composite (RGB or CMYK) channel together. By default, individual channels display in grayscale, but you can change this to see them in their own color by opening File→Preferences→Display & Cursors and checking Color Channels in Color.

Making Layer Masks Visible with Channels

Masks appear both on the screen where you create them and also on the Channels palette, where you can see them as a silhouette of the selection. The mask that you add to an image creates a new channel in your image, called an Alpha channel. Channels are Photoshop's way of storing color and mask information. (See the previous Coffee Break for more information about channels.) If you add a mask to a layer and select Window→Show Channels, you will see something like the example in Figure 12.13.

FIGURE 12.13

The Channels palette with a Layer mask at the bottom.

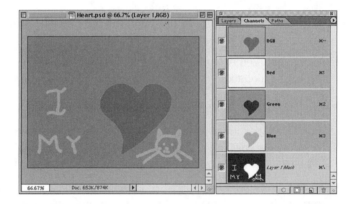

Click the eye icon to the left of the mask in the Channels palette and the mask appears as red, representing rubylith, a carry-over from the old days when this stuff was done in the real and not the cyber world. You can also edit the mask as a channel mask. More importantly, you can save it, by choosing Duplicate channel from the pull-out menu. You'll get a dialog box like the one in Figure 12.14, letting you save the mask either as part of the document, or as its own document. To turn a selection into an Alpha channel, use the menu command Selection→Save Selection. It's another quick and easy way to make a mask.

FIGURE 12.14

If you click New, the Alpha channel becomes a separate document.

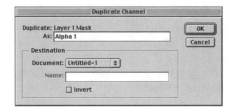

Summary

In this hour, you looked at using masks. Masking allows you to apply changes selectively, while protecting parts of the picture that you don't want to change. You learned about the Quick Mask function and how to edit a mask with the Paintbrush and Eraser. Then you learned about Layer masks and how to turn a layer into a mask. You learned how to view your mask, and save it as an Alpha channel.

Q&A

Q My picture has a lot of red in it, and the red mask is hard to see. Is there a way to change it to some other color?

A Of course. If you're working in Quick Mask mode, double-click the Quick Mask icon on the toolbox to open the Quick Mask options dialog box. If you're working on a Layer mask, Control+click (Mac) or right-click (Windows) on the Layer mask icon in the Layers menu to open a context menu that gives you access to the Layer Mask Display Options dialog box. In either one, you can set the color and amount of opacity for your mask. In the Quick Mask box, you can also set a radio button to determine whether the selection or the mask is indicated by the colored area.

Q If I'm doing catalog photos of small objects and want to mask the backgrounds, is it easier to select the background or to select the object and invert the selection?

A That depends on how complicated and/or how colorful the object is. If it's all one color, you can probably select it with one Magic Wand click and invert it to make your mask in a couple of seconds. If the background is simple and the object isn't, select the background.

Q I carefully painted in a mask, but the edges look wrong. They seem to have a dark line around them. Why?

A You probably had the brush set for Wet Edges. You can fix it, if it's an opaque mask (not painted in gray), by pouring black into the masked area.

Q **The selection tools missed some of the petals on the flower I'm trying to mask, but my hand's not steady enough to draw them in. What can I do?**

A Enlarge the image to 200% or even more. Then you can see what you're doing and draw or erase more precisely.

Quiz

1. A mask can hide
    a. An object
    b. The background
    c. Either the background or an object

2. Masks can be either opaque, semi-opaque, or transparent.
    a. True
    b. False

3. You can have up to 12 masks on a single layer.
    a. True
    b. False

4. Masks are saved with the picture and, therefore, increase file size. To save disk space, always
    a. Apply and discard the masks after you're sure you're done with them
    b. Flatten the image
    c. Hide the Layer masks

Quiz Answers

1. c. Masks hide anything you want to protect.
2. b. If the mask is transparent, it's not hiding anything. Parts of a mask can be and often are transparent, but not the whole mask.
3. b. Sorry, only one Layer mask per layer.
4. a. and b. both work. Flattening the image compresses the layers and applies the masks.

Exercises

Find a picture with several similar objects in it. Mask them separately and experiment with changing the colors of the objects, one at a time, without changing the background.

12

HOUR 13

Paths

Congratulations! You're halfway through, which is to say that you've seen only half of what Photoshop can do.

Early on, you learned about selections and how selecting part of an image isolates that part so you can work on it and not the entire image. Last hour, you learned about converting selections to masks to protect the parts of your image that you don't want to work on.

The problem with selections is that, as soon as you remove the selection marquee, it's gone. The only way to reselect something is to use the appropriate tools (Marquee, Lasso, and/or Magic Wand) and make the selection all over again, or use the History palette to revert back to the last Selection tool used. This, however, means that you lose whatever you did to the selection.

Paths solve this dilemma. With paths (also called *clipping paths*), you can create and *save* specific selections for future use. The paths get saved right within the Photoshop file, very much as a layer is saved. Because paths are vector-based rather than pixel-based, you aren't restricted to the shapes you can drag with the marquees. You can create very precise shapes and smooth curves with the Pen tools. Then you can either use them as selections, or stroke and fill them as objects or lines in your picture.

NEW TO VERSION 6 In Photoshop 6, Adobe created a new set of path shape tools. These tools can draw rectangles, rounded rectangles, ellipses, polygons, and straight lines; they have a default set of more than 60 custom shapes, ranging from stars, arrows, suns, and moons to a few I haven't figured out yet. (Is that *really* a lobster claw?) These path shapes can be filled and stroked just like the ones you draw yourself. Let's start by exploring the different ways to create paths, and then go into techniques for editing and using them in Photoshop.

Creating Paths

There are three paths you can take for creating paths (sorry, I couldn't resist):

- Create a path directly from a selection you've already made.
- Create a path from scratch by using the Pen tools and drawing the path by hand.
- Create a path using the Shape tools.

Paths via Selections

Depending on the image at hand, simply making a selection and converting it to a path can be the easiest and quickest way to create a path.

Let's look at an example. Figure 13.1 shows our test image, a cute little duck.

FIGURE 13.1

Our test image. We want a clipping path that outlines the duck.

As you remember, selection can be accomplished by using a number of tools. For this image, the Magic Wand is perfect because the subject is mostly one color. Simply set the Magic Wand tolerance to about 35 (so you're sure to get most of the yellow pixels), and select the duck. Select the duck beak by pressing the Shift key down as you click the wand on it. If there are highlights that the Magic Wand ignores, use Select→Feather to feather the edges of the selection by two to three pixels, or Select→Modify→Smooth with a setting of about 4 to even out the edges. This is usually enough to pick up highlights and edges. If not, lasso them. You may need to click in different areas to build a selection from an object that has several colors or shades of a color. Figure 13.2 shows the selection.

FIGURE 13.2

*The duck is now
selected.*

To Do: Convert a Selection to a Path

Now that you have a selection, follow these steps to convert it to a path:

1. Make sure that the Paths palette is visible. If not, choose Window→Show Paths.

2. Select Make Work Path from the pop-out menu at the upper-right of the Paths
   palette (see Figure 13.3).

FIGURE 13.3

*The pop-out menu of
the Paths palette.*

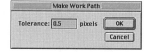

3. The only option to set in the Make Work Path dialog box is Tolerance (see Figure
   13.4). *Tolerance* refers to how closely Photoshop follows the outline of your selection in creating the path. The smaller the tolerance, the more exact the path will be.

FIGURE 13.4

*The Make Work Path
dialog box.*

> Be aware that complex paths can be resource intensive. More complexity
> means more points, angles, curves, and so on. The result can mean slower
> processing of the image, bigger files, and possible problems when printing.

For this image, I first tried a Tolerance of five pixels. As Figure 13.5 shows, the
results were unacceptable. Photoshop was too flexible and approximate in creating
the path at this setting. You can see that the smoother line of the path does not follow the outline of the duck closely enough.

13

▼

FIGURE 13.5
When the path doesn't match the selection to your satisfaction, Tolerance is set too high.

When this happens, I simply reach for my favorite Photoshop command: Undo. Undo the path conversion and try a lower Tolerance setting. After some experimentation, I found that a value of one pixel worked quite well (see Figure 13.6)

FIGURE 13.6
When Tolerance is set correctly, the path matches the selection satisfactorily.

4. Note how the path also appears in the Paths palette in Figure 13.7. Photoshop has named it "Work Path." You can rename the path by simply double-clicking it in the Paths palette. In the Save Path dialog box that appears, simply type the new path name and click OK, as shown in Figure 13.7.

FIGURE 13.7
Rename paths by using the Save Path dialog box.

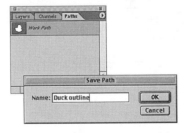

▲

Although renaming work paths isn't required, it's a good idea, especially if you might need the path again. If the path is left as a work path and you start a second path, one of two things will happen. First, if the work path is still active in the Paths palette, the new path will be added to it as a subpath. Second, if the original work path is no longer active in the Paths palette, the new path will replace it. (Undo and the History palette give you opportunities to recover the original path, but it's easier to simply rename it and transform it into a regular path at the time of creation.)

> There's also another way to create a path from a selection. Make a selection and then simply click the Make Work Path button at the bottom of the Paths palette. Photoshop creates the path automatically by using the existing Tolerance setting.

Paths via the Pen Tools

Sometimes, making a selection is too difficult or requires too much work on a particular image. In that case, consider using the Pen tools and drawing the path by hand.

If you've used vector-based illustration programs, such as Adobe Illustrator or Macromedia FreeHand, you already know about Bézier-based drawing tools such as Photoshop's Pen tools. If you haven't used these kinds of tools before, you should know right up front that it takes a little practice, but the payoff is worth the effort. In addition to the standard pens that draw a line and add or remove points on the line, Photoshop provides two additional pens. The Magnetic Pen Tool (available through the Pen Tool pop-out menu) makes drawing around a complicated object much easier. The Freeform Pen Tool gives you the power to draw any kind of line you want—straight, curved, squiggly—and turn it into a path.

NEW TERM A *Bézier curve* is a curve defined by three points: one on the curve and two outside the curve at the ends of handles that you can use to change the angle and direction of the curve. If this sounds like gibberish, don't worry, you'll see some examples.

To Do: Using the Pen Tool

▼ To Do

The best way to learn how to use a Pen tool is simply to play around with it in a new Photoshop document.

1. First, create a new Photoshop document big enough to move around in—6×6 inches sounds good, and a plain white background looks good.

2. Select the Pen Tool. (It looks like an old-fashioned fountain pen nib.) Also make sure that the Paths palette is visible.

3. Click somewhere near the left edge of the image. This is where your path begins. (Notice that Photoshop immediately creates a path called "Work Path" in the Paths

▼

13

▼   palette. This path can be renamed in the same way described in the previous
         To Do.)

    4.   To draw a straight line, simply move your cursor and click somewhere else. (Don't
         hold the mouse button down!) You've just created a *corner point*, which means that
         Photoshop connects the two points with a straight line (see Figure 13.8).

FIGURE 13.8

*Just two simple clicks
create a corner point
and a straight line.*

    5.   To continue the path (but now with a curved line), move your cursor to the middle
         bottom of the window and then click and drag left. You'll see a curve immediately
         appear and change as you drag it (see Figure 13.9). You've just created a *smooth
         point*, which means that Photoshop creates a smooth curve where two curved line
         segments meet.

FIGURE 13.9

*A click-and-drag
action creates a
smooth point and a
curved line.*

    6.   To make this clearer, draw another smooth curve. Move your cursor to a point to
         the upper right of the second point; click and drag to the right and a bit down.
         Again a smooth point and a curve are created (see Figure 13.10).

FIGURE 13.10

*Click and drag to cre-
ate another smooth
point on the same
path.*

         Notice the point you created in step 5. It creates a nice smooth curve between the
         point you just created and the point you created in step 4. That's what a smooth
         point is all about.

         As you have no doubt noticed, creating smooth points also results in the appear-
         ance of two *handles* for each point. These handles can be used to change the angle
         and direction of a curve after you've initially established it. You'll learn more about
▲   them in the "Editing Paths" section, later in this hour.

Okay, that's the basics: straight lines via corner points and curved lines via smooth points. But there's more that you have to know about each one to use them effectively.

Corner Points

Corner points are easy. No matter what kind of line is coming into a corner point, the result is always an angle, not a curve. If a curved line comes into a corner point, it's the smooth point at the other end of that line that affects the line's angle (see Figure 13.11).

FIGURE 13.11

Corner points sur-round smooth points.

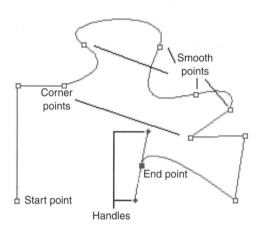

If you want to constrain corner points so they appear only at 45- or 90-degree angles, hold down the Shift key while you click to create the point.

Smooth Points

As you saw in the first Pen Tool example, the behavior of smooth points is a bit more complicated and takes some getting used to. A smooth point always tries to create as smooth a curve as it can between two meeting lines (see Figure 13.12).

13

FIGURE 13.12

Smooth points do their utmost to create curves out of any situation.

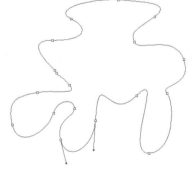

To Do: Creating a Sharp Curve

There is a less smooth kind of curve you can create when you need it. It's called a *sharp curve*, and the following steps show you how to create one:

1. In a new Photoshop document, begin a path with an initial point.

2. Create a smooth point as you normally would, by dragging after you click to set the point, making one curve.

3. Move the pointer so that it's exactly over the smooth point you just created. Hold down Option (Mac) or Alt (Windows) while you click and drag the mouse in the direction of the bump in the new curve. Release the key and mouse button. Your screen should now look something like what you see in Figure 13.13.

FIGURE 13.13

Creating a sharp curve. The rightmost line is what I just created by using the Option or Alt key.

4. Move the cursor to where you want the line to end; then click and drag opposite the direction you dragged in step 3. Figure 13.14 shows the resulting sharp curve.

FIGURE 13.14

The final sharp curve.

▲

Previewing the Path

When you're creating all these points and lines, there's a preview feature that can be very helpful. Look at the Tool Options bar. There's an option called Rubber Band. Activating this feature enables you to preview both straight lines and curves before you click to create them. Experiment to see this feature at work.

Completing the Path

To complete a path, you have two choices: *close* the path by connecting the final point to the initial point, or leave the path *open*.

A *closed path* means you have created a loop, so the final path has no beginning or end. To close a path, use the following steps:

1. Create a path by using whatever points you need.

2. After the last point, move your cursor so that it appears on top of your initial point. You'll see a small circle next to the Pen pointer.

3. Click to create a final corner point, or click and drag to create a final curve (see Figure 13.15).

FIGURE 13.15

The start and stop point is the gray one.

An *open path* means the path has a beginning and an end. Figures 13.8 through 13.14 have all been open paths. To end a path that you want to keep open, use the following steps:

1. Create a path by using whatever points you need.

2. After the last point, simply click the Pen Tool icon in the toolbar. The path now has an end.

   The next time you click in the image, you'll be starting a new path instead of continuing your previous path.

Saying that you've created a "path" is a little misleading. Actually, the path that you see consists of a number of subpaths that Photoshop has created, but for our purposes, they act as a single path. One thing to remember is that any path you create is not really *part* of the image. That is, you aren't changing the actual image at all. Think of it as adding a new layer to an image, like a layer of clear acetate that helps you manipulate an image better but that doesn't necessarily alter it in any way.

13

Editing Paths

Most of the time, the initial path you create, whether produced by converting a selection or drawing with the Pen Tool, won't be perfect. It's often too difficult to get the selection just right or the lines and curves perfectly placed on the first try. You have probably already realized this while following the previous steps in this hour.

Fortunately you can easily alter paths after they are created and, once again, you use the Pen Tool (and its associated tools) to do this.

The Path Tools

First, look at the various Path tools available in Photoshop. Click and hold on the Pen Tool (see Figure 13.16).

FIGURE **13.16**

*Photoshop's Path
tools.*

- *Pen Tool*—You already know this tool intimately. It's used to create new paths.
- *Freeform Pen Tool*—As the name suggests, you can use this tool to draw a freeform path in any shape or direction. Photoshop will add the necessary points and handles as you go, so you can adjust any part of your path that's not quite what you had in mind.

Remember the Magnetic Lasso that formed itself around what you were trying to select? The Freeform Pen has a magnetic option, on the Tool Options bar, that works the same way. Use it for tracing a shape.

- *Add Anchor Point Tool*—Use this tool to add points to a path.
- *Delete Anchor Point Tool*—Use this tool to cut points from a path.
- *Convert Point Tool*—Yes, you can even change the *type* of point after you have initially created one. For example, you can turn a corner point into a smooth point, a smooth point into a sharp curve, and so on. You'll learn more about this tool in the next section.

There are also two Path Selection Tools to help you work with paths. They're found in the toolbox right above the Pen tools. One is the Direct Selection Tool and the other is the Path Component Selection Tool. The Direct Selection Tool (represented by a hollow arrow) moves individual segments of the path. The Path Component Selection Tool (the black arrow) moves all the components of a single path at once. If you have several paths on the same layer, the Path Component Selection Tool will move one path at a time. If you want to move them all together, use the Select All command and the Hand Tool.

You can switch between the Pen tools and Path Selection tools in one of two ways: either by clicking and holding down over the Pen Tool in the toolbar, so the other Path tools appear, or by pressing Shift+P on the keyboard, which cycles between the Pen Tool and Freeform Pen Tool. Pressing Shift+A gives you the Direct Selection Tool, as does pressing Command (Mac) or Control (Windows) while using any other Path tool.

Basic Path Techniques

You've probably already figured these out on your own, but just in case, here are a few basic techniques for navigating among and using paths:

- To select a path, simply click its name in the Paths palette, just as you'd click a layer to activate it. Selected paths show up in your image, as you'd expect.
- To deselect a path, click another path name or click elsewhere in the empty area of the Paths palette. This makes the path disappear from the main window.
- To delete a path, select the path in the Paths palette and drag it to the Trash Can button at the bottom of the palette, just as you'd delete a layer.
- To create a new path, you can do one of four things:

  Simply start drawing the path with one of the Pen tools in the main image window.

  Before using the Pen Tool, choose New Path from the palette's pull-down menu.

  Click the Create New Path button at the bottom of the palette.

  Create a selection and then use the Make Work Path command or button.

- To duplicate a path, select the desired path in the palette and drag it to the Create New Path button. This works in the same manner as duplicating a layer.

Using Paths

What can you do with paths after you've gone to all the trouble of creating them? Well, a lot of things. In Photoshop, you can use paths to remember selections you want to use repeatedly. You can also fill a path area or define the color, border, and so on of the outline of the path. Paths indicate selections or lines, but they don't actually appear on your canvas unless you add some paint to them to make them show up. You can fill a path or stroke it, or both. *Stroking* adds a stroke of paint over the path. *Filling* places a color or pattern inside the path. Figure 13.17 shows a freeform path that has been stroked with black and filled with gray.

When you fill a path, you are adding pixels to the active layer of your picture. Make sure that the layer you want to put the paint on is the active one.

FIGURE **13.17**
A filled and stroked path.

Turning Paths into Selections

In Photoshop, paths are most useful as permanently saved selections. This can be incredibly helpful when you think you might want to reuse a specific selection later. When in doubt, create a path so that the selection will always be available.

To Do: Convert a Path into a Selection

▼ To Do

You already learned how to convert a selection to a path. The following steps show how to convert a path into a selection:

1. Create a path through whatever means suits your fancy.

2. Activate the path you want to convert by clicking it in the Paths palette.

3. Choose Make Selection from the pull-down menu at the top-right of the Paths palette (see Figure 13.18) or click the Make Selection button, third from the left in the bottom of the Paths palette. (This bypasses the dialog box described below.)

FIGURE **13.18**
Turning a work path into a selection.

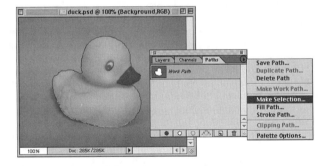

4. In the Make Selection dialog box that appears, you can set the tolerance of the selection that Photoshop creates (see Figure 13.19). The higher the Feather Radius setting, the less exact the selection will be.

▼ 5. Click OK, and you'll see the path turn into a selection.

FIGURE 13.19

The Make Selection dialog box.

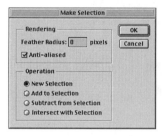

Filling a Path

Filling a path means just what you'd expect. Select a path, choose Fill Path from the pull-down Palette menu, and you'll get the same kinds of options you get for filling a selection (see Figure 13.20). In the Fill Path dialog box, you can choose a color, a pattern, or a snapshot to fill the area. You can also choose a Blending mode, opacity percentage, optional transparency, anti-aliasing, and a feathering value. If the path consists of two separate subpaths, only the one selected will be filled or stroked.

FIGURE 13.20

Fill Path dialog box.

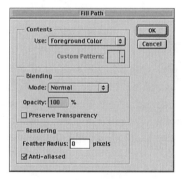

Stroking a Path

Stroking a path affects the outline of the path, not the entire area enclosed within a path. Select a path and then choose Stroke Path from the pull-down Palette menu. The dialog box enables you to choose the tool you want to use, from Pencil and Paintbrush to Blur and Sponge (see Figure 13.21).

13

FIGURE **13.21**
Stroke Path dialog box.

Whatever tool you pick, Photoshop uses that tool's current settings to create the result. So, for example, if you want to airbrush the path outline with only 60% pressure, make sure that value is set in the Tool Options bar *before* you select Stroke Path.

> There are shortcuts for filling and for stroking. Hold your mouse pointer over the buttons at the bottom of the Paths palette, and you'll see the tool tips. Press Option (Mac) or Alt (Windows) as you click a button to open its dialog box.

Using the Shape Tools

 Photoshop 6 has provided us with a handy arsenal of predrawn Shape tools. These can be used as paths and be filled or stroked as needed. They can be resized, to a certain extent reshaped, and placed wherever you need them. The rounded rectangle is great for masking photos. The polygons are useful if you need a bunch of stars or other unusual shapes. Figure 13.22 shows the Shape tools.

FIGURE **13.22**
These tools can draw filled or unfilled shapes.

To draw a shape, first specify a foreground color, which can be used to fill the shape. Select the appropriate Shape tool. (If you are using the Custom Shape Tool, you need to click the Shape window on the Tool Options bar and choose one of the available shapes.)

To create a new shape, select the Create Shape Layer, the Create Work Path, or the Fill Region option in the options bar, as seen in Figure 13.23. Use Create Work Path if you want to make a path with a particular shape. Use Fill Region to produce a filled shape. Use Create Shape Layer to draw a shape on a new layer.

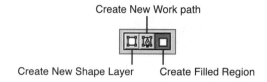

FIGURE 13.23

Select one of these options.

Create New Work path

Create New Shape Layer   Create Filled Region

To edit a shape after you've drawn it, make sure the shape layer is selected and choose the Add, Subtract, Restrict, or Invert option in the Tool Options bar. If you choose Add and draw a second shape touching the first, they'll both be filled. If you choose Subtract, you can cut out part of the filled shape. Restrict only fills the shapes where they overlap. Invert removes the color where two shapes overlap. Figure 13.24 shows some examples.

FIGURE 13.24

These options aren't available until you've drawn the first shape.

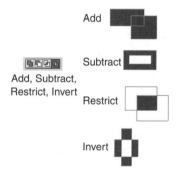

Add, Subtract, Restrict, Invert

Add

Subtract

Restrict

Invert

Dragging as you draw determines the size and orientation of a shape. Hold down Shift as you drag to constrain a rectangle or rounded rectangle to a square or to constrain an ellipse to a circle. Hold down Option (Mac) or Alt (Windows) as you drag to draw from the center of the object.

If you need a precisely sized shape, click the down arrow at the corner of the shapes window on the Tool Options bar. This opens a dialog box. Depending on the shape you chose, you can set height and width, corner radius, or the number of sides in a polygon or points on a star. Use the Tool Options bar to specify a blending mode and opacity for the shape.

Add a Shape to the Custom Shapes Palette

Create a shape using the other Shape tools, or select the path containing the shape you want to use. In Figure 13.25, I've used the duck, drawn a path around him, and filled it. To add him to the Custom Shapes palette, choose Edit→Define Custom Shape and enter a name for the new shape in the dialog box (see Figure 13.25). When you click OK, the shape will be added to the palette.

13

FIGURE **13.25**
Give the shape a name.

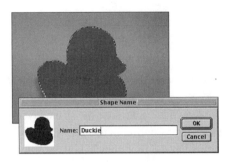

To select your new custom shape, choose it from the Shape list in the options bar. To restrict the shape to its original size, choose Fixed Size in the Tool Options bar.

Summary

The path is a magical Photoshop feature that has many applications in your daily Photoshop existence. You can use paths as permanent Photoshop selections that can be reused anytime, as the means to fill or stroke part of an image, as a way to convert areas of an image or work on an image in Illustrator, or as clipping paths to be exported into a page layout program. Photoshop provides an array of tools and options for creating paths: You can do so by converting a selection you have already made, or by drawing a path from scratch by using a Pen Tool. You can also edit existing paths with the assorted Path tools, and you can create shaped paths with the Shape tools. You can even make and use custom path shapes.

Q&A

Q How can I use paths to draw shapes onto my pictures?

A Choose the Shape Tool that's appropriate, and select Shape Layer on the Tool Options bar. Your shape will appear on a new layer in the foreground color. To draw a custom shape, select the appropriate Pen Tool and draw the path you need. Once you have placed the path, stroke it or fill it as necessary.

Q What does the Magnetic Pen do that the other Pen Tools don't?

A The Magnetic Pen bases its selection on contrast. This automates path creation to some degree, as you don't have to rely on your own hand-eye coordination to follow a complex path.

Q How do you know what tolerance to set when you convert a path to a selection?

A That depends on how smooth—or how accurate—you want the finished path to be. A tolerance of 1 pixel or less will make the path follow the selection as precisely as possible. A tolerance of 5–10 will give you a smoothed out path, following your selection to within 5 to 10 pixels.

Quiz

1. What does it mean to "stroke" a path?

    a. Using the points and Bézier handles to refine its shape.

    b. Adding a color to it so it becomes a line.

    c. Painting over it with short strokes.

2. How do you turn a selection into a path?

    a. Select it and press Command+P.

    b. Select Make Path or Make Work Path from the Paths pop-out menu.

    c. Line it with bricks.

3. What does the Rubber Band option do?

    a. Makes your paths visible before you click the mouse.

    b. Makes paths spring back to a straight line when clicked.

    c. Makes lines "stretchy."

Quiz Answers

1. b. Think of stroking it with a paintbrush.

2. b. Don't try A unless you want to make a print.

3. a. All paths are visible "as you draw them" (while you drag to set the handles), but the Rubber Band mode makes the path visible as you move the mouse.

Exercises

Start a new page and use the Pen Tool to draw a star-shaped path and a freeform path with lots of curves. Stroke both of these paths with a color. Then use the Magnetic Pen Tool to trace around them. Notice that as long as you stay fairly close to your original line, the Pen Tool places a path right at the edge of the line. Fill these shapes with a color. Draw two more paths inside these shapes, and fill them with a different color. Add a couple of shapes with a Shape tool. Try a custom shape. Practice with the Path tools, adding points and refining your paths until you're comfortable with all of them.

13

Hour **14**

Filters That Improve Your Picture

I'm not sure whether Photoshop's creators pioneered the idea of plug-in filters or just took the ball and ran with it. In either case, they've given us a wonderful tool for altering the all-over appearance of a picture. Some of Photoshop's filters are strange; some are beautiful; some are merely useful—those are the ones we'll look at in this hour.

The title for this hour's lesson doesn't really tell the story. Presumably you wouldn't apply a filter that *didn't* improve your picture. What would be the point? It might be more correct to say that the filters we'll be looking at will fix common photographic problems.

Sharpen Filters

One of the most common problems photographers face is the out of focus picture. There are many reasons why a picture might be fuzzy. Either the subject or the photographer might have moved slightly when the picture was taken. Perhaps the camera wasn't focused correctly, or possibly the picture was taken with an inexpensive camera that had a poor quality plastic lens. Some of these problems are easier to compensate for in Photoshop than others.

If a photo is way out of focus, there's not much that can be done to bring it back. If it's just a little bit soft, Photoshop can at least create the illusion of sharper focus. It does this with a set of filters called Sharpen. Like all the filters described in this chapter, they're found on the Filter menu (see Figure 14.1).

FIGURE 14.1

The Filter menu show-ing the Sharpen filters.

Sharpen, Sharpen More

Two of the Sharpen filters, Sharpen and Sharpen More, provide different levels of the same function. They work by finding areas in the image where there are significant color changes, such as at the edges of an object. Whenever such an area is found, Photoshop increases the contrast between adjacent pixels, making the lights lighter and the darks darker. Figure 14.2 shows three views of a slightly fuzzy picture of a pier. The top example is before sharpening. The middle example has had Sharpen applied, and the bottom exam-ple has had Sharpen More applied.

If you don't enlarge the picture too much, the effect looks quite good. If you take a close look, as we have in Figure 14.3, you can see that the image is really very artificial looking.

By the way, Sharpen More is the same effect as applying the Sharpen filter twice to the same picture. Keep in mind that you can do this any time a filter has less than the desired effect. The easy way to apply the same filter again is to press Command+F (Mac) or Control+F (Windows). This keyboard shortcut applies whatever filter and filter settings (if any) you applied last.

FIGURE 14.2

Before and after sharpening.

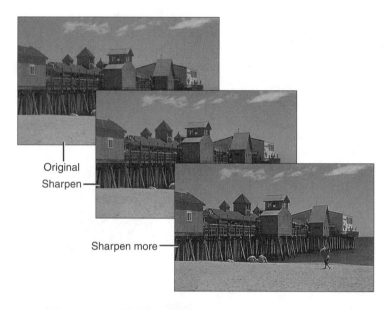

Original

Sharpen

Sharpen more

FIGURE 14.3

An image with the Sharpen More filter applied.

Try the Sharpen filter on one of your own fuzzy pictures and see what you think. Does it help? Try the Sharpen More filter also. They are great for adjusting slightly out-of-focus photographs or scans, but don't rely on these filters too much. They can only do so much. They can't add what is totally missing from an image—namely, focus and good contrast. They can, however, help bring back a photo that's just a little bit off. Don't forget that you can apply filters selectively, using masks or selections to only filter part of the image.

14

Sharpen Edges

Sharpen Edges is a truly useful filter. It doesn't affect the whole image, so you don't get as much of a sense of that harsh blocky effect as with Sharpen More. Rather, Sharpen Edges "sees" and enhances the contrast at whatever it perceives to be an edge. Figure 14.4 shows a before and after version of our pier, using Sharpen Edges. Sharpening the edges has a slight but noticeable effect on the quality of the photo.

FIGURE **14.4**
Sharpen Edges filter applied in the lower-right figure.

Unsharp Mask

Unsharp masking is a traditional technique that has been used in the printing industry for many years. It is probably your best bet for precision sharpening. It corrects blurring in an original image or scan, as well as any blurring that occurs during the resampling and printing process. The Unsharp Mask works by locating every two adjacent pixels with a difference in Brightness values that you have specified, and increases their contrast by an amount that you specify. It enables you to really control the sharpness of an image.

Set the level of sharpening you need in the Unsharp Mask dialog box shown in Figure 14.5; the dialog box appears when you select the filter. The Radius control sets the number of surrounding pixels to which the sharpening effect is applied. I suggest that you keep the radius fairly low—around 2.0. The Threshold setting controls how alike the pixels must be to be sharpened. The lower the setting, the more similar the pixels have to be. The higher the setting, the greater Photoshop's tolerance of difference will be. (Of course, as always, feel free to go wild and try all the settings. That is the best way to learn.) Be sure you check the Preview box so you can see the effect of your changes.

Many Photoshop experts recommend always applying the Unsharp Mask filter to every image that you process, whether it's going to be printed or used on the Web. (I personally don't like to say "always" or "never" because there can be exceptions to any rule.) You should probably *try* it on every image, to see whether you like the effect.

FIGURE 14.5

The preview window lets you see what effect your settings have.

Photoshop filters aren't restricted to Photoshop. Other Adobe products, such as PageMaker and Illustrator, can use many of them also. Even Macromedia's Director can employ many Photoshop filters. If you find particularly useful or interesting filters or filter combinations, try using them with other Photoshop plug-in–compatible programs.

Blur Filters

The Blur filters (Filter→Blur) are useful tools when you want to soften the effects, either of a filter you have just applied or of brush strokes in a painting. Blurring can gently smooth a harshly lit portrait or, when used on a selection instead of the whole image, can throw an unwanted background out of focus, making it less obtrusive. The Blur filters are shown in Figure 14.6.

FIGURE 14.6

The Blur menu.

14

Blur, Blur More

There are two basic Blur filters: Blur and Blur More. They do exactly as their names suggest. Blur is very subtle. Blur More is only a little less so. Figure 14.7 shows a comparison of the two filters in use, against a non-blurred original. As you can see, the changes are minor. Blurring doesn't make much difference, but it can smooth out wrinkles in a portrait or soften a hard edge.

FIGURE 14.7

Blur is applied on the top right; Blur More, on the bottom right. You have to look carefully to see the effect.

Gaussian Blur

You can apply the Blur filter several times to get the effect you want, or you can move on to Gaussian Blur (Filter→Blur→Gaussian Blur), which is a more controllable filter. It uses a mathematical formula, (the Gaussian Distribution Equation, which results in a bell curve) to calculate the precise transition between each pair of pixels. The result of this is that most of the blurred pixels end up in the middle of the two colors or values, rather than at either end of the spectrum. This produces a generalized blur that neither darkens nor lightens the image.

The Gaussian Blur dialog box, shown in Figure 14.8, lets you determine exactly how much Blur to apply by setting a Radius value from 0.1–250. You can also use it to antialias the edges of an object, and to blur shadow areas when you want to create a drop shadow effect. Even at fairly low settings, it has quite a dramatic effect. Anything greater than 5.0 would make the image incomprehensible. In Figure 14.8, notice how the subject's forehead wrinkles, obvious in the large picture, are almost gone in the Blur Preview window.

FIGURE 14.8
*Smaller numbers give
you less blur.*

The Gaussian Blur is a useful retouching tool when applied to an area within the picture that you want to de-emphasize. In Figure 14.9, the lynx is washing up after lunch, but the big wire fence behind her is distracting. The picture would be nicer if we got rid of that reminder of civilization. Obviously, we don't want to blur Natasha's spots. So rather than applying Blur to the whole image, we need to select the fence and ground around and behind it. I used the lasso to select some background and the fence, while carefully avoiding the cat. Now I can adjust the Blur radius until the fencing disappears.

FIGURE 14.9
*Selective blurring can
hide flaws, too.*

Before

After

A quick application of the Blur Tool, with Pressure set to 75%, blends the blurred and unblurred areas, and the lynx appears to be back in the wilderness again.

14

Use the Blur filters when you have a large area to blur. Use the Blur Tool when you just want to soften a small area, because it's more controllable in terms of the degree of focus change it applies.

Radial Blur

The Radial Blur filter can be interesting, if you carefully choose how to apply it. It gives you two choices: Spin and Zoom. Spin mode gives you a blur that looks as if the image is spinning around its center point. Zoom mode theoretically gives you the effect of zooming the camera into or away from the image.

In the Radial Blur dialog box, seen in Figure 14.10, you can set both an amount for the Blur effect (from 1–100) and a quality level (Draft, Good, or Best). Amount apparently refers to the distance that the pixels are moved to create the Blur. You can see the difference in the window as you set the Blur amount. You can use the same window to determine a center point for the Blur effect.

FIGURE 14.10

The same dialog box applies both Zoom and Spin.

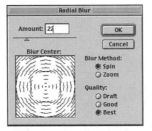

The Quality settings determine the manner in which the Blur effect is calculated; you can choose Draft, Good, or Best. There's very little difference between Good and Best in the resulting images. The biggest difference, in fact, is not in the image quality, but in how long it takes Photoshop to compute and apply the Blur in each mode. Best can take quite a long time if the image is complex and your computer is an older model.

In Figure 14.11, I've applied Spin and Zoom blurring to a picture of a yellow daisy. After experimenting with the settings, I used 10 as the amount to spin and 65 as the Zoom setting.

FIGURE 14.11
Spin and Zoom obviously aren't for everyday use, but, as a special effect, they're certainly interesting.

Spin

Zoom

Smart Blur

The Smart Blur filter (Filter, Blur, Smart Blur) is probably the most useful one of the bunch, especially for image editing and photo repair. It blurs everything in the image, or selection, except the edges. Smart Blur calculates the differences between color regions to determine boundaries, and it maintains these boundaries while blurring everything within them. It's the perfect filter when you need to take 10 years off a portrait subject's face, smooth out teenaged skin, or get rid of the texture in a piece of cloth without losing the folds.

Figure 14.12 shows the Smart Blur filter dialog box, and Figure 14.13 shows before and after views of a portrait with the filter applied on the right. You can set Radius and Threshold to determine how much blur is applied and set Quality, as done earlier, to determine how the effect is calculated.

14

FIGURE **14.12**

*The Smart Blur filter
dialog box.*

FIGURE **14.13**

*Notice how the Smart
Blur, used on the right
image, has despotted
the background, too.*

Before   After

The Smart Blur filter has three modes:

- In Normal mode, the Preview window shows the effects of the blurring.
- Edge Only shows you the outlines with which Smart Blur is working.
- Edge Overlay shows the outlines as black lines on top of the image.

You can use the Edge Overlay or Edge Only to help you determine what threshold to set.
Convert the mode back to Normal before you click OK to apply the effect.

Motion Blur

When we see lines drawn behind a car, a cat, or a comic strip character, we instinctively
know that it or he is supposed to be in motion. Those lines represent "motion blur," which
is actually a photographic mistake caused by using a slow shutter speed on a fast subject.
The image's subject appears totally or partially blurred against the background because the
subject actually traveled some distance during the fraction of a second that the camera
shutter was open.

In the early days of photography, motion blur was a common occurrence, primarily because shutter speeds were slow, and film sensitivity was not very great. Today, motion blur is unusual, unless the photographer is planning to try to capture the subject this way on purpose by using the least-sensitive film available or by using a small lens opening and a correspondingly slower shutter. If you want to try to approximate the effect of motion blur, however, Photoshop gives you a tool that can do it.

The Motion Blur Tool (Filter→Blur→Motion Blur) filter can add the appearance of motion to a stationary object by placing a directional blur for a predetermined distance. In the Motion Blur dialog box, shown in Figure 14.14, you can set both the distance and direction of the blur according to how fast and in what direction you want the object to appear to be traveling. The distance sets how much of a blur is applied—or how far the original image is "moved." The angle sets the direction of the blur. To adjust, drag the Radius icon or enter precise values into the field next to it. The trick, however, is to select the right area to which to apply Motion Blur. To get a convincing blur, you need to blur the space where the object theoretically was, as well as to where it theoretically has moved.

FIGURE 14.14

Using the Motion Blur is tricky at best.

The Motion Blur filter doesn't do much for most photos. After all, the blur caused by the camera shaking is the kind of thing we usually try to avoid—not add. But, for some special effects, and for doing tricks with type, it has interesting possibilities. Figure 14.15 shows one possible use. First, I rendered the type and applied the perspective distortion to give it some depth. Adding Motion Blur gave me a much zippier Zip, but I could even take this further.

For Figure 14.16, I took the word apart, cutting and pasting each letter to a different layer. I then applied a different number of pixels (increasing left to right) to each Motion Blur, from 6 pixels on the Z to 24 pixels on the P. The resulting Zip almost seems to be sliding into the screen, as shown in Figure 14.16.

14

FIGURE **14.15**

You can't Zip standing still.

FIGURE **14.16**

Using Layers lets you apply different filters or different degrees of filter to the same image.

Fading Filters

Filters are cool, but sometimes they just do a little too much to the image. Many, like the Motion Blur filter, are variable. You can set their effects to be as subtle or dramatic as you want. Others, like the basic Blur and Sharpen, don't have dialog boxes and don't give you the opportunity to apply any less than the full amount of effect that Photoshop thinks is right. Well, Papa Photoshop *doesn't* always know best, but you do have an option.

You can apply a filter and then open Fade to fade the effect anywhere from 1%–99%. You can also use the Fade box to set a Blending mode for the Fade effect. Even more important, you can fade whatever else you last did in the same dialog box (see Figure 14.17). You painted something, but the color was too strong? Fade it 50%. That's quicker than redoing it with a different color. You overdid an image color adjustment? Fade it. The Fade command changes whatever tool or action you just applied. Experiment with this feature. It can save you tons of time.

FIGURE **14.17**

The Fade dialog box.

To Do: Fade a Filter Effect or Color Adjustment

Let's try the putting the Fade command to practical use.

1. Open any convenient image. Apply a Blur filter or make any color adjustment (Image→Adjust).

2. Choose Edit→Fade Filter. If you're working on a selection, rather than the whole image, don't deselect it.

3. Set the Preview option so you can see the effect of the fade.

▼   4. Drag the slider to adjust the opacity.

       5. Choose a Blending mode other than Normal, if you want a particular effect.

▲   6. Click OK. Deselect the selection to merge it.

Summary

Photoshop's filters are the one tool that makes the program a "must have" for anyone working with photos. In this hour, you looked at the Photoshop filters that can help you "rescue"
a bad photo or bad scan. The Sharpen filters can restore the apparent focus of out-of-focus
photographs by increasing the contrast between adjacent pixels. The most useful of these is
the Unsharp Mask filter, which lets you set the parameters for how it finds and adjusts contrasts.

Blur filters come in several varieties and are most useful for putting unwanted parts of the
picture out of focus and for softening hard edges. The Motion Blur filter lets you create the
illusion of movement in stationary objects and can do interesting things to type.

Fade works with filters and with other Photoshop tools to decrease the effect of your action
by a percentage that you can set.

Q&A

Q What's the difference between the Blur filter and the Blur Tool?

A You can apply the Blur Tool as if it were a Paintbrush to as small an area as you
   want. The Blur filter blurs the entire image or selection evenly.

Q If I change my mind about applying a filter, can I stop the process?

A To cancel the filter as it's being applied, press Command+period (Mac) or Esc
   (Windows). To undo a filter, use the Undo command: Command+Z (Mac) or
   Control+Z (Windows). If it's too late to undo, use the History palette to revert to a
   stage before you applied the filter.

**Q I have a photo that's slightly out of focus. Is there any way to make the subject
   stand out more?**

A Select the subject and copy it to a new layer. Use Gaussian Blur on the original, and
   Sharpen on the subject only.

14

Quiz

1. Sharpen More applies _____ as much correction as Sharpen.

    a. Exactly

    b. Twice

    c. Half again

2. Gaussian Blur uses a _____ to determine how blur is applied.

    a. Mathematical formula

    b. Random memory algorithm

    c. Prismatic crystal filter

3. Many experts advise applying which filter to every photograph you bring into Photoshop?

    a. Sharpen

    b. Gaussian Blur

    c. Unsharp Masking

4. Fading a filter has this effect:

    a. It fades an action such as applying a filter according to a percentage you determine.

    b. It applies the filter at half strength.

    c. It applies a 50% gray tone over the filter.

Quiz Answers

1. b. To get the same effect, apply Sharpen twice.

2. a. The blur follows Gaussian distribution (the bell curve).

3. c. Unsharp Masking is especially helpful to scanned images.

4. a. You can fade from 99.99% down to 0.01.

Exercises

Find or shoot a picture of yourself or a friend, and load it into Photoshop. (If you don't have a digital camera or scanner, download a news photo from the Web, or a portrait from our Web site—see the Introduction for the URL.) Use the Blur and Sharpen filters to improve it. Find and remove wrinkles, eye bags, uneven complexions, and any other flaws.

HOUR 15

Filters to Make Your Picture Artistic

In Hour 10, "Advanced Painting Techniques," you saw how Photoshop's filters can help imitate other media. You looked specifically at the Watercolor, Colored Pencil, Charcoal, and Underpainting filters. But those are still just the tip of the iceberg. Under the general heading of artistic and sketch filters, Photoshop offers approximately 30 different filters that you can apply alone or in combinations to turn your so-so picture into a masterpiece. In this hour, you run through the alphabet of the Artistic, Brush Strokes, and Sketch effects. You will be amazed, boggled, confounded, delighted, ecstatic....

I've deliberately left out step-by-step To Do exercises in this chapter. You apply all these filters in the same way: Filter→Artistic, and so on. Use the dialog box and its preview window to judge the effects of the filter as you change the settings. The key to success with any of these filters is to experiment until you get the effect you want. If you don't like what you see when you apply a filter to the whole picture, undo, revert, or partially fade the filter. The command

> Edit→Fade reduces the strength of the filter, or any other tool or effect, by a percentage you set in its dialog box.

Artistic Filters

Artistic filters apply a certain amount of abstraction to your image. How much depends on the kind of filter and, to an even greater degree, on how you set the filter's variables. Many of these filters ask you to set brush size, detail, and texture. Brush size affects the thickness of the line. Detail determines how large a "clump" of pixels must be, so that the filter will, in effect, notice it and apply its changes. Texture, not to be confused with the effect of the Texturizer filter, simply adds a random smudge here and there in your image. Most of Photoshop's filters have a preview window in which you can see the effects of changing the settings before you actually apply the filter. To move the image inside the preview window, click it. The cursor turns into a hand, enabling you to slide the picture around to see the effect on specific parts of the image. If you change settings and the preview doesn't change right away, you see a thin line between the plus and minus symbols (beneath the magnification amount number). This line tells you that Photoshop is calculating the changes to apply. Click the plus or minus symbol to see a reduced or enlarged view within the preview window, but it's always a good idea to preview your image at 100% before you click OK.

For the sake of consistency, let's apply all the Artistic filters to a picture of the Old Orchard Beach pier. See Figure 15.1 for the unfiltered view.

FIGURE 15.1
Basic, nonartistic photo.

Colored Pencil

The Colored Pencil filter goes over the photo with a sort of crosshatched effect (see Figure 15.2). It keeps most of the colors of the original photograph, although any large, flat areas are translated to "paper" color, which you can set to any shade of gray from black to white. The filter's options box, shown in Figure 15.3, asks you to choose a

Pencil Width and the pressure of the Stroke. Paper Brightness can be set on a scale of 1–50, with 50 being the lightest, and 1 being completely black.

15

FIGURE 15.2
Colored Pencil filter applied.

FIGURE 15.3
Colored Pencil filter settings.

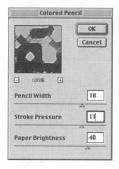

Using a narrow pencil (low number) gives you more lines. Greater stroke pressure picks up more detail from the original picture. In Figure 15.2, we used a large pencil and heavy pressure. In Figure 15.4, we tried the opposite, a small pencil and light pressure, using a Pencil Width of 3 and a Stroke pressure of 3. As you can see, the results are quite different from each other.

FIGURE 15.4
Less pencil width, less stroke pressure.

Cutout

The Cutout filter is one of my favorites. It can reduce a picture to something resembling a cut paper collage or a silk screen print. The Cutout filter does this by averaging all the colors and shades and converting them to just a handful. You can decide how many by setting the number of levels from 2–8 in its Options dialog window. You can also set Edge Fidelity (1–3) and Edge Simplicity (1–10) in the dialog box, which is shown in Figure 15.5.

Low Simplicity and high Fidelity settings produced the picture in Figure 15.6, which seems to be the most pleasing variation for this filter and photo combination. It's important to experiment with different settings every time you apply a filter to a new photo. What works with one picture might be totally wrong for another that is more or less complicated. In one combination or another, this filter manages to make almost any picture look good.

Dry Brush

Dry brush is a term used by watercolor painters to denote a particular style in which the brush is loaded with heavily concentrated pigment and dabbed, rather than stroked, on the paper. Figure 15.7 shows the Dry Brush options box with a small Brush Size and a high Brush Detail. You can see the result in Figure 15.8.

FIGURE 15.7
*Dry Brush filter
dialog box.*

15

FIGURE 15.8
*The Dry Brush filter
can look very cool
when applied to the
right picture.*

Film Grain

One reason that many commercial photographers are turning to high resolution digital photography is to get away from the problems caused by film grain. Film grain is the inevitable result of applying a layer of chemicals to a piece of plastic. When a picture is enlarged a great deal, you see the graininess of the chemicals as specks in the picture. It can add an interesting texture to your pictures, if you apply it carefully. It's often better to apply the Film Grain effect to selections, rather than to the whole photo. Figure 15.9 shows what happens when it's misapplied.

FIGURE 15.9
*Film Grain adds a
spotty texture that's
more pronounced in
dark areas.*

Notice how the Film Grain filter picks up the shading in the sky. It makes the picture look gritty. The dark specks tend to concentrate in flat dark areas, like the sky. If I use Film Grain on a more even photo, such as the roses in Figure 5.10, it works much better.

FIGURE 15.10

Grain applies dark specks to dark areas and light specks to highlights.

Fresco

Fresco is an Italian term for a mural painting done on a wet, freshly plastered wall. The results of using Photoshop's Fresco filter have little resemblance to the classical fresco works by such artists as Botticelli or Michelangelo. However, it's an interesting filter—and potentially useful. It gives a spotty but nicely abstract feeling. You need to be careful not to let the picture get too dark because the Fresco filter adds a good deal of black to the image in the process of abstracting it. Figure 15.11 shows an example.

FIGURE 15.11

A fresh approach—but not exactly a fresco.

When I first applied the Fresco filter to this picture, it turned almost totally black. To make the picture and filter combination work, I first had to adjust the curves to lighten it overall. Finally, I applied the Fresco filter with a setting of 1, for the Brush size and Texture, and a Detail setting of 3. Remember that if some filter doesn't seem to work for you with the picture "as is," you can change the filter's settings and then try again.

Neon Glow

It's hard to understand how the Neon Glow filter got its name; it has no resemblance to neon. As you can probably tell in Figure 15.12, the Neon Glow filter reduces the image to a single color negative and adds white highlights around the edges of objects. You can choose a color in the dialog box and specify the width of the "glow." If you use a very light color or gray, it can produce an interesting watermark effect. It turned the pier almost into a negative.

FIGURE 15.12
Neon Glow (?) filter applied.

The Neon Glow filter, more than most, should be applied only to certain kinds of pictures. Although it might give you an interesting spaced-out, surrealist landscape, it does nothing at all for portraits, or other photos in which you want to preserve the character of the original.

Paint Daubs

The Paint Daub filter adds a square or wavy crosshatch texture to the image. You can set brush size and sharpness, and choose among several brushes. The Simple brush was used in Figure 15.13. Experiment with the settings for this filter; some settings work much better than others. In this example, I used a brush size of 5 and set the sharpness to 3. I liked the result.

FIGURE 15.13
Paint Daub filter applied with a Simple brush.

Palette Knife and Plastic Wrap

When a painter uses a palette knife, the result is large areas of smudged color blending interestingly at the edges. The Palette Knife filter, alas, doesn't do that. Instead it reduces the picture to blocks of color by grouping similar pixels and averaging them. The result, in my opinion, is not very interesting. However, you might have better luck with it than I did. Try it. If you don't like it, there's always Undo.

Plastic Wrap is another filter that I seldom use. It places a gray film over the whole picture and then adds white "highlights" around large objects. The Plastic Wrap filter is supposed to look as if you covered the scene with plastic film. Instead, it looks more like you poured liquid latex over it. The overall effect can be overwhelming. Still, some of my friends have had good luck applying it to a smaller area, or in combination with other filter effects. It can be very effective as a way of making type look metallic.

Poster Edges

Here's a filter that *is* worth playing with. Poster Edges locates all the edges in your image, judging by the amount of contrast between adjacent pixels, and *posterizes* them, placing a dark line around the edges. It does really nice things to parts of our sample photo, as you can see in Figure 15.14. But, it's not so great on large flat areas, like sky or the side of a building. The posterizing process tends to break these areas up into patches of dark and light tone. In such a case, apply it to a selected part of the photo, rather than the entire image. For instance, the best way to use the filter on this image would be to apply it to the building but not to the sky.

FIGURE 15.14
Poster Edges filter applied.

Rough Pastels

Rough Pastels is a terrific filter with an interface that's a little bit more complicated than the others because you can specify texture as well as the stroke length and detail. Figure 15.15 shows the Rough Pastels dialog box. Choose from the textures supplied or import one from another source. (You can create textures and save them as Photoshop documents; then you can open them and apply them as textures through this dialog box or the Texturizer filter dialog box.)

FIGURE 15.15

Rough Pastels filter dialog box.

The Stroke Length and Stroke Detail settings seem to give the best results in the low to middle portion of their respective ranges, but, as always, experiment to see what works best for your image. Figure 15.16 shows the Rough Pastels filter applied to our sample picture.

FIGURE 15.16

Rough Pastels filter on Canvas, scaled to 80%.

Smudge Stick

Smudge Stick is a tricky filter. On light colored areas, the Smudge Stick filter adds a subtle, rather spotty texture that can be quite nice. On dark areas and lines, it adds a smudge, making the lines heavier and the edges blurry. Figure 15.17 shows an example.

Sponge

Have you ever tried painting with a sponge? It's a technique that's taught in some of the finer preschools and kindergartens. Basically, you dab a sponge into poster paint and then dab it on the paper. The results can be very nice, especially if you skip the poster paint and go straight to Photoshop's Sponge filter. On large flat areas, the Sponge filter gives a good imitation of a coarse, natural sponge (the kind they sell in the Sponge Market in Key West). In areas of detail, the sponge is a smaller one. You can, in fact, set the brush size, definition, and smoothness in the Sponge filter dialog box. One possible result is shown in Figure 15.18. This, again, is a filter that might be better used selectively, rather than on an entire image.

FIGURE 15.17
Smudge Stick filter applied.

FIGURE 15.18
Sponge filter applied.

Underpainting

The Underpainting filter, which you read about in Hour 10, reduces everything to a somewhat grayed out, paler, and soft-focused version of itself. Use it as an intermediate filter on the way to an effect, rather than by itself.

Watercolor

In Hour 10, you learned ways to make a photo look like a watercolor. Unfortunately, applying the Watercolor filter isn't necessarily one of them. Figure 15.19 shows this filter applied to the sample image. The look isn't really watercolor, but it might have some uses. If you like the general effect of the Sponge filter, but it distorts your picture too much, try the Watercolor filter instead. It has the same "clumping" effect, but with smaller clumps. Both of these filters—watercolor and sponge—tend to darken the image quite a bit. You might need to lighten the picture before applying the filter.

FIGURE 15.19
Watercolor filter applied.

Brush Strokes

I'm not sure why the Brush Strokes filters aren't part of the Artistic set. Artists use brushes, don't they? However, Photoshop's creators isolated these eight filters as the Brush Strokes set. What do they do? Cool stuff! Figure 15.20 is our original picture of a man playing a tuba, to which we'll be applying the next several filters.

FIGURE 15.20
Tuba Player, unfiltered.

Accented Edges

Best if applied subtly, the Accented Edges filter enhances the contrast of edges. The dialog box lets you choose Edge Width, Edge Brightness, and Smoothness. The Brightness setting darkens edges if the amount is 25 or less; from 26–50, it progressively lightens them. Figure 15.21 shows the filter applied, with settings as follows: Edge Width, 4; Brightness, 22; and Smoothness, 3.

FIGURE 15.21

Keep edge width small for best results.

Angled Strokes and Crosshatch

These filters give a crosshatched effect, similar to but darker than the one applied by the Colored Pencil filter. The Angled Strokes filter is less dramatic than Crosshatch filter. Figure 15.22 shows both.

Dark Strokes

You can use the Dark Strokes filter with many images only if you set the Black Intensity to 0 and the White Intensity to 10 in the dialog box. Otherwise, it tends to turn the whole picture black. Even with a relatively light picture, you might need to keep the black number low and the white setting high. Figure 15.23 shows you a carefully balanced

15

application of dark strokes. My settings were Balance, 5; Black intensity, 5; and White intensity, 5.

FIGURE 15.22
The Angled Strokes fil-ter applied on the left and Crosshatch filter applied on the right.

Angled Strokes filter   Crosshatch filter

I never used to like this filter, but it does surprisingly nice things to the tuba player. Perhaps it will do wonders for one of your photos, or possibly it will just muddy things up. You really never know what will happen until you try some of these filters, even though you can theoretically define what effect they'll have on specific dark or light areas. After years of Photoshop use, I am still frequently surprised (and often delighted) by what a filter like this can do to a photo.

Ink Outlines

The Ink Outlines filter places first a white line and then a black line around every edge that it identifies (see Figure 15.24). You can set stroke length and intensity in the dialog box.

Figure 15.23
Dark Strokes filter applied.

Applied to a still life or landscape, the Ink Outlines filter can give you the look of an old woodcut or steel engraving. If you use it on a portrait, however, it might add warts, blobs, and other potentially undesirable effects.

Spatter

The Spatter filter made our tuba player look like we were viewing him through pebbled glass. Possibly a useful effect, but not what I had in mind. I tried a different photo instead, a bunch of lilies. I really like the lacy effect on the flowers in Figure 15.25. My settings were Spray Radius, 15 and Smoothness, 2. Spatter is a filter that's potentially useful but, depending on the subject, might be better applied to selections rather than to the whole picture.

Sprayed Strokes

Sprayed Strokes looks like spatter—but less messy. The interesting thing about the Sprayed Strokes filter is that you can control the direction of the spray. Figure 15.26 shows what it does to our tuba player picture. The settings for this variation were Stroke Length and Spray Radius, both 14, and Direction, Right Diagonal.

FIGURE 15.24
Ink Outlines filter applied.

FIGURE 15.25
Spatter filter applied.

Sumi-e

Sumi-e is Japanese for brush painting, but the results of the Sumi-e filter looks like the work of a crazed sumo wrestler, rather than a Zen master. This filter turns any area with any sort of detail almost completely black, even at the lowest settings. It renders all dark areas in black angled strokes. Use this filter to rescue a very light picture.

FIGURE 15.26
Sprayed Strokes filter applied.

Sketch Filters

Photoshop has 14 different filters lumped under the Sketch heading. Some, such as Bas Relief, must have landed there by default. They have little or nothing to do with the process of sketching. Others, such as Conté Crayon or Chalk and Charcoal, definitely mimic sketch media. Figure 15.27 shows a sample image for these filters.

FIGURE 15.27

Statue of Frederic Chopin, University of Massachusetts at Lowell, rendered with Sketch filters.

Bas Relief

The Bas Relief filter uses the foreground and background colors to create a low relief rendering of your picture. If you choose colors carefully, it can look like copper foil, hammered metal, or carved stone. It's best used on pictures that have contrasting textures, or a textured subject against a flat background, unlike the picture of the Chopin statue. Figure 15.28 shows the result.

FIGURE 15.28

Use a dark background color for best results with the Bas Relief filter.

Chalk and Charcoal

With the Chalk and Charcoal filter, which reduces the image to three tones, you need to set the foreground to a dark color and the background to a light one. The third color, by default, is a medium gray, so choose colors that work with it. This filter can produce really beautiful drawings. Figure 15.29 shows the filter applied; notice how nicely it retained the highlights on the statue's wrist.

FIGURE 15.29

Chalk and Charcoal filter applied.

Charcoal

The Charcoal filter does much the same thing as the Chalk and Charcoal filter, but uses only the foreground and background colors. It's more difficult to control because there are only two colors. Experiment until you are satisfied.

Chrome

The Chrome filter appears to be a close relative to the Plastic Wrap filter described previously. It's only slightly more successful. As you can see in Figure 15.30, it's not really chrome-like. Perhaps, as my editor suggested, it's closer to looking into a choppy ocean of mercury. The Chrome filter removes the color from the image as part of its process. It also adds a large amount of distortion, as you can see. This filter is more useful on type.

FIGURE 15.30
Can you find the face? I can't.

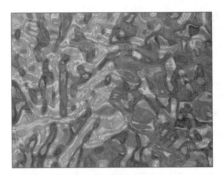

Conté Crayon

I *love* this filter—it's done good things to every picture I have ever used it on. Conté Crayon works like the Chalk and Charcoal filter described previously but with the addition of background textures, using the same interface you saw in the Rough Pastels dialog box. Figure 15.31 shows the Chopin statue rendered in Conté Crayon on a sandstone background.

FIGURE 15.31
Conté Crayon filter applied.

Graphic Pen and Halftone Pattern

These two filters do very similar things. Both reduce the image to whatever foreground and background colors you set. Graphic Pen then renders the image in slanting lines, whereas Halftone Pattern renders it in overlapping dots. On the proper subject, the

Graphic Pen filter can be very effective. Halftone, however, merely looks like a bad newspaper photo.

Note Paper and Plaster

I don't understand the name of the Note Paper effect. I'd have called it Stucco or maybe Flocked Wallpaper. See for yourself in Figure 15.32. The Note Paper filter uses the background and foreground colors, plus black for a shadow effect. Interesting, but...note paper? The Plaster filter is very similar but smooth instead of grainy with the look of wet, runny, freshly poured plaster.

FIGURE 15.32
Note Paper filter applied with a low relief setting.

Photocopy, Reticulation, Stamp, and Torn Edges

These four filters can be grouped together. Like many of the filters in this set, they all convert an image to a two-color copy of itself. The Stamp filter loses most of the detail, attempting to replicate a rubber stamp—but not very successfully. Photocopy keeps most of the detail, resulting in the somewhat confusing image in Figure 15.33. Reticulation adds dot grain to the Stamp filter, so it looks as if you stamped the picture on coarse sandpaper. Torn Edges is the Stamp filter again, only with the edges of the image roughened.

FIGURE 15.33
Photocopy filter applied.

Water Paper

The last filter in the Sketch set is a strange filter. Once again, I don't know how they named it. To me, the Water Paper filter produces an effect more like needlepoint, at least in the background. Unlike most of the filters in the Sketch set, Water Paper keeps the colors of your original picture, adding cross-hatching in the background and softening what it identifies as the subject of the picture. Figure 15.34 shows this filter applied to the statue of Chopin.

FIGURE 15.34
Water Paper filter applied.

Summary

None of the filters described in this chapter can produce a work of art from a lousy photo. The old proverb about silk purses and sows' ears applies. However, these filters can, when carefully and thoughtfully applied, elevate an ordinary picture to something quite extraordinary. Photoshop's filters are well worth taking the time to master. Spend some time with this hour's activity to work through the filter sets, so you can see—with your image in color and enlarged—exactly what the filters can do.

Q&A

Q How do you decide what filter to try?

A As you've seen, you can't always judge a filter by its name. If you want an "art" effect, decide first whether you want full color or limited color. For the latter, look at the Sketch filters. Consider how abstract you want to get.

Cutout and Conté Crayon are both successful with most pictures.

Q Is there a way to tone down a filter that does what I want, but does too much of it?

A Yes. Near the top of the Edit menu is a command called Fade Filter. It enables you to change the strength of the filter from 100%–0%.

Q Are the filters that come with Photoshop 6 all there are?

A Nope! There must be literally thousands of filters that have been created by individuals or companies. You can locate them by searching for "Photoshop filters" or try the following Web pages:

`http://www.flamingpear.com/blade.html`. (This site has several awesome sets of shareware plug-ins.)

`dir.yahoo.com/Computers_and_Internet/Software/Graphics/Filters_and_Plug_ins/`. (This site links to many pages of filters and other useful Photoshop goodies.)

Quiz

1. The colored pencil filter applies

    a. Colored outlines around edges

    b. A crosshatched effect

    c. The color-wheel opposite of any color to which you apply it

2. Sumi-e is Japanese for

    a. A kind of painting

    b. Raw fish and rice

    c. Photoshop

3. Photoshop Artistic filters, in general, tend to _____an image.

    a. Lighten

    b. Darken

    c. Sharpen

4. The Chrome filter is best used with type.

    a. True

    b. False

Quiz Answers

1. b. Try applying it twice with the image rotated 90 degrees between applications. It's a very cool effect.

2. a. If you knew sushi....

3. b. If an image is dark to start with, it might turn black.

4. a. At least, in my opinion...

Exercises

Use a picture you already have, or download one of the three used in this chapter, and try the Artistic, Brush, and Sketch filters. (You can find them at the Macmillan Web site mentioned in the introduction.) Experiment with different settings and then try applying the same filter a second time. Also, see how fading a filter can make its effect more useful. Try applying a second filter over the first. Some combinations work better than others. See whether you can find a combination that turns your photo into a work of art.

HOUR 16

Filters to Distort and Other Funky Effects

So far, the Photoshop filters described have been more or less useful. They corrected a fuzzy image or blurred a distracting background. Or they did something to turn your photo into an imitation drawing, painting, or mixed media construction. In this hour, we'll play with some filters that are mostly just for fun. These filters distort, stylize, and pixelate your picture. Most of these are meant for special effects. They're not for every day, but you are sure to find one or two that are helpful.

The key to success with these filters is to try as many different combinations of settings as you can with each filter and each new image that you bring into Photoshop. When you encounter a filter that relies on background and foreground colors, try several different color combinations. Try a dark background and light foreground, and then reverse them. It's simple enough to do, if you just click the double-headed arrow next to the color swatches in the toolbox.

Distort Filters

Distort filters run the gamut from gentle glassiness to image-destroying twirls and even more. Want to make your picture look like it's going down the drain or being blown off the page? These are the filters for you. In this section, we'll try out filters on the picture of a pink flower shown in Figure 16.1.

FIGURE 16.1

Pink hibiscus.

Diffuse Glow

Not all the Distort filters actually distort. The Diffuse Glow filter adds a gentle haze of the background color over the lighter areas of a picture. This creates a glow that blends into the image. Hard to say why it is in the Distort family of filters, but it is cool, nevertheless.

The controls are Graininess, Glow Amount, and Clear Amount. Try to balance the Glow Amount and Clear Amount. For soft glows, I suggest that you keep the Graininess setting low. Higher numbers increase the graininess. This might be useful if you want a somewhat speckled look. In Figure 16.2, I used a hot pink as a background color, with graininess of 3 and glow amount of 4 to place a bright pink glow on the flower.

FIGURE 16.2

The Diffuse Glow filter applied.

Displace

The Displace filter is one of several Photoshop filters that requires the use of a displacement map, which works like a texture map. You can find a collection of these in the Photoshop Plug-ins folder. Set the amount, in a percentage, for horizontal and vertical displacement in the dialog box. Higher percentages have a greater effect. After you set the amount of displacement, you're asked to choose a displacement map. Figure 16.3 shows a partial list of maps, and Figure 16.4 shows the results of applying the Schnable Effect map. The effect you get from this filter depends on which map you choose. You need to try them out to see their effects because the names aren't necessarily helpful.

FIGURE 16.3
Choosing a displacement map.

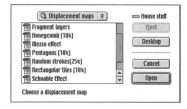

FIGURE 16.4
The Displace filter applied.

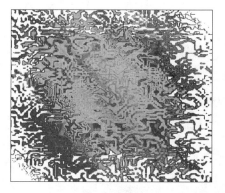

NEW TERM *Displacement maps* are images or patterns that are saved in the Photoshop format and applied as part of a mathematical formula that moves each pixel in the original image according to the values in the displacement map.

Glass and Ocean Ripple

I decided to lump the discussion of these two filters together because of the similar effects they can have on an image. They both create displacements that make the image seem as if you are looking through glass or water.

The Glass filter offers you a greater amount of control (see Figure 16.5). You can select a type of texture, such as Frosty, Tiny Lens, or Canvas, and you also can load a texture of your own. Just select Load Texture from the drop-down menu at the bottom of the dialog box.

Use the Smoothness slider to increase the fluidity of the image. Keeping the Distortion low and the Smoothness high will create a subtle effect. Try the opposite for a much more distorted image. The scaling slider adjusts the scale of the distortion from 50%–200%.

The Invert button at the bottom of the dialog box replaces the light areas of the texture with dark areas, and vice versa. Figure 16.6 shows the results of applying the Glass filter.

FIGURE 16.5
The Glass filter dialog box.

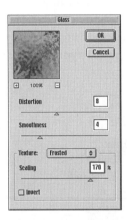

FIGURE 16.6
The Glass filter applied.

The Ocean Ripple filter is quite similar. It creates an effect that makes your image appear as though it is under water. It is an effective filter and easier to use than the Glass filter because it has only two options on its dialog box.

Pinch, Spherize, and ZigZag

The Pinch, Spherize, and ZigZag filters are lumped together, not so much because they do the same thing but because their interfaces are so similar. Figure 16.7 shows the dialog box for the Spherize filter.

FIGURE **16.7**

The Spherize filter dialog box.

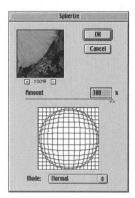

16

Keep an eye on the grid provided at the bottom of the box as you drag the Amount slider higher or lower. It can give you a good indication (as can the preview box) of what is going on in the image. See the final version in Figure 16.8. It makes our flower look as if it's reflected in a Christmas tree ornament.

FIGURE **16.8**

The Spherize filter applied.

This is a tough filter to master, but a good one to have in your bag of tricks. The Spherize filter can be very useful on occasion, but don't try to force it. If it doesn't look right, try something else.

Also, you can set a negative amount in the Amount slider box to generate a hollow instead of a bump. And if this doesn't satisfy your needs, try the Pinch filter or the ZigZag filter. The latter creates very neat pond ripples, too.

Shear

You can tell a great deal about most filters just by their names, but this isn't one of them. The Shear filter warps images horizontally. (It moves them in relation to the vertical line.) Drag the line in the Shear dialog box, as shown in Figure 16.9. Watch the preview to see the effect of shearing the picture. You also can add more control points on the curve by clicking it at different areas. These control points are like joints; they enable you to redirect the motion of the curve.

Figure 16.10 shows the results of the Shear filter. I've set the image to Repeat Edge Pixels, so it now looks as if the warping left a smudge of pixels behind.

FIGURE **16.9**
The Shear filter dialog box.

FIGURE **16.10**
The Shear filter in use, with Repeat Edge Pixels applied.

The Shear filter works only in one direction. If you want something to shear vertically instead of horizontally, simply rotate the image before you apply the filter. Then, rotate it back again.

Twirl

The Twirl filter does precisely what its name suggests—it spins an image. You can control the amount of spin with the slider within the dialog box. This is a great filter for creating special effects. So far, I haven't found very many subtle uses for the Twirl filter, but if you can, go to it. It creates wonderful, kaleidoscopic effects and can also simulate a swirling drain. It looks great with our flower, as shown in Figure 16.11.

FIGURE 16.11
The Twirl filter applied.

Pixelate Filters

When one is "pixilated," according to my dictionary, he's intoxicated, but in a charming, bemused, whimsical, pixieish way. Pixelation can be equally whimsical and bemusing, if applied to the right subjects. Misused, it just turns everything into a bunch of dots. *Pixelation* happens when similarly colored pixels are clumped together to form larger units, which might be square (pixel-shaped), round, or rounded off by anti-aliasing to whatever form they take. It happens, unasked for, if you're printing a picture at too low of a resolution. You end up with large pixels forming jagged shapes that look like they were built out of a child's plastic block set.

When controlled, the effect can be quite interesting. Photoshop includes a set of Pixelation filters that produce different effects all based on the notion of clumping together similar pixels. It's best to apply these effects to simple subjects and to those with strong contrasts, such as the photo of the orange in Figure 16.12.

FIGURE 16.12
Orange halves.

Crystallize

Most of the Pixelate filter set looks best if the effect is applied with the cell size quite small. Otherwise, the crystals, facets, and so on get so big the image becomes unrecognizable. In Figure 16.13, I applied the Crystallize filter at a Cell Size of 10. It adds reasonable distortion without destroying the shape of the fruit. In Figure 16.14, I pushed the Cell Size up to 50, destroying the picture. You can even set the Cell Size as high as 300, but it turns the entire picture into one or two cells.

FIGURE 16.13
The Crystallize filter applied.

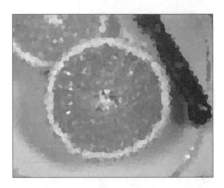

FIGURE 16.14
Same filter, over applied.

Pointillism and Mosaic

As a former art student, it's fun to go back and recall the first time I was introduced to the work of Georges Seurat. It was a revelation (especially after studying some of the "sloppier" French impressionists) to see these dabs of paint all neatly clustered, forming elegant scenes from a distance and forming equally elegant abstract patterns up close. It would be nice if the Pointillism filters did the job as neatly and scientifically as M. Seurat. They don't.

This is, however, one case where the smallest setting doesn't work as well as some of the larger ones. I first tried the picture using 3 pixels as the Dot Size. I got a spotty picture, as I expected, but it looked more like video noise rather than pointillism. Using a slightly larger dot size produced an image a little closer to what I was looking for. But when I tried a much larger size, approximately 25, I ended up with baseballs. Figure 16.15 shows all three effects. Be sure to set your background and foreground colors to something appropriate to the image because Photoshop uses them in creating the dots.

FIGURE 16.15

From top to bottom, cell sizes 3, 8, and 25.

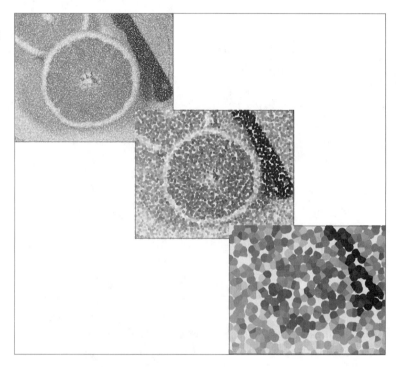

16

There's a Mosaic setting in the Pixelate effects, but all it does is to make larger pixels out of the smaller ones. The result is the sort of thing used to hide the faces of the people being arrested on all those late night police shows (see Figure 16.16).

FIGURE 16.16

Alleged perpetrator, concealed by the Mosaic filter.

Stylize

The Stylize filter family offers some wonderful effects. They are creative, and you can use them to add final effects or touches to an image. This section touches on the most interesting of the filters, including the Find Edges filter, the Glowing Edges filter, and the Wind filter.

Find Edges, Glowing Edges, and Trace Contour

These three effects sound as if they should look alike. They actually do look somewhat alike, with Glowing Edges and Find Edges being much more dramatic than Trace Contour. The Find Edges filter removes most of the colors from the object and replaces them with lines around every edge contour. The color of the lines depends on the value at that point on the original object, with lightest points in yellow, scaling through to the darkest points, which appear in purple. The picture looks like a rather delicate-colored pencil drawing of itself. Find Edges works best, naturally, on photos that have a lot of detail for the filter to find. In Figure 16.17, I've applied it to a digital photo of Chinese dragon dancers. Find Edges sometimes becomes more interesting if you apply it more than once to the same picture. If you apply it once and don't like the result, try it again before you move on to a different filter.

FIGURE 16.17
Notice how it picks up the detail of the dragon mask.

Unfortunately, you cannot set the sensitivity of the Find Edges filter. In practical terms, this means that you have to prepare the picture before you trace it. Begin by despeckling, so Photoshop won't attempt to circle every piece of dust in the background. If you don't want the background to show, select and delete it, or select your object and copy it to a separate layer first. You can also use the Edit→Fade command to back off the strength of the filter. Using this filter with different blending modes can produce some spectacular effects.

Glowing Edges is more fun because it's prettier, and because you can adjust it to have maximum impact on your picture. Glowing Edges turns the edges into brightly colored lines against a black background. The effect is reminiscent of neon signs. You can vary the intensity of the color and the thickness of the line.

In Figure 16.18, I've applied Glowing Edges to the same picture. It works especially well with "busy" pictures with lots of edges. The more it has to work with, the more effective the filter is.

16

FIGURE 16.18

Some of the color remains, but the background goes black.

Trace Contours, like several of the previous filters, works better on some pictures if you apply it several times (see Figure 16.19). The Trace Contour dialog box has a slider setting for the level at which value differences are translated into contour lines. When you move the slider, you are setting the threshold at which the values (from 0–255) are traced. Experiment to see which values bring out the best detail in your image. Upper and Lower don't refer to the direction of the outline. Lower Outlines specifies where the color values of pixels fall below a specified level; Upper Outlines tells you where the value of the pixels are above the specified level.

FIGURE 16.19

The image was traced several times with different settings.

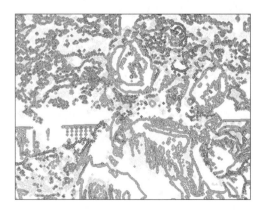

I like to use this filter to place different tracings on different layers and then to merge them for a more complete picture.

Wind

The Wind filter creates a neat directional blur that looks, strangely enough, like wind. You can control the direction and the amount of wind in the dialog box (see Figure 16.20). This is a great filter for creating the illusion of movement and for applying to type. It works best when applied to a selected area rather than to the entire picture.

FIGURE **16.20**
The Wind filter and its dialog box.

One of this book's editors adds, "My favorite Wind filter effect is making a brushed metal look by adding noise to the basic metal color and then hitting it with wind from both directions, followed by a bit of tweaking for the perfect illusion." Thanks, Jon!

Emboss

Honestly, the Emboss filter doesn't do much for most photos. It turns an image into a bas-relief, though not as well as the Bas Relief filter does. In the process, the Emboss filter converts the image to medium gray. Like the Wind filter, it works very well on type. You can adjust the Shadow Angle and Amount in the dialog box. Figure 16.21 shows a piece of embossed type.

FIGURE **16.21**
Embossing.

Occasionally, you come across a photo, like this picture of Florentine stonework, which almost begs to be turned into a corporate logo or advertising image (see Figure 16.22). In such cases, the Emboss filter can do wonders to make the picture just abstract enough to be useful. In working with this photo, I found that the angle at which the filter is applied can make a major difference. Figure 16.22 shows two different angle settings applied to the same picture. The Height and Amount settings were the same for both.

FIGURE 16.22
On the left, the knight's leg appears to come forward. On the right, it recedes.

16

Combining Filters

Some people like things plain. I'm not one of them. I want the whipped cream, marshmallow, nuts, and cherry on my ice cream, and I'm seldom satisfied with using just one Photoshop filter. And with an arsenal of 99 different Photoshop filters (plus dozens of third-party add-ons), why shouldn't we take advantage of as many as possible? In the remaining few minutes of this hour, let's look at some interesting combinations.

Texturizer

You can add a texture to any photo, no matter what you have already done to it. The Texturizer filter (Filter→Texture→Texturizer) places a pattern resembling canvas, burlap, brick, or sandstone over your image, making it look as if it's on paper with that texture. The canvas texture is particularly nice if reduced in scale. Figure 16.23 shows a photo of a seascape, first treated with the Dry Brush filter and then texturized.

FIGURE **16.23**
*Dry Brush on
Sandstone applied.*

Rough Pastels and Film Grain

The Rough Pastels filter adds a strong directional quality to Figure 16.24, a photo of a
Japanese drummer. A single filter is applied to it.

FIGURE **16.24**
Pastel drummer.

In Figure 16.25, I added Film Grain over the pastels, which lightened the image, and
came up with what I think is an even more interesting result.

FIGURE **16.25**
*The drummer with
added Film Grain.*

The possibilities are endless. If you can imagine a style or treatment for a picture, chances are excellent that Photoshop can do it. As a final picture and final filter combination, here's how you can turn a photo into instant stained glass. Start with any picture that has reasonably large areas of flat color. Figure 16.26 shows my original picture, a tropical bird.

FIGURE 16.26
Unfiltered parrot.

16

To Do: Convert a Photo to Stained Glass

To turn this picture into stained glass:

1. Apply the Crystallize filter (Filter→Pixelate→Crystallize) with a moderate Cell Size. I used 15 as the Cell Size in Figure 16.27.

FIGURE 16.27
Crystallized parrot.

▼

2. Next, apply the Ink Outlines filter (Filter→Brush Strokes→Ink Outline) with the Stroke length set to approximately 4, and the light and dark intensity balanced at approximately 15. Figure 16.28 shows the result—a reasonable rendering of a stained glass window. You can, of course, draw in any lines that Photoshop didn't trace completely, and you can go over the "glass panels" and change their colors if you want.

▲

FIGURE 16.28
Stained glass parrot.

At the risk of sounding like a broken record, let me leave you with a final reminder to keep experimenting. You never know what a filter or combination can do to a particular picture until you try it. The way that Photoshop calculates the filter effects means that some filters can look very different, according to the kind of picture to which they are applied. You can't always predict what will happen, but the unexpected effects are frequently wonderful.

Summary

This hour has been devoted to some of Photoshop's stranger filters: the Distort, Pixelate, and Stylize filters. They're not for everyone—and certainly not for every image—but they're fun to play with and can occasionally create some interesting, unusual, and beautiful effects. Filters can add interesting dimensions to type, also.

Don't hesitate to add a second filter over the first. Many times, the second filter or second application of the original filter can turn a ho-hum picture into something marvelous. At worst, you can always Undo.

Q&A

Q I am bored with the textures that the Texturizer adds. Can I make my own?

A Of course. One way is to scan items with interesting textures or make digital photos of them. Save as a grayscale file in .psd format, and apply them from the Texturizer filter dialog box by selecting Load Texture from the Texture pop-up menu and opening the texture file you want to use.

Q What kinds of things make good textures?

A Look around you. Napkins—either cloth or paper—, fabrics of any kind, barn boards, sandpaper, uncooked pasta, practically anything semi-flat that you can photograph or scan.

Q Does the Glass filter include more than one kind of glass?

A This is Photoshop; your choices are virtually unlimited. In addition to the textures provided, you can choose Load Texture from the pop-up menu and open any Photoshop document to apply as a texture.

Quiz

1. A displacement map is
   a. Another name for a texture map
   b. A pattern applied as a mathematical formula to move individual pixels in an image
   c. A chart showing how colors shift between your monitor and printer

2. The Spherize filter can make your picture appear to bump ____.
   a. Out only (convex)
   b. In only (concave)
   c. Either way

3. Pointillism was originally a painting style introduced by
   a. Jean Luc Pontille
   b. Georges Seurat
   c. Leonardo da Vinci
   d. Jean Luc Picard

4. The shear filter can be used either vertically or horizontally.
   a. True
   b. False

16

Quiz Answers

1. b. Some, like the Schnable filter, are named for their creators.
2. c. It depends on how you apply it.
3. b. See an example at `www.moma.org/collection/paintsculpt/seurat.html`.
4. b. If you want to apply it vertically, you must rotate the image.

Exercises

Start with a simple picture and add filters, one by one until you can't recognize the image. See how many different filters you can apply on top of each other before the picture disappears.

Go back to your original picture, and use the Colored Pencil filter. This should give you an interesting image. Save it. Try the other filters over it until you find at least three that work well with the Colored Pencil filter. Whenever you have time, repeat this exercise, starting with a different filter.

HOUR 17

Adding Type to Pictures

If a picture's worth a thousand words, how many more is it worth if we add words to the picture? Well, never mind…. The fact is, though, sometimes you have to add type to a picture for one reason or another. If you've used previous versions of Photoshop, you might recall that type was never its strong point—until now. In Photoshop 6, Adobe's engineers and programmers have finally given us the kind of control over type we have learned to expect from PageMaker, Illustrator, and other Adobe products. Now, you can add type directly onto a page, edit it, and control its leading, tracking, and kerning. You can set type vertically as well as horizontally, and you can warp it onto a predetermined path. You can set text either by clicking a start point on the page, or by dragging the Text Tool to create a bounding box and then filling the box with type. Let's start with the basics.

A few things haven't changed. Photoshop still places your type on a separate type layer. Type must still be rendered, or *rasterized*, before you can apply filters. You can apply layer styles such as drop shadows, bevel, and emboss, plus gradient fills either before or after type is rasterized.

At this point, a few words about type might prove helpful. There are two kinds of type that you'll be dealing with: outline type and bitmapped type. *Outline type*, which is also called *vector type*, consists of mathematically defined shapes, in either Postscript or TrueType language. Outline type can be scaled to any size without losing its sharp, smooth edges. *Bitmapped type* is composed of individual pixels. The sharpness of bitmap type depends on the type size and the resolution of the image. If you scale bitmapped type to a larger size, you'll see jagged edges, or "jaggies."

When you enter type on the screen in Photoshop, the letters are drawn as vector type. That's why you can edit them, reshape them, and play with them as much as you like. Anything you do just changes the numbers, and computers are very good with numbers. However, Photoshop is a bitmapped program. It manipulates pixels, not vectors. In order to make the type part of the picture, it needs to be converted from vectors to pixels, or *rasterized*.

Think of it this way—vector type that you set on a type layer is sort of floating. It's not nailed down, therefore it's easy to edit words or to move letters closer together. It's there, but it's not completely part of the image yet. When you rasterize type, you are, in effect, nailing it onto the layer. When you print a Photoshop image that has a type layer, the printer actually receives the image with rasterized text, even if you haven't rendered the layer.

The Type Tools

Because Photoshop 6 does so much more with type than its predecessors did, we now have three different ways to control type in Photoshop. When you select the Type Tool (the capital T in the toolbox), the Tool Options bar will display the basic type options: font, size, alignment, and a few other controls. The Type Tool options are shown in Figure 17.1. (I had to cut the bar into two pieces so it would fit on the page.) There are also Character and Paragraph palettes that give you even more control. Let's look first at the Type Options bar.

Starting at the left side of the bar, you'll see a filled letter and an outline, and then two T's with arrows. The arrows indicate horizontal or vertical type, and the outline indicates that type set with that tool will be created as paths rather than as actual letters. The capability to set paths enables you to do one of Photoshop's neatest tricks—cut type out of pictures.

After that comes a scrolling menu listing all your available fonts, styles, and font sizes from 6–72 points. You can set larger or smaller type by typing the point size into the window. Next, you can set the amount of anti-aliasing to apply: none, crisp, smooth, or strong. Anti-aliasing produces smooth-edged type by partially filling the edge pixels. As a result, the type edges appear to blend into the background. Generally speaking, anti-aliased type looks better, especially if you are working with small type sizes. (Anti-aliasing can make small type sizes appear more readable when viewed online.) Select from three levels of anti-aliasing to modify the appearance of type online. Crisp makes your type sharper, Smooth makes it smoother, and Strong makes it look heavier.

FIGURE 17.1

The Type Tool Options bar.

The next set of three icons let you select flush left, centered, or flush right alignment. The color swatch, which is the same as your current foreground color, lets you set a color for the type. Clicking the swatch opens the color picker, just like clicking any other swatch.

The T... icon with the curved line under it represents one of Photoshop 6's most welcome additions. It's called Warp Text, and it gives you access to 15 preset type paths ranging from arcs and flag to fisheye. We'll go into greater detail on this tool later on in the hour.

Finally, there's a button called Palettes, which opens the Character and Paragraph palettes; we'll consider these palettes next. But first, let's set some type.

To Do: Getting Started with Type

Start a new page in Photoshop. Make it about 5-inches square and give it a white or colored background.

1. Click the Type Tool.
2. Use the Tool Options bar to select a font and size.
3. Set flush left alignment.
4. Click the Type Tool on the left side of your page. You'll see a blinking black line. That's the insertion point.
5. Type your name.
6. Drag the cursor over the type to select it.
7. Click the colored square in the Tool Options bar and change the color of the type.
8. Change the point size.
9. Change the font.

▼   10. Click anywhere in the toolbox to deselect the Type Tool.

11. Click the Type Tool again. Click the Tool Options bar icon with the solid T and downward pointing arrow.

12. Click somewhere near the top of the page, and type your name. It's vertical.

▲   13. Play with the type options tools until you understand them.

The Character Palette

The Character palette (see Figure 17.2) gives you control over letter spacing, kerning, tracking, and shifting the baseline, in addition to the font, style, color, and size options also found on the tool bar. You can either decide your type options with the Character palette before you set the type on the page, or you can use the palette to reformat type you've already entered.

FIGURE **17.2**

The Type palettes.

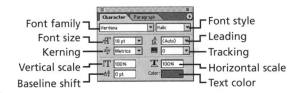

The scroll down menus on the Character palette give you access to your installed fonts, font sizes, and styles, just as on the Tool Options bar.

The window indicated by the A\V and arrows tag controls kerning. *Kerning* refers to the amount of space between adjacent letters. Most fonts, in larger sizes, require some kerning to adjust the spaces between letter pairs such as AV or WA. Otherwise, you'll notice a gap. The default setting for kerning is Metrics, which means that Photoshop will apply the font metrics information built into the font. If you decide to override this, you can do so by entering a different kerning amount in the window. *Tracking* is similar to kerning, but involves evening out the amount of space between letters in a word or phrase rather than just in a pair. Tracking can be tight (enter negative numbers) or loose (enter positive numbers). Setting 0 in the tracking window means that no tracking is applied.

Leading (pronounced to rhyme with *heading* or *bedding*) determines the amount of space between lines of type. If you're setting a single word or one line of type, you won't need to deal with this. As soon as you add a second line, leading becomes important. Because leading is measured from the baseline of a line of text to the baseline of the line above it, the amount of leading has to be greater than the point size of the type to keep the lines from touching or overlapping. (The *baseline* is the invisible line on which type is placed.) Photoshop's default for leading is 120%, which is to say, 10-point type gets 12-point leading, and so on up the scale.

Finally, on this palette, you can set a distance from the baseline for subscript and super-script types. Why you'd be using subscripted footnotes in Photoshop, I'm not sure. Using superscript to correctly set an equation like Einstein's Theory of Relativity could prove useful, though.

The Paragraph Palette

What Photoshop defines as a paragraph would horrify grammarians. In Photoshop terms, any line followed by a carriage return is a *paragraph*. The Paragraph palette sets options that relate to the entire paragraph, such as alignment, justification, indentation, and line spacing (see Figure 17.3).

FIGURE 17.3

The Paragraph palette.

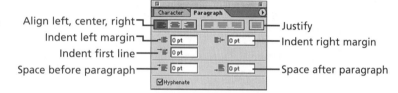

Align left, center, right · Justify
Indent left margin · Indent right margin
Indent first line
Space before paragraph · Space after paragraph

The icons at the top of the palette display the possible alignments: left, centered, and right. You also have these options on the Tool Options bar. Additionally, there are icons to let you set justified type with the last line flush left, centered, or flush right, or fully justified. These latter options are only available if you have set text in a bounding box.

The other icons and windows on the Paragraph palette let you set paragraph indents, first line indents, right indents, and additional space before or after a paragraph. These, obviously, are most useful when you are dealing with a block of text.

Setting Type

As mentioned earlier, there are two ways to set type in Photoshop 6. The first and simplest way is to click the page where you want the type. If you select flush left on the Tool Options bar or the paragraph palette, your text will stream right from the insertion point. If you select centered, Photoshop will center the words around your insertion point as you enter them. Flush right sends the text shooting off to the left from your right side insertion point. Figure 17.4 shows examples of each.

FIGURE 17.4

Text flows from the insertion point.

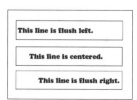

This line is flush left.

This line is centered.

This line is flush right.

The other way to position type, when you have to set a lot of it, or when you need to fill a specific area, is to drag a bounding box. Simply select the type tool, click it on the corner point of the box, and drag until the box is approximately the right size and shape (see Figure 17.5). You can go back after you've entered the type and resize the box, if necessary.

FIGURE 17.5

The Type Bounding Box.

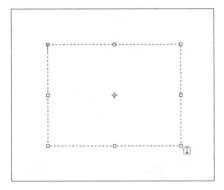

Enter the text by typing it, or by copying and pasting from another program. Type always appears on a new layer. Type layers are indicated in the Layers palette by a large letter T, as you can see in Figure 17.6. Type layers are named according to the first word(s) you type. If you want to edit your type, click the T icon in the type layer (Mac) or double-click the Type layer in the Layers palette (Windows) to select the Type Tool and the tool options you've previously set for that line. Clicking the T also selects the type so you can apply changes, as does clicking with the Type tool on the type you want to change. If the type's not selected, you can't edit it.

If you have set a lot of text into a bounding box, now's the time to adjust the leading, paragraph spacing, and indents, if any. The Type Layer palette will only show you the first few words of the type you have set, so be sure you have selected the right type layer, if you have several.

FIGURE 17.6

Each line is on a different type layer.

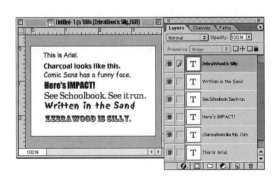

After you create a type layer, you can edit its text and insert new text, or delete some. You can make changes in the text itself or in the font, style, or size. You can change the orientation of the type from horizontal to vertical; you can apply or change the type of anti-aliasing. You can move, copy, or change the order of layers, or change the layer options of a type layer as you would for a regular layer. You can use Layer Effects. You can apply most of the transformation commands from the Edit menu, except Perspective and Distort. (To apply the Perspective or Distort commands, or to transform just part of the type layer, you must first rasterize the type layer to convert it to a regular layer.)

There's one more step to go through before your type is part of the page. The type must be rendered before you can apply the full range of filters to it. (You can apply distortion and effects to the layer before it's rendered.) Before type is rendered, it's as if it were placed on a separate layer but not stuck down. *Rendering*, in effect, sticks it to its layer. After the type is rendered, you can't go back and edit it again. To render type, select the type layer, and use Layer→Type→Rasterize. You can rasterize type layers one at a time or all layers at once. Or simply flatten the image, if you're sure you are finished making changes to it.

After you place the type on the screen, you can have some fun with it. Apply filters to your heart's content. Pour paint into selected letters. Select the type and distort it. Figure 17.7 shows just a few of the things you can do.

FIGURE 17.7

Filtered, stretched, and distorted type.

 Filters are most successful on bold type. Thin, delicate letters tend to get lost.

Creating Drop Shadows

As soon as you start looking for drop shadows, you'll find them everywhere: in magazines, television ads, Web sites, and in every other form of media you can imagine. Everyone is discovering that as soon as you put a shadow behind some text or an image, it takes on added dimension that can really make it pop forward into view. It's a nice and easy special effect for giving something more visual weight and making people pay attention. Drop shadows are a layer effect rather than a filter, so you can apply them before or after you render the type.

The following are some tips for effectively using drop shadows:

- Don't use them all over the place! If you use too many shadows, everything pops forward equally, and you lose the benefit of using shadows to draw attention to one particular object.

- Make sure all your shadows look alike! If you use shadows on multiple objects in the same area, make sure the shadows all go the same way, and make sure the "depth" of the shadow is appropriate. If the shadows are all different and haphazard, people will notice.

- Don't make the shadows too dark. It's easy to go overboard and create deep, saturated shadows that overwhelm what's supposed to be getting all the attention—the foreground image. Keep shadows light and subtle. Figure 17.8 shows what can go wrong (and right).

FIGURE 17.8

A too dark shadow, a too blurred shadow, and a dark and badly positioned one, and finally one that gets it right.

Photoshop 6 includes a powerful and easy Drop Shadow tool, along with Glow, Bevel, Emboss, Satin, and Overlay tools that will do wonders for type and graphics alike. You will find these tools on the Layer, Style submenu. Remember that you can use drop shadows and other effects on objects as well as on type. You can't apply a layer effect to anything that's not on its own layer, though. Painting on the background, and then trying to add an effect won't work.

To Do: Creating a Drop Shadow for Text

Follow along to create a cool drop shadow.

1. Create a new Photoshop document with a white background.

2. Select the Type Tool and enter some words. Choose any font that appeals to you. For now, don't worry about color, kerning, or setting a baseline. Figure 17.9 shows the basic type.

FIGURE **17.9**

The original art in need of a drop shadow.

The shadow of your smile...

17

3. Open the Layer, Layer Style, Drop Shadow dialog box, as shown in Figure 17.10. Check the Preview box so you can see your work as you create it. The trickiest part of this operation is getting the screen arranged so you can see both the dialog box and the type you're working on.

FIGURE **17.10**

Applying a Drop Shadow in the Layer Styles dialog box.

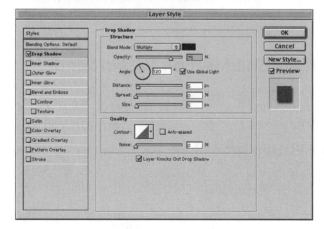

4. Set the Blend Mode to either Normal, Multiply, or Darken. Otherwise, you won't see the shadow. Click in the color swatch next to the Mode menu to change the color of the shadow. This opens the Color Picker.

5. Adjust the shadow's Opacity and Angle as desired, by clicking the slider and dragging on the clock face to change the angle, or typing numbers into the boxes.

6. Set the Distance to how far away you want the shadow to be from the word or object. Set the Size according to the amount of shadow you want to see. Set the Spread according to how distinct you want the edges of the shadow to be. Click OK when you are happy with your drop shadow. You can still change it, of course. Until you merge the layers, or render the type, you can make any changes you want. I've added a lightly textured background to create the finished effect you see in Figure 17.11.

FIGURE **17.11**

Drop shadow type, on a lightly textured background.

I find that shadows often work better if they're *below* the original image, that is, moved down instead of up when they're offset. When the shadow falls downward, the object looks more like it's popping up.

Drop shadows can be tricky. When it looks right, you know it. Trust your eyes to tell you what looks realistic and what looks fake, and be willing to experiment with settings. Try making your shadow twice as blurred as your original setting, or twice as far offset. You might be surprised!

Variation: Shadows on Backgrounds

Of course, drop shadows don't have to occur just over white or solid-color backgrounds. You can have a drop shadow fall over a texture, an image, or anything else that strikes your fancy.

To Do: Placing Drop Shadows on a Background

Follow these steps to apply drop shadows from text onto a background image and add depth to the background itself.

1. First, create the Photoshop image. I started with a photo of a bowl of gumdrops. I added some type, and copied two of the gumdrops onto a new layer. The important thing to remember is to create a *new layer* for each element for which you want to have a drop shadow (see Figure 17.12). For a refresher on layers, refer to Hour 11, "Layers."

FIGURE 17.12

The original image before drop shadows. I've attached the Layer palette so you can see the separate layers.

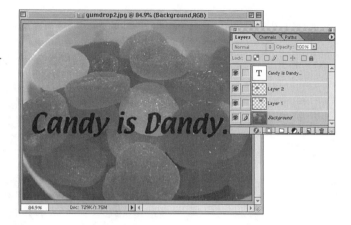

2. Add a shadow to the text first, by following the steps in the previous section (see Figure 17.13).

FIGURE 17.13

A drop shadow applied to the text.

Notice how you can actually see the texture of the background right "through" the new shadow. The result is a pleasant, realistic effect. You can make even more of the background show through by adjusting the Opacity slider in the Layers palette. Give it a try.

3. Now create some depth in the background itself. I'll start by adding a drop shadow to the two gumdrops. It's subtle, but it's there. To make the candy stand out even more, I'll drop a piece onto the lettering. And I'll add a larger drop shadow because it's higher up. Figure 17.14 shows the final version.

17

▼

FIGURE 17.14
Drop Shadows at work.

Tasteful Typography

There are thousands of typefaces available. Buy them in CD-ROM collections, download them online, use the ones that come with other applications, and so on. Trying out wild typefaces can be so much fun that you might lose sight of the goal—to communicate. Before committing to a design, print out a sample page and hold it up at full arm's length. If you can't read it easily, maybe even with your reading glasses removed, try to figure out why and consider tweaking the design. It might be a simple matter of making the type larger or giving the lines of type more space (leading). You might need to rethink your background or add an outline. A drop shadow might help—or might make matters even worse. Try combinations of different type and image treatment.

Remember to use "curly" quotes and apostrophes rather than the straight kind. You're setting type, not using a typewriter that has only one kind. The pros don't use underlining very often, either. The underline habit also comes from the old manual typewriter days, when no other typographical tool was available to give emphasis to words. Use bold or italic type styles instead.

Cutting and Filling Type

The words you paste onto a picture might be filled with meaning. They can also be filled with pictures. Here's how to do some of my favorite Photoshop tricks.

Half the battle is finding a picture to work with. The other half is finding a nice fat typeface that leaves plenty of room for your pictures to show through. I'm doing a cover for our town's annual report. I found and scanned a very old surveyor's map that I'll use as a background for my cut out letters.

First, I click the Type Tool and select the outline icon on the Tool Options bar. I've selected a bold face called Cooper Black. To make it even bolder, I'll select Faux Bold from the Character palette's pop-out menu, shown in Figure 17.15. Check out the other character options on this menu, too.

FIGURE 17.15

Faux Bold adds extra boldness to any character, whether already bold or not.

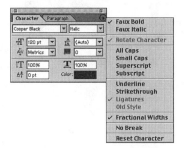

When I position the cursor and start to place my letters, something surprising happens. The screen goes into Quick Mask mode, and turns pink. As I enter the letters, they appear to be in a contrasting color, but when I finish typing and deselect the Type Tool, they turn into paths and the temporary mask goes away. Figure 17.16 shows how this looks onscreen.

FIGURE 17.16

The letters are active selections.

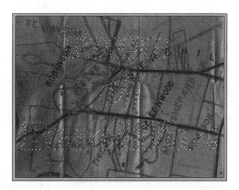

Now I can click Command+X (Mac) or Control+X (Windows) and cut out the letters. I'll quickly open a new page and paste them on it for safekeeping. Figure 17.17 shows the cut out lettering and the map.

If you open a new page after having copied or cut a selection, Photoshop will automatically insert the dimensions of the selection in the New dialog box.

17

FIGURE 17.17

*The type's cut out of
the map.*

Next, I'll work on the cut out letters, first using Image→Adjust→Invert, to make them
look like a blueprint. Then I'll use Image→Adjust→Auto Contrast to darken them.
Finally, I'll copy them and paste them back on the original, sliding them a bit so there's a
white outline behind them, adding some dimension. A bit of drop shadow completes the
picture. Figure 17.18 shows the final logo, after all of these tricks.

FIGURE 17.18

*The letters jump
right out.*

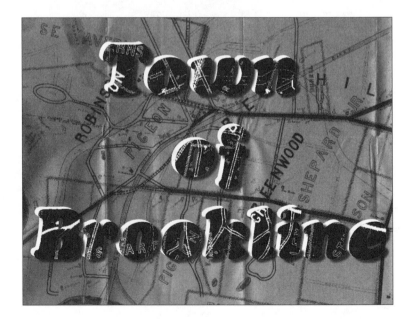

Adding Glows

There really are other effects on the menu besides drop shadows, fun though they are. Let's try a glow effect this time. We'll use the Layer, Effects menu to put a glow—or in this case an outline—around your type. You can also apply an inner glow to make it appear as if the letters themselves are glowing. This is a great effect to add emphasis around a piece of text or to make it stand out from a busy background. Figure 17.19 shows a fairly ordinary text and photo combination. (It's a title for a slide show.)

FIGURE 17.19
The letters don't quite stand out enough.

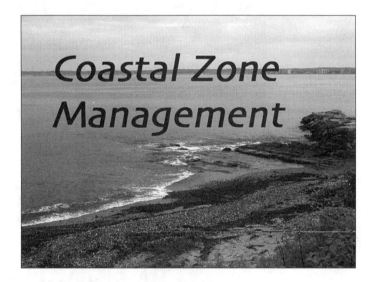

In Figure 17.20, I've applied a light Outer Glow around the letters. It's simply another way of defining them from the background and is useful when a drop shadow isn't appropriate. Other objects can glow, too, and we'll discuss these in more detail in the next hour.

Creating Bevel and Emboss Effects

These two tools are found in the Layer Style box. Both produce raised type: Bevel affects the edges of the type, producing a raised, but flat, letter surface; whereas Emboss gives the appearance of curved or rounded letters. Figure 17.21 shows examples of both. I added a little noise to the beveled "stone" with the Noise filter, and applied some Plastic Wrap to the embossing for more highlights.

FIGURE 17.20
The glow helps sepa-rate the text from the background.

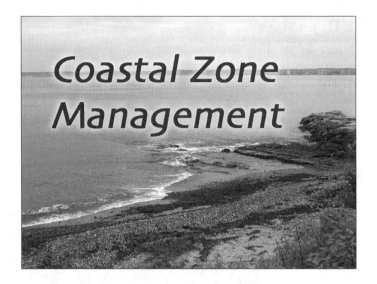

FIGURE 17.21
The difference is obvious.

You can vary the effect of these tools by changing the blending modes, by varying the opacity, and by changing highlight and shadow colors. As always, the best way to see what they do is to experiment with different settings.

Warping Text

One of the major complaints about Photoshop used to be that you couldn't set type on a path within the program. If you wanted, say, a wavy line of text, you could either position the letters one by one or set the type in Illustrator or something similar and import it into Photoshop. It was a nuisance, at best. About two years ago, Extensis published a plug-in called PhotoGraphics, which drew shapes and paths and let you drag your text onto them. It's still worth investing in, although Photoshop 6 has added both Shape tools and a new feature called Warp Text. It's not quite text on a path, but it's close.

Instead of drawing your own path, the Warp Text dialog box enables you to select from 15 preset paths. You can also warp and distort the paths as necessary. Figure 17.22 shows a list of the presets.

FIGURE 17.22

Use the multiline presets with two or more lines of type.

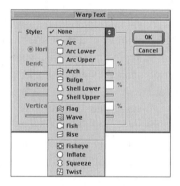

The dialog box settings, shown in Figure 17.23, are a little bit tricky at first. Use the sliders to increase the amount of Bend applied to the path. Moving to the right bends words up; to the left (minus numbers), bends them down. Distortion makes the line of type appear to flare out on one end (Horizontal Distortion), or from top to bottom (Vertical Distortion).

FIGURE 17.23

Move the sliders left or right to change the settings.

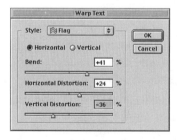

In Figure 17.24, I've applied some of the warp styles to various bits of type. The best way to master this tool is to play with it. Set a line or two of type and try the different kinds of warp on it. Move the sliders around. You can't break anything.

FIGURE 17.24
Can you guess which wave forms were used on these words?

Summary

Photoshop doesn't have all the type capabilities of a more traditional desktop publishing program, but it can handle most of your typographic needs, whether it's producing a single headline or a block of text precisely placed over a photo. Of course, getting the letters into the picture is only the beginning. After you have the type on the page, you can apply all Photoshop's filters, blending modes, and tools to it. You can warp it, distort it, punch it out of a graphic, or make the letters out of a picture. With Photoshop, your words can come alive. If all you want to do is set type, use a program such as InDesign. If you want to do strange and wonderful things to type, Photoshop has all the tools you need.

Q&A

Q Is there any way to improve the appearance of small type online? Anything less than 20 points looks like it's run together.

A By default, Photoshop displays type using fractional character widths. This means that the spacing between characters varies, with fractions of whole pixels between some characters. In most cases, fractional character widths provide the best spacing for type appearance and readability. However, for type in small sizes displayed online, fractional character widths can cause type to run together, making it hard to read. Use the fly-out menu on the Character palette to turn off fractional character widths. Using a full width character will keep small type from running together.

Q I have a lot of fonts installed on my Macintosh, and it takes forever to scroll down the list to find the one I want. Any suggestions?

A Use a font management program such as Suitcase, ATM Deluxe or Font Reserve to sort your fonts into suitcases. Keep a suitcase for serif type and separate ones for sans-serif faces, display faces, and special purpose fonts such as Handbill, StarTrek, or Wild West. Only open the suitcases with fonts you're likely to need.

Q I've typed in the text I want and have rendered it. The problem is I found a typo and when I try to go back and edit the text, I can't. What can I do?

A After you render text, it's converted from an editable text layer to a graphic that can't be edited by any of the Type tools. Make sure that you have the type you want and that it's all spelled correctly before you render it. To save your project, you might be able to go back in the History palette to a state before you rendered the type.

Q Is there a way to use cut out type to reveal another picture underneath?

A Certainly. Place the photo you want to see through the cutouts on a layer underneath the layer that will be cut. Enter your letters as outlines and cut. To enhance the effect, apply a drop shadow to the top layer.

17

Quiz

1. Photoshop 6 can set type horizontally or vertically.

    a. True

    b. False

2. Every piece of type needs a drop shadow.

    a. True

    b. False

3. Photoshop places type on

    a. The background.

    b. Special type layers.

    c. Regular layers.

    d. Adjustment layers.

4. If there's a T in the box on the layer palette, it means

    a. You can double-click it to open the Type Tool.

    b. That the layer is a type layer.

    c. Effects have been applied to the type.

    d. Both a and b.

5. There's no way to set small caps in Photoshop.

    a. True

    b. False

Quiz Answers

1. a. And if you want it diagonal, rotate it.

2. b. Use them sparingly.

3. b. Type layers are editable until they are rasterized.

4. d. The italic F symbol indicates layer effects.

5. b. Small caps is one of the options in the Character palette fly-out menu.

Exercises

1. Download the photo of the sandy beach from our Web site. It's called
   `Biloxi1.jpg`. To get to the Web site point your Web browser to

   `http://www.mcp.com/sams/detail_sams.cfm?item=0672319551`

   After the main book page has loaded, click the `Downloads` link to get to the files.
   Set the word "Biloxi" in a dark blue in the sky. Add a drop shadow.

2. Using the same photo and the Type Outline Tool, cut the letters "Beach" out of the
   sandy part of the photo and place them over the sky below the word "Biloxi." Add
   the same kind of drop shadow. Download `Biloxi2.jpg` if you want to see my version.

3. Try using a glow instead of the shadow. Which do you like more?

HOUR 18

Special Effects and Useful Tricks

This hour is going to be a little different. We're going to kick back and explore some of the cool things you can do with the awesome tool known as Photoshop. Think of this hour as a collection of recipes—some special effects that you can add to your mental list of Photoshop tricks and use again and again, along with some timesaving tricks. You'll learn about extracting backgrounds, using stickies, and making contact sheets and picture packages. Just follow the steps, and you'll be a Photoshop wizard in no time.

The following are the special effects covered in this hour:

- Glows
- Lighting effects
- Reflections

> Very detailed instructions will be given in this hour, and I'll use very specific settings along the way. It's important to realize that, as you create these special effects with your own images, my settings might not be the best settings for you. Different resolutions, sizes, and colors call for different settings. So when you see specifics, feel free to play with them a bit and see whether you can get even better results with your artwork.
>
> Truly, that's the real secret of getting better and better at Photoshop: *Never stop experimenting!*

Glows

Using the Glow Tool produces an easy special effect. It's essentially a drop shadow that isn't offset at all from the original object and is often in a color other than black. In Hour 17, "Adding Type to Pictures," you learned how to use Photoshop's Glow Tool to apply a glow to lettering. Here's a different way to do it.

To Do: Create a Glow Around an Object

Let's create a basic glow around an object. You can download this image at the book's Web site. To get to the Web site, point your Web browser to:

```
http://www.mcp.com/sams/detail_sams.cfm?item=0672319551
```

When the main book page has loaded, click the Downloads link to get to the files.

1. Select an image to which you'd like to apply the effect. I took a picture of a lit match. (Actually, I took several and assembled them.) It just doesn't look right because the flame isn't shedding any light. Figure 18.1 shows the original photo.

FIGURE **18.1**

The original match, sans glow.

▼ 2. First, you need to select the object that will glow, in this case, the flame. The
      Magic Wand tool does a fine job of this. If there are cutouts, be sure they're
      selected, too.

   3. Copy the object, and paste it onto a new layer. Now you have two layers: one with
      the complete image and one with just the selected object.

   4. Return to the background layer and reselect the object by pressing
      Shift+Command+D (Mac) or Shift+Control+D (Windows). Cut it out and paste it
      on a new layer.

   5. Expand the selection (Select→Modify→Expand) by 45 pixels (or whatever's
      appropriate for your image). Feather the edges by 10 pixels.

   6. Use the Path menu to make a work path around the selection. Use the Fill Path
      command to fill the work path with an appropriate Glow color. Use the Delete Path
      command to lose the line around it. Now, only the color remains on the layer.
      Figure 18.2 shows this step.

FIGURE **18.2**

*Just the Glow layer
and background.*

18

   7. Make sure the glow is selected. Use the Gaussian Blur filter to diffuse the glow.
      Try a setting around 10, for a big glow.

   8. Assemble the layers, so the glow is beneath the object. If the shadows interfere
▼   with the glow, remove them. Figure 18.3 shows the final product.

FIGURE **18.3**

The match with the glow effect added.

▲

We've only scratched the surface of glow effects, so I encourage you to try all sorts of settings and colors. Experiment with the brightness and size of the glow. Also try other Blur filters for glows that imply movement or dimension. Have fun!

Lighting Effects

Lighting effects refers to a whole range of special effects that are all related to how objects are lit. By illuminating objects in a unique way, you can change the entire feel of an image, drawing attention exactly where you want it.

To Do: Generate Lighting Effects on an Object

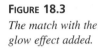

Our primary tool, as you might expect, is Photoshop's Lighting Effects filter.

1. Start with an original image. Perhaps this is an image that is fairly "flat" as far as brightness is concerned. Perhaps it's an image that simply needs to be more three-dimensional to match its content. Figure 18.4, showing a stuffed dog toy, is such an image. (If you want to follow along, download the image Huskie.jpg from the Macmillan Web site discussed earlier.)

2. At this point, I need to decide whether I want to light the entire scene or just the dog. Lighting just a selected object is more dramatic; lighting the whole canvas is more natural. I opted for spotlights.

3. Choose Filter→Render→Lighting Effects to bring up the Lighting Effects dialog box (see Figure 18.5). Under the Style pull-down menu near the top, select Triple Spotlight. You'll see the preview of your image in the left with the new spotlight effect.

▼

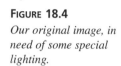

FIGURE 18.4
Our original image, in need of some special lighting.

FIGURE 18.5
The Lighting Effects dialog box.

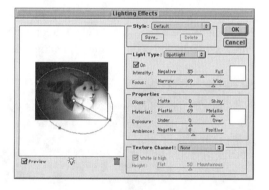

4. Although Photoshop ships with a number of neat default settings, it's fun to play around with the various sliders and values. Don't be intimidated by the number of choices here. For one thing, I don't like how the spotlights are falling on the image. I want them to overlap more.

   To change the direction and/or shape of the Spotlight, simply grab the handles around the oval you see on the left side of the dialog box. You can move them around as you want. You can even move the center point. Move everything around so that it looks something like what you see in Figure 18.6.

5. Now it looks like the non-lit parts of the image are too dark. I need to bring the overall lighting up a bit, so I adjust the Ambience slider up to 6, and change the color of the spotlights to a light blue.

▼

FIGURE 18.6
Three lights, one puppy.

6. Sometimes, a fancy effect like this one is overkill. I can also use this dialog box to create a simple spotlight. Here's the Two O'clock Spot, with some very basic settings. (see Figure 18.7) I think, on the whole, I like this one better.

FIGURE 18.7
Sometimes simple effects are best.

▲

Reflections

If you often find yourself bringing various images together in Photoshop (and I predict you will), you can't simply toss the images together and have the new image look realistic. As we've seen, effects like shadows are essential to create a realistic-looking environment. Creating reflections is another technique for doing this.

To Do: Add Reflections to a Surface for Realism

Let's look at an example to see how you can add reflections to your toolkit of special effects:

1. Let's say I have an object (which I do) that I want to insert into an image I've created. First, I need to create a background. I'll use the Gradient Tool to lay down a very simple gradient from dark to light. Then I'll add some noise from the Noise filter so it has a little texture. I want this to look like a photographer's seamless background, so I'll use Transform→Distort to drag the bottom out wide. Figure 18.8 shows this stage.

FIGURE 18.8

A very simple "studio" backdrop.

2. The sides of the top part should be vertical, so I'll select the backdrop part way up and distort again to straighten the side borders (see Figure 18.9). As a final touch, I'll apply the Plastic Wrap filter to make the surface look like hammered metal.

FIGURE 18.9

All ready to put something on.

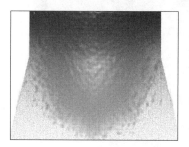

3. I have a lemon wedge that I'll set onto this background. (You can download the lemon from the book's Web site.) I think you'll agree that the effect isn't very realistic. It looks like the lemon and background came from two different sources (which they did, but I don't want it to be so obvious!).

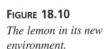

FIGURE **18.10**
The lemon in its new environment.

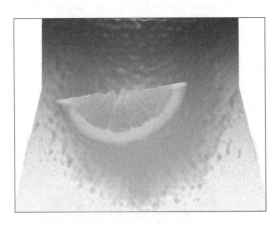

4. To start working on a reflection of the lemon on the background, duplicate the lemon layer. In the Layers palette, move this new layer (I named it Reflection) below the original lemon layer, because we want the reflection to appear "underneath" the original lemon.

5. With the Reflection layer active, select Edit→Transform→Flip Vertical. This flips the reflected lemon onto its head.

6. Select the lemon's reflection and use the Move tool to move it down. (Hold down the Shift key as you move the selection, so that it moves straight down and not at all horizontally.) The adjacent edges of the "two lemons" should meet precisely without much backdrop visible between them (see Figure 18.11).

FIGURE **18.11**
The lemon flipped and moved down into place.

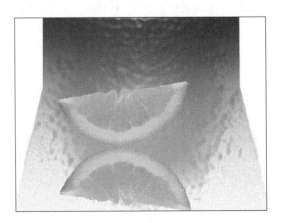

It looks like a reflection, right? Well, sort of. It looks like a reflection only if the surface is *perfectly* reflective, like a mirror, which obviously it isn't.

▼ 7. To make the reflection realistic, some of the background has to show through, just as we saw with drop shadows. Adjust the Opacity slider for the Reflections layer, until the reflection looks more realistic and blends in with the surface (see Figure 18.12).

FIGURE **18.12**

With Opacity reduced, the reflection looks much more realistic.

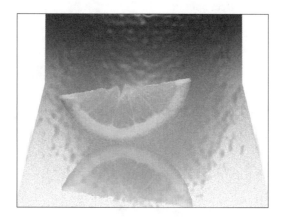

If you're satisfied with the reflection as it is now, you're done. Unfortunately, I'm picky and seldom satisfied. The reflection still looks too perfect to me. The background isn't that smooth.

8. To introduce a little "dirtiness" into the reflection, it's time for another trip to the Plastic Wrap filter. I use settings of Strength, 4; Detail, 7; and Smoothness, 10 to get the effect I like. (see Figure 18.13).

18

FIGURE **18.13**

Looks good enough to eat.

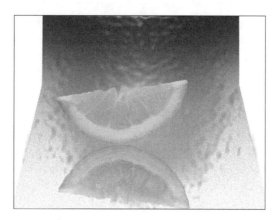

▼ Okay, now it's looking good. The lemon image is now interacting with the floor image, creating a realistic effect. There's just one more thing bugging me—the

▼ wall behind the lemon. Shouldn't the lemon and wall interact? Shouldn't the lemon be casting just a bit of a shadow on the wall? I think so.

9. I can use the Layer Style→Drop Shadow effect to add this shadow, being sure to move the light source so the shadow falls on the wall, not on the reflection. Figure 18.14 shows the effect applied.

FIGURE **18.14**

Now the lemon casts a shadow onto the wall as well as a reflection.

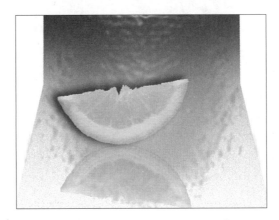

▲

Well, I'm satisfied. The image now looks like one piece instead of three disparate images thrown together. That's what special effects like Reflections can do for you.

Extracting Selections

Some selections are easy to do; some are like pulling teeth. That's why Photoshop includes an extraction tool. The Extract command (Image→Extract) enables you to isolate a foreground object from its background. Even objects with fuzzy, soft, or hard-to-define edges can now be separated from their backgrounds with very little difficulty.

To extract an object, choose Image→Extract to bring up the Extract dialog box. You can either pre-select the object with the Magic Wand or use the Extract Edge Highlighter Tool to draw around the edges of the object. Then you define the object's interior by using the Paint Bucket to fill in the outline. Click the Preview button to preview the extraction. You can refine and preview the extraction as many times as you want. Figure 18.15 shows the Extract window. I've partially selected the lemon, using the Extract tools to refine the selection. When you are ready to perform the extraction, Photoshop erases the background to transparency, leaving just the extracted object.

FIGURE 18.15

Many of the Extract window's tools look like the regular Photoshop tools.

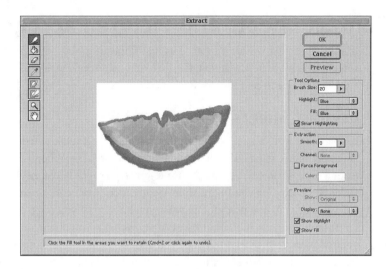

Notepad

NEW TO VERSION **6**   If you've ever used those sticky notes (and is there anyone who hasn't?), you're going to love Photoshop's Notepad. Click the Notepad icon in the toolbox, and then click the picture where you want the note to be referenced. You can even put notes outside the picture. Your Notepad stretches to fit long notes, and it's even personalized with your name on top. This is a great feature if you pass pictures back and forth with other members of a workgroup. I also use it when I download a bunch of photos and want to make notes about what to work on, when I have time. Figure 18.16 shows one of my current projects.

FIGURE 18.16

If you close a note, its icon remains. Clicking reopens it.

If a note covers something you want to see in the image, you can drag the actual note to another location. To get rid of a note, drag its icon completely off the screen.

Contact Sheets and Picture Packages

In this automated world, it's only fair that Photoshop should provide ways to automate some of the more noncreative tasks that we must occasionally do. Two of my favorites are Contact Sheets and Picture Packages.

Contact Sheets

If you come from a background of darkroom photography, as I do, you're already used to making contact sheets of every roll of film you process. When you download images from a digital camera, you might use a transfer program that displays your photos as slides in a sorter, or you might simply copy them from card to hard drive. If you follow the latter course, you don't know what you have until you open each picture in Photoshop and look it at. That takes time. Suppose you could simply scan thumbnails of your pictures, and choose the ones you wanted to use without deciphering the cryptic numbers from the camera or having to open each picture separately. Much easier? You bet.

All you need to do is to save the images for the contact sheet into a folder. You can even place several subfolders inside one main folder. Then select File→Automate→Contact Sheet to open the dialog box in Figure 18.17 and select the folder you want to make contacts of.

FIGURE 18.17

Click Include All Subfolders if you want their contents to be included in the contact sheet.

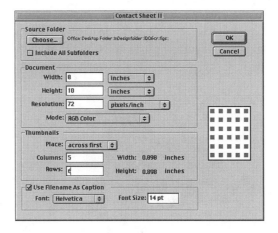

If you're going to print your contact sheets, be sure the document size is no larger than the paper in your printer. Low resolution (72 dpi) is usually good enough to see what's going on, and saves time and space. Decide how many thumbnails you want per page, and set them up across or down as you prefer. Finally, if you want them identified on the contact sheet (which I strongly recommend), click the Use Filename As Caption check box and select a font and size for the caption, which is the name of the file. When you click OK, Photoshop will automatically open your files one at a time, create thumbnails, and paste them into a new document. You can then save and print this contact sheet just like any other page. Figure 18.18 shows a typical contact sheet.

FIGURE 18.18

Each little photo has its filename as a title.

DSC00041.JPG   DSC00042.JPG   DSC00043.JPG

DSC00044.JPG   DSC00045.JPG   DSC00046.JPG

DSC00047.JPG   DSC00048.JPG   DSC00049.JPG

DSC00050.JPG   DSC00051.JPG   DSC00052.JPG

18

Picture Packages

Remember school pictures? You got a page with one 5×7, a couple of "stick-on-the-fridge" size for the grandparents, and a couple of wallet-size photos for mom and dad. Around the holidays, your local discount store or department store offers similar deals. You don't need to bother with them. You can do your own, and save a bundle.

Use File→Automate→Picture Package to open the dialog box. Choose a photo, or click the check box to use the current one. Choose a paper size according to whatever your printer can handle. In Photoshop 6, you have options for 11×17 paper as well as smaller sizes. Figure 18.19 shows the dialog box with the size selection menu open to show you the many options.

FIGURE 18.19

Portrait sizes, wallets, little tiny ones, even passport sizes—what more could you want?

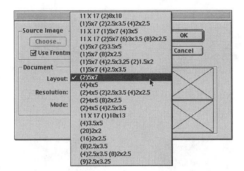

Set the resolution as appropriate for your printer, and click OK. Photoshop will assemble the package for you, just as it does with the contact sheets. When you're ready, save it and/or print it. Figure 18.20 shows a sample layout.

FIGURE 18.20

Be sure you retouch your photos before you assemble them.

Summary

Creating a special effect isn't about specific instructions and narrowly defined settings—it's about experimenting with all that Photoshop has to offer and being pleasantly surprised by new discoveries. As you use Photoshop's features (especially its filters) more and more, you'll uncover an endless stream of special effects. This hour is just a small taste of what's possible. Have fun creating your own special effects!

The tricks in this hour are also just a taste of what Photoshop can do. Explore the menus. If you see a command you don't understand, try it. You might find something you can use.

Q&A

Q How would you place a reflection in water?

A Much the same as we did on the metal backdrop, except that I'd apply an appropriate Ripple filter to the reflection, as well as blurring it. Depending on the kind of water, you might want to apply Blur first, and then Ripple, or vice versa. Try both and see which looks more realistic.

Q I'm a schoolteacher, and I have taken photos of my class, which I'd like to post on the bulletin board. Is there an easy way to print them all at the same size, with the kids' names underneath?

A That's not hard. Make sure the child's name is the name of the file, and put all the files in one folder. Then open Contact Sheet and set it for an appropriate number of columns and rows, determined by how large you want the final photos. If you want them as large as possible, print only one image per sheet. Choose a font and size for the names and assemble the contacts. When they're ready, hit Print. Ta da! There they are, and I bet they're all cute!

Q Just how did you learn how to do all this?! It all seems so complicated—filters, effects, selecting things, changing colors, modifying options. Argh!

A I learned the way you're learning—one step at a time. I studied my pictures and decided what effect I wanted to achieve and then kept trying things until I got the picture to look the way I wanted. When I have some free time, I like to turn on Photoshop and use it like a video game. I open a picture and see how long it takes me to completely lose the original image. It sounds silly, but I learn a lot from these sessions.

18

Quiz

1. How many kinds of lighting effects are there?

   a. Three: Spot, Omni, and Directional

   b. Seventeen, including colored spots and multi-light patterns

   c. Two: On and Off

2. A glow is a drop shadow that's not offset.

   a. True

   b. False

3. Which direction do reflections face, in relationship to the reflected object?

   a. The same horizontal direction, but the opposite vertical direction

   b. The same vertical direction, but the opposite horizontal direction

   c. Either a or b could be correct. (It depends on where the Mirror surface is.)

4. How many images can you put on a contact sheet?

   a. Up to a dozen

   b. 10

   c. It depends on how small you make them. One hundred is possible. However, if the images are at less than a half-inch wide, you might have trouble seeing them.

Quiz Answers

1. b. Take an image that's basically flat lit and try them all.

2. a. (And in a color other than black.)

3. c. Think about it.

4. c. A reasonable number is 24–30.

Exercises

Take some time and study reflections. Look at yourself in your coffee table. (You might have to polish it first!) Go outside and see the reflection of trees in water—even in a puddle or a pothole in the road. Find a book (or look on the Internet) of M.C. Escher's drawings and etchings and look in particular for "Three Worlds," "Puddle," and "Rippled Surface."

Download the photo of the rubber duck from our Web site, and place it in water. Position the reflection beneath it and a shadow behind it. Experiment until both look natural.

HOUR 19

Photoshop Plug-Ins and Add-Ons

By now, you have seen, if not used, most of the 99 filters that came with your copy of Photoshop. There couldn't possibly be any more, could there? Well, Photoshop is kind of like those fashion dolls or action figures that kids of a certain age demand. You can't just buy Batman and Robin or Barbie. You need the Batmobile, Stately Wayne Manor, and Barbie's Dream House, Yacht, and Sport Utility Vehicle… After you see how much fun you can have with the basic filters, you'll want Eye Candy, Xenofex, KPT 6, BladePro, and at least several dozen of the latest shareware filters, too. And the list goes on.

You've probably also considered buying a graphics tablet and more RAM. (You can never have too much.) Maybe you also need a faster computer to make all these tools work a little more efficiently. Of course, none of these plug-ins or add-ons is absolutely necessary, but for the next hour, let's pretend we're kids in a candy store. We'll sample everything possible.

Where to Get Plug-Ins

Commercial plug-in sets, such as the KPT, Chromatica, and Eye Candy packages described in this hour, can be found in mail order catalogs or at your friendly local computer dealer (who'll be even friendlier when you start buying all these goodies).

On the other hand, you needn't spend a lot of money. It often amazes me how very many talented and generous people there are who not only write useful software, but then turn around and give it away or sell it for such a pittance that they might as well be giving it away. I am speaking, of course, of shareware, and its authors who spend many long nights polishing a program and then upload it to CompuServe or AOL, or to the Web. If you go searching in appropriate areas for Macintosh or Windows software, you should find plenty of new and useful Photoshop plug-ins.

I did a Lycos search on *Photoshop filter* and got back a list of hundreds of sites that were triggered by that combination of keywords. The following are some good ones to get you started:

pluginhead.i-us.com/

www.pixelfoundry.com/

www.mediaco.com/nvr/ (Windows only)

How to Install Plug-Ins

Few things could be simpler than installing an individual filter. Simply drag it into the Photoshop filter folder if you're using a Macintosh. Windows users, place it in the `Photoshop 6\Plug-Ins\Filters` directory. Then launch Photoshop, and the new filter will appear in the list under the Filter menu. If you purchase a set of filters, such as Alien Skin's Eye Candy, there's an installer included, which automatically places the filters where they belong. Installed third-party filters appear in the filter list after Photoshop's native filters. Figure 19.1 shows my current collection.

FIGURE **19.1**

The Filter menu.

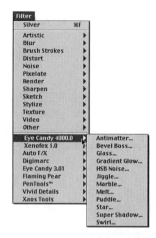

Alien Skin's Eye Candy

I love this company. Not only do Alien Skin's designers produce great products, but they have a wicked sense of humor. Their latest T-shirt reads, "Saturate the Industry with Freaks." Whether or not you qualify as a freak (and I'm sure I do), you're going to love Eye Candy. It comes in both Macintosh and Windows flavors, and can be found at your local software store or mail order source for about $125. Some of the Eye Candy effects are probably not for everyday use, unless your day job is designing covers for a science fiction magazine. Others, however, like Bevel Boss and Perspective Shadow, could be very useful.

The Alien Skin interface changes according to the effect you're applying, but the basic screen (shown in Figure 19.2) remains the same.

19

FIGURE **19.2**

Alien Skin's Eye Candy.

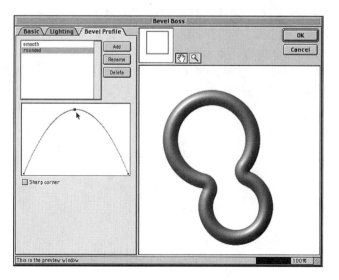

As of version 4.0, there are 23 Eye Candy effects, including chrome, fur, drip, puddle, smoke, fire, jiggle, squint, swirl, and a lot more. You can adjust all possible parameters of each of these effects, making the chrome shiny or dull; the fur wavy, long, or curly; the smoke dense or wispy; or whatever you can think of.

Applying many of these effects requires first selecting an area to which the effect will be applied, or adding a layer for it. A few, like Antimatter, simply do their thing. Antimatter inverts the brightness without affecting the colors or saturation value. Darks become light, and lights go dark. Figure 19.3 shows the Swirl effect being applied to a crate of watermelons.

FIGURE 19.3

You might not use this every day, but it's fun.

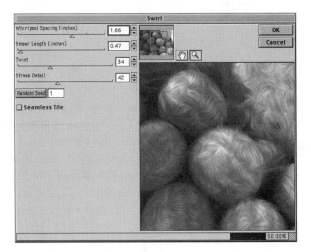

How to Create Glass Distortion

The Glass filter is one of the more useful filters in the Eye Candy set. It places your image behind a sheet of beveled glass and makes a wonderful glass distortion effect when combined with Photoshop's Glass filter. In Figure 19.4, we're looking at the watermelons again, only through a sheet of bumpy glass. The Glass effect is achieved by simulating three different effects: reflection, refraction, and light filtering.

FIGURE **19.4**

Using Glass distortion.

To Do: Create Glass Distortion Effects

To use the Glass distortion effect, follow these steps.

1. Start with an image that is basically simple. Glass works best on uncomplicated photos. Select the Glass filter from the Eye Candy list.

2. Set the bevel width. This controls both the width of the smooth outer edge of the glass and the apparent thickness of the glass. Larger values, used with high refraction, make your glass seem thicker. Smaller values, with low refraction, make the glass appear thinner. If you make the bevel as thick as possible and set a high refraction amount, you see your image through a prism.

3. Use the color box to select a color or shade of "dirt" for the glass. A very light gray suggests a dusty window without affecting the colors of the original picture. Use the Opacity slider to determine how much of a color tint is applied to the glass. Higher values add more color; lower values let the picture show more clearly.

4. Set the Edge darkening. This controls how much of the bevel you actually see.

5. Set the refraction. Refraction is the most important control for "glassiness." It controls the amount that the glass warps your picture. The scale runs from 0%–100%, but only the low end lets your image remain intelligible. Setting refraction higher than 50% reduces the edges of the underlying photo to vague shapes.

19

▼   6. Go to the Advanced mode and set the Highlight Brightness and Sharpness.
         Highlight Brightness and Sharpness affects only the white highlights that appear on
         the edges of the bevel. Higher values here give a glossier effect. Direction and
         Inclination can be set by typing numbers into their boxes or by dragging the ball
         around until the lighting looks right.

      7. Watch the effect of each change in the Preview window as you make it. When you
         like what you see, click the check mark to confirm it and return to Photoshop, or
         just press Return or Enter. If the overall effect is too much, undo it and lower the
         settings or use Photoshop's Fade command to moderate it.

      8. When you're done with the edges, click OK to apply the filter. Then go to the
         Photoshop Glass filter (Filter→Distort→Glass), and draw a selection box just
         inside the beveled frame. Apply the Photoshop Glass filter to the selection with a
         distortion of about 7 and a smoothness of around 5. (I like the effect of the Canvas
         texture, scaled to 70%.) Click OK to apply the filter. Your image now looks like
▲   you're seeing it through a bumpy glass window.

      Eye Candy's Star filter, shown in Figure 19.5, is another of my favorites. It draws stars,
      blats, and little pointy things, with as many points as you want, shading them in three
      dimensions. These are great for pepping up a Web page. Create them in Photoshop, and
      then jump over to ImageReady and assign rollover actions. (You'll learn how to do this
      in Hour 24, "Photoshop for the Web.")

FIGURE 19.5

How many points on a star? With this filter, you can have up to 50.

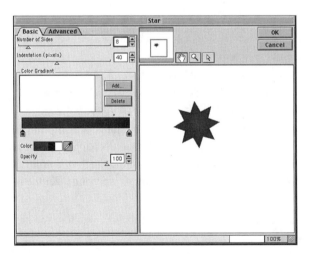

As is true of any of these tools, the more you explore, the more you'll learn about working with it. Some filters can take quite a long time to apply (and this is true of both
third-party and Photoshop-native filters). Don't assume your system has frozen if you

don't see any movement for as much as a minute. The math involved in remapping each pixel in a swirl effect would make Einstein choke. Be patient. The computer is thinking as fast as it can.

Kai's Power Tools

Kai Krause is a legend in the field of computer graphics. He's the guiding genius behind Kai's Power Tools, Bryce, Convolver, Vector Effects, Final Effects, Goo, Soap, and probably many more goodies yet to be announced. The current edition is KPT 6, distributed by Corel Corp. KPT 6 has 10 new filters, most of which are potentially useful, unlike some of Kai's earlier and stranger creations. (Sadly, earlier toolsets might not be available much longer. When stocks of KPT 5 are sold out, there's no guarantee that Corel will reissue it, and KPT 3 and Convolver are long gone.)

The interfaces are designed to be as intuitive and as interesting as possible (see Figure 19.6). There are excellent help screens available within each filter (look for a question mark and click it). The goal of these filters, besides allowing you to do interesting things to your photos, is to change your way of working with the computer. By the way, you can find KPT 6 in mail-order catalogs or on the shelves of your local software store for about $129.

FIGURE 19.6

The interface for the KPT tool collection.

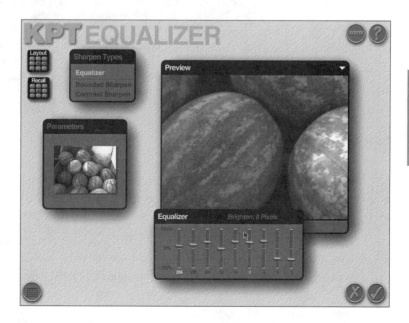

19

When you open any of the KPT toolsets, your screen will go blank except for the KPT logo. Then it will open with a futuristic control panel. Within the panel are smaller panels that control individual actions as parts of the filters' functions. For example, in Figure 19.6, when you slide the mouse over the panels or click a triangle, other panels drop down. The Equalizer filter enables you to selectively sharpen, smooth, or blur parts of a photo without affecting the rest. Clicking the question mark opens the PDF user guide for the selected filter. Clicking the www button takes you to Corel's home page. The button in the lower-left corner, which looks a bit like a calculator, takes you to presets for the filters.

Materializer, shown in Figure 19.7, is my favorite KPT filter. It adds a texture by following the contours of the objects in the photo, rather than simply covering the whole canvas with a texture.

FIGURE 19.7

Materializer gave my watermelons a third dimension.

There are lots more KPT filters to play with. Some can even make QuickTime movies of your actions, let you swirl and stretch the image, put it into perspective, and insert the resulting animation into a PowerPoint presentation. You can then put your movie on the Web, or do whatever you can think of with it (as long as it's QuickTime-compatible).

One last KPT filter that's incredibly cool lets you create your own sky. Figure 19.8 shows the interface. You can add haze and fog to your sky and define up to four separate layers of clouds. If you'd rather make a moonlit sky, that's there too.

FIGURE 19.8

Tilt the camera to see more (or less) sky.

AutoF/X Photo/Graphic Edges

This filter package puts the finishing touch on your pictures: textured edges. AutoF/X has four CD volumes of edges, with more than 10,000 different textures in all. You can customize them with the controls in the filter's dialog box, shown in Figure 19.9.

FIGURE 19.9

You can add color, change the size, and make any other adjustments with AutoF/X Photo/Graphic Edges.

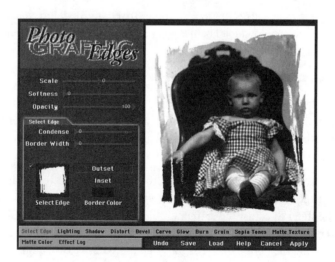

19

You can download a demo version of this filter from www.autofx.com, along with some other interesting and useful plug-ins. Be sure to check it out.

Flaming Pear

Here's another company with an interesting name and a collection of useful plug-ins. My favorite in this set is called India Ink. It gives a pen-and-ink drawing texture to your photo. This filter is especially effective on portraits. It mellows out the details without making the person unrecognizable. Figure 19.10 shows it being applied to the watermelon picture.

FIGURE **19.10**

This works equally well in black & white and color.

Among the other filters in the Flaming Pear set are BladePro, Lacquer, Silver, and Swerve. You can download demo versions of these at www.flamingpear.com.

Vivid Details Test Strip

If you really like tweaking colors, Vivid Details Test Strip is the plug-in you'll enjoy most of all. Like Photoshop's Variations, it's used for color correction. But Test Strip allows—in fact, *demands*—that you be the judge of when the color's right. When you open Test Strip, you'll see a window like the one shown in Figure 19.11.

Much like a photographer's test strip from the darkroom, Test Strip gives you samples of your image with various kinds of corrections applied. Color Balance comes first. You can use the slider to adjust the amount of color added or subtracted. Click the version that looks right and move on to the next setting, which lets you change the amount of a single color within the photo. Too red? Take out a percent or two, adjust Brightness and Contrast, and finally change the Saturation, if you like one of the options. The final choice on the Test Strip tool bar lets you see before and after versions of your picture, so you can see how much of a change you've made before you click the button to apply it.

FIGURE 19.11

Click the version that looks best to you.

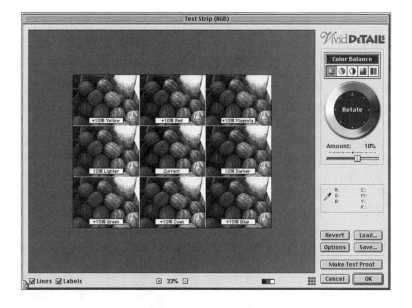

You can download a demo version of Test Strip at www.vividdetails.com/ Test_Strip.html. It's available for both Windows and Macintosh platforms. You can buy it online or from the usual mail order sources. By the way, the Web site has an excellent tutorial on monitor calibration using Test Strip. Monitor calibration is vital if you want accurate color reproduction.

If you think you have a good eye for color, and know what you want, Test Strip is a good choice.

Genuine Fractals

This plug-in is a necessity if you intend to rescale images that you have scanned or imported from a digital camera. It allows you to save files at low resolution and then repurpose them as needed in high resolution, with no loss of quality. I can work at a comfortable 72 dpi, rescale to 300 dpi for a high-quality Iris print, and you'd never know that the file wasn't always high-resolution.

Xenofex

Last in this hour, but far from least, is a very cool plug-in set from our friends at Alien Skin. Xenofex makes textures. Of course, that's sort of like saying that Beethoven wrote pretty tunes.

Xenofex features 16 terrific effects plug-ins. Among my favorites are Little Fluffy Clouds, which adds clouds all the way from snowflake-like wisps to a hurricane; Flag, which adds ripples to your selection; and Baked Earth (see Figure 19.12), which places your selection on a rough, cracked surface that could be either a terrazzo floor or sun-parched clay. Other effects include Puzzle, Shower Door, Stain—which creates the look of a coffee stain—and Stamper—which fills your selection with copies of any TIFF image.

FIGURE 19.12

I've applied the Baked Earth filter over a plain background to create a useful texture.

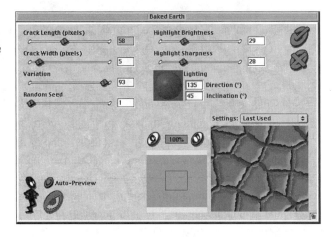

Two other Xenofex plug-ins produce electrical effects: Electrify causes glowing bolts of lightning to radiate from your selection, and Lightning generates everything from static and Vandergraff generator effects to flower stems inside the selected area. Figure 19.13 shows the Lightning filter being applied, and Figure 19.14 shows both Electrify and Lightning applied to a picture of one of my cats.

FIGURE 19.13

These filters, like all the Xenofex series, are extremely flexible. Poke around the dialog boxes and you'll find even more variables.

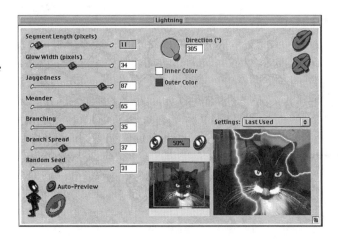

FIGURE 19.14
Static cat. He feels like this all winter.

Most of the plug-ins give you lots of options for customizing the effects. For instance, Electrify lets you set the arc lengths, how much they'll branch out, and the size and color of the glow. Baked Earth lets you choose the depth and width of the cracks, as well as how the light hits them. Preset textures include Tile Floor and Scaly Skin. Xenofex is a tool with which you can have a lot of fun. The more you explore, the more you'll discover tricks like using the Puffy Clouds very small to make snowflakes, or Stain with Dissolve as a blend mode to create a speckled surface.

Summary

In this hour, we checked out some of the cool third-party filters you can use with Photoshop. The most versatile and complete package is still Kai's Power Tools (KPT 6.0), although it's probably not the easiest to use. My personal favorite, Alien Skin's Eye Candy filter set, includes a great many really odd filters, such as Fur and Fire, as well as very simple-to-apply drop shadow and glow filters. Test Strip will save you time compensating for bad scans or lousy photography. Genuine Fractals makes image scaling simple. Finally, Xenofex gives you the power to add textures, ripples, and electrifying effects to your art.

Q&A

Q Is there a way to design your own Photoshop filters?

A There's an old plug-in called Filter Factory, which supposedly lets you do so. I've found it on the Web, but haven't really tried to do anything with it. It's a fairly complicated procedure, and the documentation is lacking. If you're really good at programming, Adobe makes specifications available for software developers who want to create plug-ins for Adobe products. Visit `partners.adobe.com/asn/ developer/gapsdk/PhotoshopSDK.html` for more information.

Q Do these weird filters, such as Fur and Squint and Water Drops, have any practical uses?

A Just today, I saw a sign that featured a frosty bottle of Coca-Cola on a red background. The entire image was made to look wet with Alien Skin's Water Spot filter. Anything's practical if you have enough imagination to make it work.

Quiz

1. Where do plug-ins appear?

   a. On the Plug-ins palette

   b. At the bottom of the Filter menu

   c. At the top of the Window menu

2. Which of the following is NOT an Eye Candy effect?

   a. Fur

   b. Fire

   c. Squint

   d. Slime

Quiz Answers

1. b. (If you have many plug-ins, you may have to scroll down to see them all.)

2. d. (But if you start with Green Glass, you can create a reasonably slimy effect.)

Exercises

Download some of the great plug-ins from Flaming Pear and Alien Skin at www. flamingpear.com and www.alienskin.com. See which ones you can't live without.

Hour **20**

Compositing

Compositing can be known by other names. It can be "combining" or making a collage, or photo-montage. Whatever it's called, the goal is the same: To make one picture from pieces of other ones. Photoshop is the ideal program for this kind of work for several reasons. First, it has the tools to assemble pieces of different pictures. Second, it gives you the ability to work in layers. Third, its filters enable you to blend pictures and add shadows and reflections more easily and effectively than any other graphics program can.

You can use the techniques described here, along with the ones you've already learned, to produce all sorts of surrealistic images, and (for many people) this is what Photoshop is all about. For others, myself included, compositing is more often a way of making up for deficiencies in the original picture.

Sources for Images

Pictures are everywhere. You can download thousands of images from the Web. You can buy CD-ROMs full of photographs and line art. And, of course, you can either scan conventional photos or import pictures from a digital camera into Photoshop.

When you start thinking about combining images, you'll probably realize that some pictures are more suitable than others for this kind of use. You can even classify some as backgrounds, others as objects, and some as the raw materials from which to create special effects. As you browse through your own pictures and look at collections of stock photos, some images will jump out at you, and you'll begin to see possible combinations.

Stock photos? If you're not familiar with the term, you should be. *Stock photos* are pictures that are made available to you for a fee (a flat fee or sometimes a per-use royalty) to do with as you see fit. You can use them in your reports, in ads, or practically any way you want, as long as you're not reselling them as is or using them in any way that's libelous, defamatory, pornographic, or otherwise illegal. Be sure you read and understand the licensing policies before you use them.

Point your Web browser to http://www.comstock.com/ to see some really good stock photography. Alas, you can't use any of the pictures in the Comstock libraries without paying for them. The screen versions download as low quality JPEGs, but you can get a feel for what's available and how much it costs.

Comstock is typical of stock photo collections. The Comstock collection includes more than 50,000 pictures of everything you can imagine. Figure 20.1 shows a page from the Comstock catalog. There's no reason you can't use these kinds of images in combination with your own. If you need something basic, like a slab of concrete to use as a background, it will be faster, cheaper, and just as effective to use one from stock. Let's start compositing with a couple of images from my own stock collection.

FIGURE 20.1

Stock photos.

Of course, as you wander around town with your digital camera in your pocket, you can start your own stock collection, too. In fact, it's one of the ways you can make money with your pictures, allowing you to invest the profits in more software and higher resolution cameras.

Making One Picture from Two

Remember the rubber ducky from the selections in Hour 13, "Paths"? He always wanted to be a big duck in a little pond. Well, I have a nice shot of a pond, so let's put him in there. Start by downloading the duck and separating him from his background. (The duck and the pond are available for download at the usual source, if you'd like to work along.) Figure 20.2 shows the duck, selected.

FIGURE 20.2

Just ducky...

Then open the water picture, copy the duck, and paste it in. Figure 20.3 shows the duck after this step.

FIGURE 20.3
I scaled him up a bit, too.

He still doesn't look natural, but we have a few tricks that should help. Before we start, let's duplicate the duck layer and then click on its eye to close it. (We'll come back to that shortly.)

First, put a drop shadow on the duck. The sun is coming from in back of him, so the shadow has to be in front. Figure 20.4 shows the Layer Style/Drop Shadow dialog box. Notice the settings, particularly the distance. This controls the amount of offset and places the shadow under the duck, as it ought to be. Instead of using a black shadow, I've set the shadow color to match the darker parts of the waves. That will also help the shadows match.

FIGURE 20.4

FIGURE 20.4

*The drop shadow needs
to be below and in front
of the duck because the
light source is at the
back of the pond.*

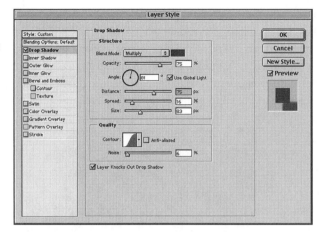

There's no way to determine which settings to use, other than trying them to see what
works best. The only one I could set arbitrarily was the angle. That's because I knew
where the light was, and shadows are usually directly opposite the light source. Setting
the other parameters gives you a chance to play with the shadow, to make it harder or
softer, bigger or smaller. Figure 20.5 shows the shadow I applied.

FIGURE 20.5

*He looks more real
when he casts a
shadow.*

20

Now we're about halfway there. Water reflects, and the duck is bright enough to reflect pretty well. To make the reflection, open the duck layer you copied and hid. Select the duck and apply Edit→Transform→Flip Vertical. Now you have an upside-down duck superimposed over the first one. Use the Move Tool to slide the duck reflection down. Figure 20.6 shows the results of this step. Because the duck is on a separate layer, you don't have to worry about damaging the background.

FIGURE 20.6

It's a reflection, but it's not quite right.

Reduce the opacity to 35% so that the water and drop shadow show through, and erase the part of the reflected duck that overlaps the other one. It's a bit too well-defined, so add a 6-pixel Gaussian Blur (Filter→Blur→Gaussian Blur). Figure 20.7 shows this step.

FIGURE 20.7

A generous amount of blur helps blend the overlap between the duck and its reflection.

We're almost done. As a final touch, let's make the reflection match the waves. Temporarily, bring the layer opacity up so you can see what's going on—75% will do. Open the Glass filter (Filter→Distort→Glass) and set the Distortion and Smoothness to about 12 and 10, respectively. Make sure the selected texture is Frosted. Apply the filter and reduce the layer opacity again to about 33%. Figure 20.8 shows the final image.

FIGURE 20.8

Now the duck lives here.

Controlling Transparency in Overlaid Images

It's extremely simple to paste one opaque image over another one—you just do it. Transparent images are harder to work with, though Photoshop makes it a little easier by giving you Transparency control.

When you're creating a multi-layered picture, as in Figure 20.7, you have two ways to control the way the layers blend. One is the Opacity slider. You can set any degree of opacity, from 100% all the way down to zero, at which point whatever's on the layer has completely disappeared. You can also control the effect by using the Blending Modes menu. By applying different modes to different layers, you can control the way each layer overlays the others.

20

Realistic Composites

Creating an image that's not meant to be completely realistic is relatively easy. Faking realism is a lot harder. The main tasks to consider in making composites are

- Keep your backgrounds simple.
- Isolate the elements on different layers for easier editing.
- Make sure the pieces you combine are in the proper scale for each other.
- When you're done, merge the layers for a smaller file.

> Remember also that adding shadows, reflections, or other special effects can make a big difference in the end result. Watch out for perspective, too. If it's wrong, you'll know it, although you might not know why exactly.

The series of pictures that follows shows a problem that I encountered with perspective and how I solved it.

Figure 20.9 is a photo I shot of one of Miami's Art Deco buildings. On the same trip, I shot a lighthouse a few miles south of the city. I thought it might be fun to put the lighthouse tower in place of the silo-shaped thing.

FIGURE 20.9
Not very exciting.

First, I'll work on the building. The Handicapped parking sign doesn't add anything to the composition, so I'll take it out. With the Rubber Stamp Tool and a bit of copy and paste, it's gone. See Figure 20.10 for this step.

FIGURE 20.10

*No more sign, just the
building and the car.*

20

Now, let's look at the lighthouse. In Figure 20.11, I've cropped it out of its background.
The palm branch that cuts across it should blend in with the palms in the other picture.

FIGURE **20.11**
The lighthouse minus everything else.

I'll make a new layer on the original picture and copy the lighthouse into it. First, though, I'll check the height of the silo and make the lighthouse approximately the same height by resizing the image. Pasting it in is simple. Then I need to select and remove the sky that imported along with it. With the lighthouse moved into position, I see one minor problem (see Figure 20.12). The buildings are crooked because I used a wide-angle lens, but the lighthouse is straight. Time for some perspective adjustment.

FIGURE **20.12**
What is it, the tiltin' Hilton?

I can fix this easily by selecting the background layer and applying Transform→Perspective to pull the sides of the building out. Remember that you can drag beyond the frame of the photo. With the building straight, it's easy to blend in the lighthouse so that it looks like it belongs there. I'll flip it horizontally so the branch comes in on the proper side, and then smudge the branch and copy a few palm fronds from the top of the picture to fill in the gaps. I can even paint some extra ones and remove the branch against the building that doesn't look right. Figure 20.13 shows the final photo, which is much different from the original.

FIGURE 20.13

Downtown Miami is a strange place for a lighthouse, but why not?

Replacing a Background

Remember that lynx with the chain link fence in her background? We hid the fence, but it would nice to put her somewhere more comfortable. How about in bed with my stuffed sheepdog? Figure 20.14 shows the lynx, and Figure 20.15 is the new background.

FIGURE 20.14

Natasha, a Siberian lynx.

20

FIGURE **20.15**
A nice friendly sheepdog.

The first thing to do is to isolate the cat, but, because the background is so complicated, the Magic Wand won't be much help. For now, I'll just loosely trace around her with the lasso and paste her into the other picture so I can see whether the concept works. Figure 20.16 shows that it does.

FIGURE **20.16**
Yes, she fits pretty well.

There are several ways to get rid of the edges of the outdoors around the lynx. I could erase it, bit by bit. I can remove some, but not all, by selecting it with the Magic Wand. I could use Image→Extract. But the easiest way is to use a tool called the Background Eraser. It pops out from the toolbox when you click and hold on the regular Eraser, and it erases pixels to transparency as you drag it.

To Do: Use the Background Eraser Tool

Let's do some practicing with this useful tool:

1. Go to the Layers palette and select the layer containing the areas you want to erase. (It's often easier if you hide the other layers.)

2. Select the Background Eraser Tool.

3. Set an appropriate brush size and shape from the Brush menu in the Tool Options bar.

4. Choose an erasing mode:

   • Discontinuous erases the sampled color anywhere it appears in the layer.

   • Contiguous erases areas that contain the sampled color and are connected to one another.

   • Find Edges erases connected areas containing the sampled color, while better preserving the sharpness of object edges.

5. Set the tolerance by entering a value or dragging the slider. A low tolerance limits erasing to areas that are very similar to the sampled color. A higher tolerance erases a broader range of colors.

6. To determine how erased colors are treated, select a sampling option:

   • Continuous samples colors continuously as you drag. Use this option to erase adjacent areas that are different colors.

   • Once erases only areas containing the color that you click first. Use this option to erase a solid-colored area.

   • Background Swatch erases only areas containing the current background color.

7. Select Protect Foreground Color to protect areas that match the foreground color in the toolbox.

8. Drag the eraser through the area you want to erase. If you have set Brush Size Cursors in the Preferences box, the Background Eraser Tool pointer appears as a brush shape with a crosshair indicating the tool's hot spot. Otherwise, it's a block eraser with a pair of scissors on top, just like its icon. This process is easier if you zoom in on the area to be erased.

▼ To Do

20

In Figure 20.17, I've erased most of the background. It still needs a bit of cleaning up with the regular Eraser, though.

FIGURE 20.17
Pause to clean the paws.

Finally, apply a little gaussian blur all over. And just for fun, copy the dog's paw and paste it on the cat's back. Figure 20.18 shows the lynx in her new bed.

FIGURE 20.18
Ah, domestic bliss...

So you see, combining pictures isn't at all difficult. You simply need to prepare them by removing unwanted backgrounds or other bits, and then assemble them in layers. Don't forget to merge the layers when you're sure that you're done working on the picture. Otherwise, your files, if they have several layers, can be quite large, and you won't be able to save them in specialized formats like .jpg or .pcx. Save copies unmerged on a Zip or Jaz disk, hard drive, or CD-ROM, so you can go back and improve on your work later.

Composites from Nothing

You've seen in some of the earlier hours that Photoshop can create art "from scratch," as well as editing and altering existing photos. As a final attempt at compositing, let's see what we can make out of nothing.

To Do: Create a Composite Image from Scratch

I'll start with a new page and apply a gradient as a background.

Gradients can be linear, radial, angled, reflected, or diamond-shaped, and can have as many transparent or opaque colors as you want. To create a gradient, follow these steps:

1. Select the Gradient Tool and look at its Options bar, which is shown in Figure 20.19.

FIGURE 20.19
Gradients and the Gradient Options bar.

2. I want to use a linear blend, which applies the colors in a straight line from one point to another. Select that icon, and then select the very simplest dark-to-light gradient from the pull-down menu.

3. Set the foreground color to a medium dark blue and the background color to white. Then position the crosshair cursor at the top of the screen and drag a line straight down. Figure 20.20 shows the gradient.

FIGURE 20.20
The gradient.

4. Now turn the image into a cloudy sky. Filter→Render→Clouds gives you a nice set of clouds, although they cover up the gradient. Use Edit→Fade Filter to make the sky a bit less cloudy (see Figure 20.21). Changing the mode to Multiply also helps bring back the dark-to-light gradation.

FIGURE 20.21
The cloudy sky.

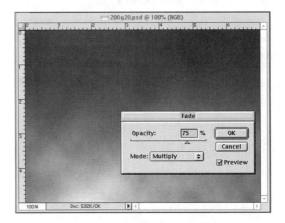

5. Having gotten this far, we need to put something in the sky. NASA makes some amazing photos available to anyone who wants them. I went to their Web site and found a shot called "Full Earth." It's shown in Figure 20.22.

FIGURE 20.22
Earth, courtesy of NASA.

6. I selected the Earth with the elliptical marquee (holding down Shift to keep the selection round) and pasted it into the sky. Now I can get silly and turn it into a balloon or a soccer ball, draw a rocket ship heading for us, or whatever else I want. Figure 20.23 shows one possibility.

Figure 20.23

The Earth on a string.

If you're interested in playing around with NASA's uncopyrighted, royalty-free images, check out their Image Exchange Web site at
`http://nix.nasa.gov/`.

Be sure to read the guidelines for use. Basically, they say that you should credit the photo to NASA, and that the use of NASA's photos doesn't imply its endorsement of any product or service.

Summary

Composites, montages, whatever you call them—they're simply combinations of two or more images, carefully merged. Use your own pictures or stock photos from collections, or create images by combining techniques and filters. It's fun, and it's effective. It's one of the things Photoshop does exceptionally well. Be sure to spend some time playing with compositing.

Q&A

Q Can I apply a filter to a gradient?

A Certainly. It's easiest if the gradient is on a separate layer. Just make the gradient the active layer and apply any filter or combination you like. The results often make an interesting background for other pictures, too. Start by trying the Texture filters and some of the Brushstroke ones. These are generally successful.

Q I tried importing a building into another photo, but it just doesn't look right. Why not?

A There could be a dozen different reasons, but the three most obvious are scale, perspective, and lighting. The import might be too big or too small for where you put it. It might need to be skewed into a different perspective. You might also be trying

20

to put a shadowless, noon-time picture into a late afternoon background. When you select pictures to combine, try to match sizes, orientation, and time of day. If that's not possible, you can still make it work, but you will have to do more correcting.

Q There's usually a difference in sharpness between the object I want to add and the background. It makes the object stand out like a sore thumb. Any ideas?

A If you don't want to blur the sharper image, try feathering the edges of the object. As little as four pixels should be plenty.

Q This is fun, but my files get so big that they take forever to save or apply a filter to. Any ideas?

A Be sure to merge down layers when you're done with them. Save frequently. Save different stages if you think you might want to go back further than the History palette can take you.

Quiz

1. Any picture you download from the Web can be considered a stock photo.

    a. True

    b. False

2. Photoshop has _____ different kinds of gradients.

    a. Two

    b. Three

    c. Five

3. Name one thing you'll have to master to make good composite images.

    a. Zen

    b. Filters

    c. Layers

4. What's the easiest way to remove a plain background?

    a. Erase it

    b. Select it and delete

    c. Fill it with clear paint

Quiz Answers

1. b. Be careful because many images are copyrighted, and you could get into legal trouble if you use them commercially. If you're just messing around with Photoshop at home, you're probably safe.

2. c. Can you name them? If not, start Photoshop and explore the toolbar where the Gradient tools reside.

3. c. You'll have to know several Photoshop techniques to create composite images, but being a pro at using layers is indispensable.

4. b. Depends on the situation, but generally a plain background is easy to select.

Exercises

To experiment with compositing, find two of your own pictures or two stock photos—one landscape and one portrait. Remove the background from the portrait subject, and place him or her into the landscape. Add shadows or reflections if necessary to make the person look as if he or she were photographed "on location."

20

HOUR **21**

Photo Repair— Black-and-White

Fixing damaged or "just plain lousy" pictures is the number one reason why most people buy Photoshop. It can really work miracles on old, torn, faded photographs, and it can also make up for most, if not all, of the flaws in your snapshots. Photoshop can be used to recompose a picture that's off-center, tilted, or has too much empty space. You can edit out the power lines and trash cans that spoil the landscape. You can even remove unwanted former spouses, or that awful boyfriend your daughter finally dumped, from family portraits. It's nowhere near as difficult to get rid of them onscreen.

Easy Fixes

Let's start by looking at some of the things you can do to fix up an old picture that might have faded, yellowed, or been damaged. First, we'll consider a couple of old family photos that need a little bit of adjusting and touching up. We'll run (literally) through the steps involved in fixing them and the tools you'll need to know how to use. (Remember, you can always flip to the front of the book to refresh your memory about these tools, too.) Finally we'll take an extremely damaged picture and work through it step by step, until it looks like new again.

Some pictures don't need very much work. The photo in Figure 21.1 was taken in 1905 but has been kept in an album away from sunlight for most of the past 95 years. It's turned a little yellow, but, all in all, it's remarkably well preserved.

FIGURE 21.1
This needs only minor touch-ups.

To fix this picture, we first crop the borders to remove any unnecessary edges. Then we set the mode to Grayscale, which removes any color information that the scan picked up. Doing this immediately eliminates the yellow and brown tones. Next, we use Curves (Image→ Adjust→Curves) to tweak the contrast a little. By using Curves, we can lighten the light tones without affecting the darks. In Figure 21.2, the very slight curve in the window lets you see just how subtle this adjustment is. Figure 21.3 shows the result of the steps we've taken.

FIGURE 21.2
*The curve adjustment
is very slight.*

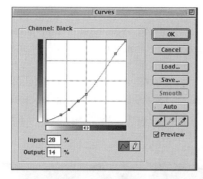

FIGURE 21.3
Much improved.

21

A couple of spots in the picture could use some minor enhancement. We'll apply the Burn Tool and Dodge Tool to darken and lighten some areas where the contrast could be a little better. By applying the Burn Tool only to the shadows and with a low percentage setting, we can darken the features on the baby's face, so her surprised expression shows up better. Similarly, applying it to midtones separates the lady's jawline from her high whalebone collar. Finally, a pass with the Dust and Scratches filter cleans up any spots and a pass with the Unsharp Masking filter gets rid of the softness the scan might have brought in. Figure 21.4 shows the final result.

FIGURE 21.4

Well-preserved photos, regardless of age, can be digitally enhanced.

Many Photoshop users make a habit of applying the Dust and Scratches filter (Filters, Noise, Dust and Scratches) to every scanned photo. This is often a mistake because, although it does make dust particles less obvious, it also softens the focus of the picture. If you decide to try it, evaluate the results carefully. Use the Preview check box to toggle back and forth, turning the filter preview on and off until you're certain that it's an improvement.

Here's another fairly old photo, shot in 1947. (I know. It's me.) This one is in much worse shape. It is both yellowed and faded, and it comes complete with a set of scratches on the negative where someone tried to indicate cropping. Even when it was shot, the contrast wasn't very good. The untouched photo is shown in Figure 21.5. Can we rescue it?

FIGURE 21.5

This one needs more serious work.

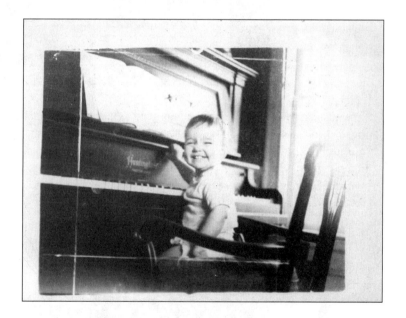

Again we'll start by cropping and then go to Grayscale to get rid of the yellow tones. There's a good deal that can be cropped out of the background of this photo, improving the composition. (see Figure 21.6).

21

FIGURE 21.6

Cropping can remove some of the problem areas.

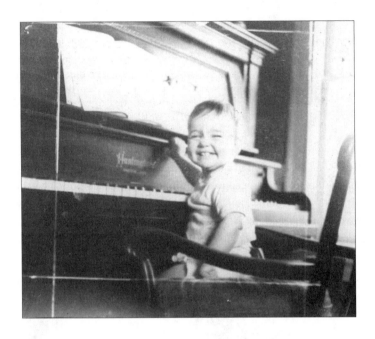

The contrast ratio in this picture isn't as good as in the previous one, so our next step will be to attempt to improve it. The Levels window shows the histogram for this picture, which tells us that the whites are too white and the darks not dark enough. The best way to learn to make these adjustments is to work on a copy of a "bad" picture, and simply experiment with the settings until you see the picture looking the way you want. Notice what happens when you move the sliders to the right or left. Figure 21.7 shows the corrections so far.

FIGURE 21.7

Changing the Levels adjusts the contrast.

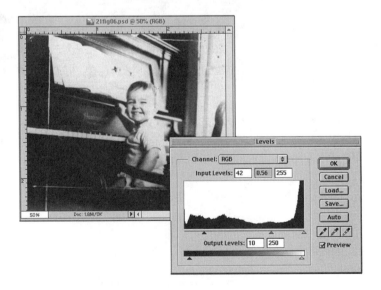

Using the Eyedropper

Taking a closer look, I'm aware of some dust as well as the scratches. You can see them in Figure 21.8, in the "before" sample. I'll have to do some touch up work to get rid of those.

Sometimes you need to paint over part of the image, either to fill in scratches or to remove unwanted lines, spots, or in-laws. Use the Eyedropper Tool to select a color with which to paint. Simply click the Eyedropper on any color (or in this case, shade of gray) in the image that you want to replicate, and that color becomes the foreground color, ready to apply with the Paintbrush, Airbrush, or whatever Painting tool you choose. You can also hold down the Option (Mac) or Alt (Windows) key while a Painting tool is selected to turn it temporarily into an Eyedropper, so you can change colors as you paint. Clicking the Eyedropper opens its Options toolbar. A pop-up menu gives you the choice of using a single pixel color sample or of taking an average color from either a 3×3- or 5×5-pixel sample.

With the Eyedropper, Brush, and Smudge tools, we'll repair the damage. All we need to do is to pick up the appropriate background grays from elsewhere in the picture, paint or rubber stamp them or ruor in, and smudge the area a little bit so it blends.

Before

FIGURE 21.8

You can see the changes in this photo from Before to After.

After

21

Using the Eyedropper Tool in a situation like this is much easier than trying to match an existing color or shade of gray on the color wheel. All you need to do to paint in the background is to find another spot in the picture where the color or gray shade is the one that you'd like to use. Select the Eyedropper and click it to make that color the foreground color. Then use your brush to paint in the selected shade. Smudge the edges very slightly if necessary to blend in the new paint. When the area to work on is very small, I like to use a single pixel brush as a Smudge Tool, and set it for only 20% pressure so I don't overdo the smudges. When you are working on corrections this small, it's much easier to apply them gradually and let the effect build up, rather than trying to do it all in one pass.

Using the Rubber Stamp

The Rubber Stamp Tool is perfect when you need to copy small pieces of a picture and paste them elsewhere. Technically, it's a cloning brush. It samples from a chosen point in the image and duplicates the selection, exactly as if you'd made a rubber stamp of it. Figure 21.9 shows the Rubber Stamp Tool and its options bar. Choose a brush shape, blending mode, and opacity as you would with any other tool. When you select a reference point, the Stamp creates a duplicate of the image anywhere you start painting, expanding the duplicated portion of the image as you go. Conceivably, you could reproduce the entire image if you had enough blank canvas.

If you don't choose Aligned, the stamp behaves differently. After you select your reference point and start painting, the duplicate portion of the image expands only while you continue to hold down the mouse button. When you release it and press it again, you start painting another duplicate image from the same reference point.

Figure 21.9

The Rubber Stamp Tool's icon looks just like a rubber stamp.

To select a point to clone from, press Option (Mac) or Alt (Windows) while you click the mouse on the spot you want to copy. Then release the key and start stamping by moving the mouse to the new spot and clicking. You can stamp as many times as you want. The crosshairs show the spot you're cloning from and the brush shows where you are stamping (see Figure 21.10).

FIGURE 21.10

If you move the stamp slightly as you click it, it will smudge, just like a real one. This can be useful.

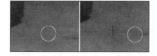

FIGURE 21.10

If you move the stamp slightly as you click it, it will smudge, just like a real one. This can be useful.

You can define a pattern and stamp it with the Rubber Stamp Tool. Use the Rectangular Marquee to select a piece of an image to use as a pattern, and select Define Pattern from the Edit menu. Now when you use the Pattern Stamp Tool, if you choose Aligned, the pattern will be tiled as if from the upper left corner of the document, no matter where you drag. If you uncheck Aligned, the pattern will tile from wherever you start dragging each time.

When you use the Rubber Stamp Tool to retouch, always choose a soft-edged brush in a size only slightly larger than the scratch or blemish you're hiding. Retouching is generally easier if you enlarge the image first.

In the following exercise, we'll use the Rubber Stamp Tool and probably all the tricks in the book.

Cleaning Up a Picture, Step by Step

As you can see in Figure 21.11, this picture has been folded, ripped, faded, and generally beaten up. We'll go through this one step by step, so you can see exactly what happens at each stage. You can download this one from the Web site mentioned in the introduction and follow along. It's called `Friends.jpg`.

FIGURE 21.11

This will take some work. (Photo courtesy of Susanna Pyatkovskaya)

21

To Do: Restore a Badly Damaged Photo

To make this picture, or any other, look like new:

1. Crop the image to remove the border and any unnecessary parts of the image. (Anything you remove doesn't have to be retouched.) Select the Cropping Tool from the toolbox. Drag it across the picture, holding the mouse button down. Use the handles on the Cropping window to fine-tune the selection, and then double-click inside the window to crop the image.

2. Set the mode to Grayscale (Image→Mode→Grayscale) to remove the colored stains.

3. Open the Histogram window (Image→Histogram). Look at the histogram to see what needs to be done to equalize the contrast (see Figure 21.12.) In this case, both the white and dark points need to be reset. To make these changes, we'll need to adjust the levels.

FIGURE 21.12

The histogram shows a lot of light points and not many dark ones.

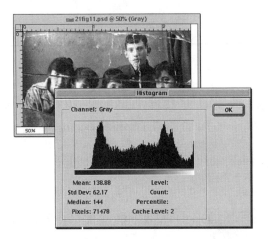

4. Open the Levels window (Image→Adjust→Levels) and adjust the levels by dragging the dark point to the right until it's under the beginning of the dark peak of the histogram. Drag the white point to the left until it's under the beginning of the white peak. Figure 21.13 shows our adjustments.

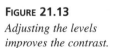

FIGURE 21.13

Adjusting the levels improves the contrast.

5. Now we'll try the Dust and Scratches filter (Filters→Noise→Dust and Scratches). In this case, it seems that the harm it does outweighs the improvement. In removing the dust, it removes too much detail, even at a low setting. (see Figure 21.14 to see the filter applied.) Click OK to apply the filter or cancel if you don't want to use it.

FIGURE 21.14

Removing dust can also remove detail.

6. Because the Dust and Scratches filter didn't work, we'll have to remove the dust and scratches by hand. Use the Rubber Stamp Tool to cover them. Select the tool and open the Brushes and Options windows (Window→Show Brushes and Window→ Show Options). Choose a small brush and set the opacity to 90%. Choose Clone non-aligned, pick the dark tone adjacent to the scratch, and start stamping it out. Remember to set a spot to use as a stamp, and press Option (Mac) or Alt (Windows) while you click the mouse on the spot you want to copy. Figure 21.15 shows the partially treated photo. Remember to change your stamp selection as the areas the scratch runs through change value.

21

▼

FIGURE 21.15
*Help stamp out
scratched photos!*

7. The best way to remove the scratches across the faces is to use a Paintbrush and repaint each face, rather than trying to stamp them. To make the task easier, enlarge the picture to at least 200%. Click the Magnifying Glass Tool at the bottom of the toolbox to enlarge the picture.

8. Select the Eyedropper Tool and click the closest gray adjacent to the scratch. Choose a small Paintbrush and paint over the scratches, changing shades of gray with the Eyedropper as needed. Figure 21.16 shows before and after views of this step.

9. At the same time, you can use the Smudge Tool to remove any light spots and to fill in the background between Rubber Stamp impressions.

FIGURE 21.16
*Be careful not to apply
paint too evenly.*

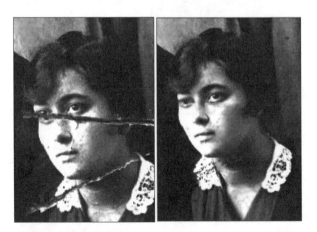

10. Next apply the Dodge and Burn tools as needed to bring out details. Dodging lightens the image, and burning darkens it. Sponging increases or decreases the saturation of colors. Select the Dodge Tool and set its exposure to 25%, so the

▼ effect will be gradual. Dodge the dark shadows out of the girls' eyes. Figure 21.17 shows our progress to this point.

FIGURE 21.17
It's looking better.

11. As you can see, I've saved the worst for last. The girl on the left has had her eye pretty much destroyed. Repainting would be difficult, because there's nothing to go by. Fortunately, one of her sisters has an eye that should match fairly well. I can copy it, paste it in, and rotate it or scale it as needed. See a close-up in Figure 21.18, and the final results in Figure 21.19.

FIGURE 21.18
I've borrowed an eye from the girl on the far right, rotated it to be in line with the other eye, and scaled it down to fit.

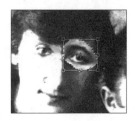

FIGURE 21.19
Maybe not as good as new, but darned close.

21

Applying Tints

It was common in the early days of photography for pictures to be brown, blue, or silver instead of plain black and white. Sepia toning, which gave a warm reddish-brown color, was the most common, and the one we tend to associate with most "old time" photos.

If you want to restore the sepia tone to a picture you've been working on, Photoshop gives you several ways to accomplish this. Perhaps the easiest is to reset the mode to CMYK or RGB, depending on whether the finished photo will be viewed onscreen or printed, and then use the Hue/Saturation window (Image→Adjust→Hue) to add color. After you open the window, as shown in Figure 21.20, check the Colorize box and the Preview box. Then move the sliders until the image looks the way you want. Click OK when you're satisfied with the color.

FIGURE 21.20

Don't forget to check Colorize.

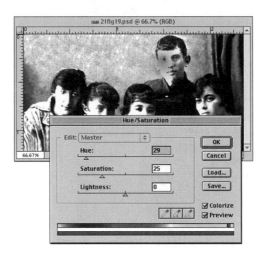

Duotones

A somewhat richer tone can be achieved by using Duotone mode, which combines the grayscale image with a colored ink. Duotones are often used to extend the gray range of a photograph because a typical printing press is capable of reproducing only about 50 shades of gray. Photoshop can generate 256.

To create a duotone, start with a grayscale image. (You needn't convert it back to RGB or whatever colorspace you usually work in.) Open the Duotone window. (Image→ Mode→Duotone) Within Duotone mode, you also have the option of adding additional colors to make a tritone or quadtone. Although duotones are usually composed of black plus a single color, as shown in Figure 21.21, there's no good reason why you can't use two colors instead, especially if the end result is to be displayed on a Web page or as part of a desktop presentation, rather than in printed form.

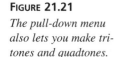

FIGURE 21.21

The pull-down menu also lets you make tritones and quadtones.

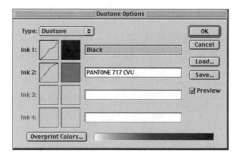

To Do: Create a Duotone from a Grayscale Image

Because it has a nice range of grays, our next touch-up job, a very old photo of an unknown baby (possibly my grandfather), should make a good duotone. (If you want to work along, download the photo called Baby.jpg.) To make a duotone from a grayscale image, follow these steps:

1. Open the Duotone Options window (Image→Mode→Duotone).

2. Select Duotone from the Type pop-up menu, if it's not already selected (refer to Figure 21.21). This menu is in the upper-left corner of the dialog box.

3. Choose colors for your duotone by clicking the Color swatches. Choose black or a dark color for Ink 1 and a lighter color for Ink 2. (Figure 21.21 shows my choices.) You must select the Photoshop Color Picker, rather than the system Color Picker, to access the Custom colors (that is, process colors such as PANTONE, Focaltone, Toyo, Trumatch, and so on). If you need to switch to the Photoshop Color Picker, close this window temporarily by clicking Cancel, and open the General Preferences window (File→Preferences→General or Command (Mac) or Control+K (Windows). Set the Color Picker to Photoshop and click OK. Reopen the Duotone Options window and proceed.

4. Use the curve windows within the Duotone Options window to adjust the curves for your two colors. (They're the small windows with diagonal lines, just to the right of the words "Ink 1" and "Ink 2.") If you click on of the small windows, it expands to a full size curve grid, which works just like the one on the Image→Adjust menu (see Figure 21.22). Click to set points and drag to adjust the curve. You can't see the effect on the image, but you can see it on the strip of tone in the Duotone Curve window.

5. Click OK to apply the duotone to the image. Unfortunately, there's no preview box available. If you're not satisfied with the result, undo it and try again.

21

FIGURE 21.22

*Here we're adjusting
the curve for Ink 2.*

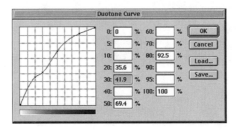

Using blue as the color with black gives you an image that replicates an old, black-and-white TV set. Using a light-to-medium brown with black gives a pretty good imitation sepia, as does a combination of red and green.

"Hand-Tinted" Photos

Years ago, before color film was readily available, it was common to see hand-tinted photos. These had been painstakingly overpainted with thinned-out watercolors to add a pale suggestion of color to the picture. The Photoshop Paintbrush and Airbrush are well suited for re-creating the look of a hand-colored photograph. You can even do the whole Ted Turner routine and colorize stills from your favorite Marx Brothers movie or Bogart classic. (You can find lots of movie stills and movie star pictures on the Web to practice on.)

After you have cleaned up the image that you want to hand-tint, change the mode back to color, either RGB or CMYK, as you did previously for the duotone. Make a new layer and set the Layer opacity to between 10% and 30%. Set the Brush opacity to 100% and paint your tints.

If you have large, uncomplicated areas to tint, use one of the Selection tools, such as the Lasso or the Magic Wand, to select the area. Select a foreground color and choose Fill from the Edit menu; a dialog box will appear as shown in Figure 21.23.

Set the Opacity to about 25% and choose Multiply from the Blending Mode option. Set Foreground Color on the Use pop-up menu. Click OK to fill all the selected areas with your chosen color at that opacity. If it's not enough, either reopen the Fill window and apply it again, or undo it and set a higher percentage. If it's too much, undo and set a lower percentage.

FIGURE 21.23

*Use Fill for large areas.
It's faster and smoother
than painting.*

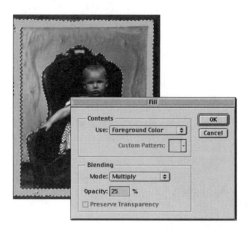

Vignetting

When you're working with old photos, or with new photos that you would like to have "look" old, vignetting is often the trick that makes the difference. It gives that sort of cameo look as the portrait subject comes forward and the background fades to nothing. Here's an easy way to do it.

Draw an oval marquee around the portrait subject. Invert the selection, so the background is selected. Feather the selection by about 15 pixels. (Select→Feather). Use Edit→Fill and set the Background color to white, the blending Mode to Normal, and the Opacity to 100%. Figure 21.24 shows the effect.

FIGURE 21.24

*No more annoying
backgrounds.*

21

Summary

We have been looking at ways to repair photographs that need help. When you have old, cracked, torn, or faded pictures, you can use a variety of Photoshop tools to cover up the imperfections and restore the image. The Eyedropper Tool enables you to select a color or gray tone and apply it with any of your Painting tools. The Rubber Stamp clones a selected piece of the picture and places it wherever you want it, as much or as little as needed to cover a crack, fill in an empty space, or cover objects you want to hide.

Tinting old photos can be managed in any of several ways. Toning can be applied by colorizing or by turning the picture into a duotone, tritone, or quadtone. Hand-tinting can give you a different "old" picture look. Vignetting adds to the "old" look.

Q&A

Q How can I remove my ex-husband from a group shot of the family? He's right in front.

A Perhaps you can find some other face the right size and colors to hide him. (Brad Pitt, perhaps?) Adjust the size and position of the new face on a separate layer. Blur the face you want to hide and use the Opacity slider to bring in the replacement. If you leave it at about 80%, it should merge right in.

Q Printing these old photos on plain paper just doesn't look right. What should I use?

A If you want to duplicate the look of the original photo printed on glossy paper, invest in a package of glossy photo-quality paper for your inkjet printer. If the photo was originally printed on a matte surface stock, try printing on card stock.

Q Okay, I've retouched all the old family photos. What do I do now?

A The next logical step is to buy a package of photo-quality glossy paper and print them out as photos. Kodak, HP, and Epson all sell glossy paper for inkjet and bubblejet printers. It's about the same weight as photo paper, and it makes your pictures look really good. If you don't have a reasonably good color printer, take your photos to a service bureau and have them printed on a color laser or high quality inkjet.

Be sure to save the files for future use, too. CD-ROMs and Zip disks can hold several generations of family photos and can be stored in very little space. If you keep a backup copy in a safe place, like a bank safe deposit box, your precious family history is fire- and flood proof. You can also place a family album on your Web page, so distant relatives and friends can see how the kids have grown.

Quiz

1. Burning is the opposite of

    a. Covering

    b. Filling

    c. Dodging

2. The Rubber Stamp Tool prints

    a. Text

    b. A clone of whatever you have selected

    c. Random shapes and designs

3. How many colors of ink are in a duotone?

    a. One

    b. One plus black

    c. Any two, not necessarily including black

4. To remove the sepia toning from an old scanned photo

    a. Change the mode to Grayscale

    b. Adjust the colors to add more cyan

    c. Click Bleach

Quiz Answers

1. c. Dodging lightens the image. Burning darkens it.

2. b. Though c. might be fun…

3. c. Although black is usually one of the two colors, it needn't be.

4. a. This also helps gets rid of colored ink, coffee, or other stains on a black-and-white print.

Exercises

Find a picture in need of retouching, or download one from this book's page on Macmillan's Web site. Clean it up as much as you think necessary and save a copy. Convert the copy to a duotone. Hand-tint the original using transparent tints. Notice how the duotone looks like rotogravure pages from the 1930s, whereas the hand-colored version looks like photos from the '40s or '50s. Think about how you might use these techniques with your own work.

21

HOUR 22

Photo Repair—Color

Last hour, we worked on some black-and-white pictures that needed help. This hour we'll do the same with color pictures. You can adjust the colors to fix a picture that's faded with age or has too much red, green, or some other color in it. You can compensate for slight to moderate underexposure or overexposure, but you can't put back an image that's just not there, unless you paint it in.

You can take the red out of your daughter's eyes or the unearthly green out of the cat's eyes. Does your teenager wonder how she'd look with orange or green hair or a half-shaved head? Try it on the screen first. Maybe she'll settle for a second set of earrings.

Color Retouching

So far, all the pictures we've worked on are old, black-and-white photos. You can use most of the same tools and tricks in color. You might find that color retouching is even easier than working in black-and-white. The color tends to disguise some of the manipulation.

Figure 22.1 is a picture that was taken sometime in the early 1960s. I don't know what happened to it. Perhaps it was left on a radiator or something like that. The colors have turned from normal to nothing more than shades of purple. (I know, it's hard to see this in black-and-white. Use your imagination or download the picture from the Macmillan Web site and work along. It's called `purplegirl.jpg`.)

FIGURE 22.1
This picture turned purple with age.

To Do: Apply a Simple Color Correction to a Photo

▼ To Do

First, look at the Channels palette, shown in Figure 22.2. You can immediately see that the darkest channel is the green one. This means that very little green is visible in the image. The blue channel is the strongest, and the red channel is close behind it.

FIGURE 22.2
We need to add more green to balance the red and blue.

Using the Curves window, as shown in Figure 21.3, I can adjust the green channel to remove most of the unwanted color. Rather than trying to remove all of it, which would take away the flesh tones, it's better to compromise and leave a faint warmth. To adjust a single color with the curves window:

1. With the image open, open the Curves window (Image→Adjust→Curves).

2. Choose the color closest to, or the complement to, the color that needs adjusting from the pop-up Channels menu. Choose Red, Green, or Blue if those colors need lessening. If there's too much yellow, add blue. If there's too much magenta, add green. If there's too much cyan, add red. In this case, we obviously need to add green.

3. Drag the curve up to increase the amount of the color. Drag it down to decrease the amount by adding the complement. Watch the preview as you drag. Click OK when the colors look right. (See Figure 22.3)

FIGURE 22.3
After correcting the green, you can also adjust the red and blue as needed.

This photo needs some additional tweaking to increase the saturation now that we've taken out the excess magenta. It also needs some brightness and contrast adjustment and some cropping to improve the composition. The final version can be downloaded from the Web site, as notpurple.jpg. It's not perfect, but it's a lot better.

Fixing Red Eye

You've seen red eye. It's not a problem in black-and-white photos that you colorize, but it's often a problem in color pictures of people and animals taken with a flash camera.

Basically what happens is that the flash reflects off the blood vessels at the back of the eye and puts an eerie, red glow into the pupils of anyone looking straight at the flash. Some cats, by the way, can also display a similar phenomenon called "green eye," caused by the flash reflecting off crystals in the back of the eye. You can avoid this if you make sure your portrait subject, human or otherwise, isn't looking directly at the flash. Also, make sure that there's plenty of light in the room so the subject's pupils have contracted as small as possible.

Figure 22.4 shows a portrait of a cat suffering from serious red eye. This one was shot in a dark room and the flash caught the cat staring wide-eyed. If we correct the off-color eyes, it will be a nice picture.

FIGURE 22.4

Even printed in black-and-white, the eyes look wrong.

▼ To Do

To Do: Correct Red Eye

The correction is actually quite easy. Here's how to do it:

1. Open the image and zoom in on the eyes by clicking the Magnifying Glass.

2. Use the Magic Wand to select the parts that need to be corrected (see Figure 22.5).

FIGURE 22.5

Cat's eye selected at 200% magnification.

▼   3. Choose the Paint Bucket Tool. Set the foreground color to black. Double-click the tool icon to open the Tool Options window and set the Paint mode to Darken with an Opacity of about 80%. This setting darkens the eye while maintaining the detail.

▼   4. Pour the paint carefully into the pupils of the eyes, making sure not to pour it into any white or colored highlights in the pupil. You might need to click different selected parts of the pupil to cover all of it. If you accidentally fill one of the highlights, undo. If you want to accent the highlights more, use a single pixel pencil (select the smallest possible brush size) and touch up as needed.

5. Press Command+H (Mac) or Control+H (Windows) to hide the selection so that you can evaluate the effect of the change. Figure 22.6 shows the finished cat.

FIGURE 22.6

Highlights in the pupils are called catchlights.

▲

The semi-opaque black that we poured in effectively darkened the pupils without losing detail. You can use this technique any time you have a small area in a picture that needs to have the color changed drastically. Be careful not to select any part of the image that you *don't* want to change.

How Much Change Is Okay?

Editing a picture to improve the composition is entirely reasonable, if it's a picture for your own use, but this is precisely what got the esteemed *National Geographic* magazine in trouble some years ago. They were doing a piece on Egypt and sent a photographer to get pictures of the pyramids. The art director studied the pictures and decided the composition would be better if he moved one of the pyramids closer to the next. As soon as the issue was published, astute readers began calling and writing to the magazine to complain. An apology appeared in the following issue, but simply knowing that the manipulation was possible waved a red flag for many people both inside and outside the publishing industry. The question has been debated ever since. How much change is okay? How much is too much?

It's clear that you can't always believe what you see. The supermarket tabloids frequently feature pictures that stretch the bounds of believability. Remember the one of the President shaking hands with the "space alien?" Or the "Big Foot" carrying off the scantily clad woman. (Why was she

22

dressed like that in the snow anyway?) On the other hand, if a model is having a bad hair day or her face breaks out, retouching is required and expected. Where do you draw the line?

The answer depends on how the picture is to be used. Reputable newspapers and magazines tend to have strict guidelines about what they'll allow for photo manipulation. The general rule seems to be that, if a change affects the *content* of the photo rather than its appearance, you can't do it. You can lighten a too dark picture of the politician, but you can't change the soda can in his hand into a beer can (or vice versa).

Drag and Drop Repairs

Some photos are almost perfect, except for one annoying flaw. Maybe it's power lines running through the sky, or as in this example, a misplaced trashcan. (see Figure 22.7.) Because the area directly behind it is essentially the same at the rest of the foreground, I can get rid of the can by simply lassoing a piece of beach and dragging it to cover the offending object. This technique also works well when you have things like power lines or cellphone antennae sticking into the sky.

FIGURE 22.7

The trashcan adds nothing to the composition, so we'll take it away.

To Do: Use the Lasso Tool to Retouch a Photo

To use the Lasso for this purpose:

1. Select the Lasso Tool from the toolbar. Open the Feather dialog box (Select→Feather) and set the Feather radius to somewhere between 3 to 6 pixels. This will help the copied sand blend in.

2. Select a piece of sand by circling it with the Lasso.

3. With the dotted line Marquee flashing, choose the Move Tool and press Option (Mac) or Alt (Windows) as you drag the selection. (See a close view of this in Figure 22.8)

FIGURE 22.8
Be sure to cover all of the area.

4. Repeat as needed, selecting different pieces of the picture to drag over whatever you need to cover. You can also use this trick to hide any other parts of the picture that you don't want.

5. Press Command+D (Mac) or Control+D (Windows) when you're finished dragging and copying to deselect the selection. Figure 22.9 shows the cleaned-up picture.

FIGURE 22.9
No more ugly trashcans.

▲

"Editing" a Picture

There are times when you have to remove more than a scratch or a small imperfection from a photo. Sometimes you have to take out larger objects to save a potentially good picture. Figure 22.10 shows just such a photo, a picture from when my two adult sons were young boys playing in Central Park. It's called `josh&dan.jpg`, if you want to work along.

To Do: Remove Unwanted Items

1. First let's crop the picture to improve the composition. Select the Cropping Tool from the toolbox and drag a rectangle that includes the kids and the rock, and some of the buildings, but cuts off the top and sides of the photo (see Figure 22.11). Double-click inside the rectangle or choose Image→Crop to remove the non-selected part.

▼   2. The next step is to straighten the tilting building. I'll use Edit→Transform→Skew
        to fix this (see Figure 22.12).

FIGURE 22.12

Drag guides so you can see what's straight.

3. I don't like the tree branches sticking out of Joshua's head, so I'll remove them.
    The easiest way to do this is to copy and drag pieces of adjacent space to cover
    them. First, use the lasso to select a small piece. Then click the Move Tool (it's the
    pointer with crosshairs at the top-right corner of the toolbox). Hold down Option
    (Mac) or Alt (on PCs) and drag the selection. This copies it as you go. (See Figure
    22.13) I also used Transform→Flip Horizontal to make one of the pieces of branch
    look different.

FIGURE 22.13

Can you tell where I copied bits of tree?

4. Now is a good time to do any last minute color adjustments. I checked the Levels
    on this picture and decided that they didn't really need any tweaking, but I used the
    Dodge Tool to lighten both boys' faces. Figure 22.14 shows the final photo, ready
▼   to go in the family album.

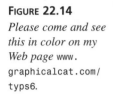

FIGURE 22.14

Please come and see this in color on my Web page www. graphicalcat.com/ typs6.

Removing Uncle Eddie's Indiscretion

It happens in the best of families—someone creeps into the family portrait who really shouldn't be there. Maybe it's your former spouse, or your kid's current attraction with the green punk hairdo, leather vest, and nose ring. Well, whoever it is, you can usually get him or her out of the picture more easily with Photoshop than in the flesh. Figure 22.15 is a typical group photo, in black-and-white, but because of the advanced techniques used, it really belongs in this chapter.

FIGURE 22.15

Three happy couples, until his wife saw the picture...

We're going to remove the second woman from the left. We'll also clean up the rest of the picture. I'll start by cropping out the table in front of the group and a little off the top of the wall. Then I'll place a selection rectangle that just includes the lady we want out (see Figure 22.16).

After deleting her, I'll cut the couple on the left to a new layer and slide them over so the bit of her shoulder I left lines up with the middle man's suit jacket. Then I'll crop again to get rid of the whitespace. Figure 22.17 shows the picture at this stage.

After a lot of rubber-stamping, copying and pasting, and some airbrushing to even out the differences left by the Rubber Stamp, I came up with the result you see in Figure 22.18—an even happier family portrait.

FIGURE 22.18
His wife likes this version much more.

22

Putting "Back" What Was Never There

I shot this photo of the horse and carriage at Mystic Seaport in Connecticut. Unfortunately, some tourists wandered into the picture just as I shot it. I'd love to get rid of them, but there's not much to replace them with. Figure 22.19 shows the original picture. Can it be saved?

FIGURE 22.19
Darned tourists...

I don't want to just crop out the people because one is right up against the horse, and because I'd like to see some empty space on the left where they were. In Figure 22.20,

I've started by selecting the narrow strip of road between the man and woman, and have dragged it across their legs. This easily gets rid of everything below their waists.

FIGURE 22.20
"Drag and drop" is ideal for this kind of coverage.

There's not too much background to work with. Therefore, instead of just dragging and copying the background, I'll cut and paste to as many new layers as needed. I copied the left side of the window, pasted and then flipped the selection to make the right side. The bricks copy and/or rubber-stamp quite nicely. In Figure 22.21, I've completely hidden the man on the right.

FIGURE 22.21
He's history, but what about his friends?

More copying, pasting, rubber-stamping, and painting gives us the result shown in close-up in Figure 22.22. It's a little bit contrived, but it's only a small part of the picture. Figure 22.23 shows the final result.

22

FIGURE 22.22
Good enough approximation of the building.

FIGURE 22.23
Horse and wagon minus tourists—much better.

The point of these exercises is that there's no picture too damaged, or too full of interlopers to rescue. The only limit to what you can do with your pictures is your own imagination.

Summary

Color repair isn't much different from black-and-white photo repair, except that you need to be a little more aware of the colors and color blending modes. Off-color photos are fixed with Photoshop's regular color adjustment tools. Retouching to get rid of obvious flaws and red eye is best accomplished with the Brush and Eyedropper and with the image enlarged so you can see what you're doing. Use layers to protect your original while you're working, and merge the changes when you are satisfied with the results.

Q&A

Q If the picture I need to repair doesn't have enough background to copy, or doesn't have a good background, what should I do?

A Remember that Photoshop allows you to have more than one file open at a time. You can "borrow" from another picture and copy the selection onto a new layer of the picture that needs fixing. Shrink it or enlarge it so the texture is in scale with the rest of the scene, and then copy and paste it as much as needed. If you have a digital camera, shoot lots of backgrounds and keep them in a special file on your computer or on a zip drive. Then when you have a problem photo, you have ready-made scenery to drop the subject into.

Q What color mode should I be working in—CMYK, RGB, Indexed, Lab, or Grayscale?

A If the image is grayscale, such as a black-and-white photo, and is going to remain grayscale, stay in that mode. If the image is intended for the Web or an inkjet printer, stick with RGB. If the image will be sent to a commercial print shop for four-color process printing, convert to CMYK after you've done your retouching.

Quiz

1. "Red eye" is caused by

    a. Excessive consumption of caffeine

    b. Impossible deadlines

    c. Light reflecting off the back of the eye

    d. Trying to finish this book in 24 hours straight

2. If a picture is too yellow, add more

    a. Cyan

    b. Blue

    c. White

3. Old color photos most often look too

    a. Blue

    b. Red

    c. Washed out

Quiz Answers

1. a., b., c., and d. Mine are almost too red for Photoshop to correct.

2. b. Blue is the color wheel opposite of yellow.

3. b. Color dyes often shift toward red as a print ages.

Exercises

Find some of your own photo portraits that have bad "red eye." Scan them into the computer and use the tricks you have learned to restore normal eye colors.

Find a group photo and remove one member of the group.

HOUR 23

Printing

We're almost done…. You've created some wonderful Photoshop art, and you'd like to hang it on the walls and send copies to your friends. (You'd probably also like to add these masterpieces to your Web page, but you'll learn that in the next hour.) Even in this brave new world of the Internet, CD-ROM, and other electronic media, printing isn't going away, and it never will. Getting your image to output correctly is as important as any other step in the process of image creation, and that's why it deserves its own hour.

Printing should be easy, right? Click the Print command and watch your image emerge on paper. Unfortunately, getting Photoshop images to print well can involve quite a few variables and decisions. In this hour, we'll look at what those are, from choosing a printer through setting up inks, separations, halftones, and other issues.

Be warned. Some of this stuff gets into detail and gets very technical, and some of it is irrelevant if you only print to one kind of printer. Feel free to ignore the sections that don't relate to the kind(s) of printing you do. If *none* of it makes sense, stick with the default settings. Your pages will be, at the very least, adequately printed.

Choosing a Printer

You know this already: Lots of printers, as well as lots of printing technologies, are out there. How you print obviously depends a lot on what printer you're using. In fact, the printer you use can and should influence how you work in Photoshop and how you prepare your image because you'll want to create a final image that will print best from your particular printer.

An entire book could be written about all the varieties of printers. In this section, we'll make do with a snapshot of what's available: inkjet printers, laser printers, dye-sublimation printers, thermal wax printers, and imagesetters.

Inkjet Printers

At the inexpensive end of the spectrum are home and office inkjet printers, almost all of which can deliver acceptable quality color printing. Examples of inkjets (sometimes also called "bubble jets") include HP's DeskJet series, Canon Bubblejets, and Epson's Stylus printers.

Inkjet printers are not necessarily PostScript-compatible. This means that some of them can't print *PostScript* information that might be in your non-art documents. For most Photoshop images, however, this isn't a problem unless you've chosen to save them as EPS (Encapsulated PostScript) or Adobe PDF.

NEW TERM *PostScript* is a page-description language that lets any two devices (computer and compatible printer) describe and reproduce exactly the same page.

The quality of output varies tremendously between inkjet printers, ranging from fair to excellent, depending on how much you want to spend. A lot depends on the size of the ink dot a printer applies and whether it's a four- or six-color process. Most inkjets use a four-color ink cartridge, with cyan, magenta, yellow, and black inks. Many can produce photo-quality pictures. The six-color inkjet adds two more inks, a light magenta and light cyan. In the four-color process, if you have a broad light area, like sky, you might see the dots of cyan and magenta that color it because they're quite far apart. Using lighter values of those inks lets the printer place more color, less visibly.

High-end inkjets, like the Iris, can cost tens of thousands of dollars but can be perfect for graphics professionals. Iris and similar "art quality" printers are sometimes found at service bureaus or art studios. They can produce very large prints, up to 33"×46", with remarkable detail and quality. You can have an Iris print made of your work, but they tend to be expensive. Prices average around $150 for a single 16×20 print.

Laser Printers

The laser printer is the professional standard and a good balance of price, quality, and speed. Laser printers abound from well-known companies such as Apple and Hewlett-Packard.

Most laser printers output 300 to 600 dpi (some up to 1200 dpi), and they are particularly good with halftone and grayscale images. Some can subtly alter the size of the printed dots, thus improving quality. Laser printers are generally faster than inkjet printers, but they tend to be more expensive.

Color laser prints can be very good, if you like bright colors and don't mind the shiny surface that you're likely to get in areas where the toner is quite dense. Laser printers work by fusing powdered toner to the paper. Color lasers use a four-color toner cartridge.

23

Dye-Sublimation Printers

Dye-sublimation printers are expensive photographic-quality printers, but you get what you pay for. Image quality is superb, but these printers use special ribbons and paper. You can't use ordinary paper with them, and the specially coated paper is expensive. You can often find these printers at a service bureau, where you can get a single dye-sub print for a modest fee.

Thermal Wax Printers

Thermal wax printers also provide excellent quality color output, but at prices comparable to laser printers. Because of the materials they use, thermal wax printers are especially useful for producing transparencies. For a short time, they were very popular as portable printers because all they require is a ribbon and some mechanics and electronics to move the ribbon and paper in the right directions. I remember trying out one that was about the same size as a three-hole paper punch—about a foot long by three inches square. The quality was surprisingly good. These printers have gotten much harder to find because the price of inkjets has come down and their portability has improved.

Imagesetters

Imagesetters are printers used for medium- or large-scale commercial printing jobs. These large, expensive machines burn the image onto photographic film or paper. That film is then developed and used to make printing plates that are used for the actual printing. We're talking high resolution here: 1,200–2,400 dpi, or even better.

Imagesetters don't print in color per se. Instead, you have to create a separate image for each color you want printed. These are called *separations*; we'll talk more about them later.

Preparing to Print

It's possible to go very deeply into the theory and methodology of printing. Professionals know the power of having color-compensated monitors and color-printing profiles, which guarantee that what you see on the screen is as close as humanly possible to what you will see on the paper. For the rest of us, most of the time pretty good is good enough. We'll delve into some of the mysteries of color printing in this hour, but before we do, let's start with the most basic of the basics.

Printers (the hardware kind) use software called *printer drivers* that function as part of your operating system, whether it's Mac or Windows. The driver converts the output from Photoshop (or your word processor, or whatever printable software you're using) into a form that the printer can understand and reproduce on paper. (Okay, on silk or transparency, too…) So before you can print, you need to have a printer hooked up and the appropriate driver loaded.

If you have more than one printer available, be sure you've selected the one you intend to use. If you're on a Mac, use the Chooser. On a PC, select a printer from the File→Page Setup pop-up list.

Photoshop has three print-related dialog boxes. Page Setup is part of the printer driver. Print Options is specific to Photoshop, and it's new in version 6. Print is where you verify everything you've set in the other two boxes and click OK to create the actual print. You can make many of the same settings in either the Print Options or the Page Setup dialog box. It doesn't really matter which one you use. Let's start with Page Setup. It's shown in Figure 23.1.

FIGURE 23.1

The Page Setup dialog box looks different depending on what printer you're using.

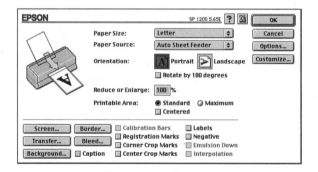

Each printer's page setup dialog box looks a little different, but they all provide the same basic functions. (Note that not all options will be available in every situation.) A Page Setup dialog box will display the following information and options:

- *Printer*—The name of the printer always appears at the top. Make sure it's correct!

- *Properties*—On Windows machines, you can click this button to access a dialog box that enables you to change things such as paper size, layout, printer resolution, and halftone settings.

- *Paper Size*—Choose the size of the paper on which you're printing. If you change the paper size on a Macintosh, the preview in the upper-left corner of the screen changes accordingly.

- *Source*—If your printer has two paper trays or gives you a choice of tray or single-sheet feed, you can choose the paper source for the printer to use.

- *Orientation*—Choose how you want the printed image to be placed on the page: portrait (narrow dimension at top and bottom) or landscape (wider and shorter).

- *Reduce or Enlarge*—Want the image to print smaller or larger? Adjust this percentage appropriately.

23

Later, when you actually choose the Print button (see the next section), you might run into a problem with files that are large in dimension. If the image dimensions are larger than the dimensions of the page you're printing on, Photoshop tells you. You can then choose to print anyway, resulting in only part of the image being printed, or you can cancel and adjust the Reduce or Enlarge value so the whole image fits on the page.

You can set other options in this dialog box, too, but I prefer to set them in the Print Options box so I can see exactly what I'm doing. Take a look at the Print Options box in Figure 23.2.

The first option here is Position. If you uncheck Center Image, which is checked by default, you can then slide the picture around on the page, placing it wherever you want. This is a big change from previous versions of Photoshop, which could only print an image centered. If you drag on a corner of the image, you can rescale it. The Scaled Print size values will change accordingly. You can also scale the image by typing a number into the Scale percentage window. Scaling is done relative to the original image size. If you have a photo that's 6 inches wide and you want it to print 9 inches wide, scale it to 150%. This setting can be made either here or in the Page Setup box.

When you click Show More Options, you can choose between Output options and Color Management options. Output options are the same here as in the Page Setup box, except that you can see them on the preview screen as you apply them. In Figure 23.3, I've added crop marks, calibration marks, and a caption line to my photo.

FIGURE 23.2

*Notice that I've
checked the Show
More Options box.*

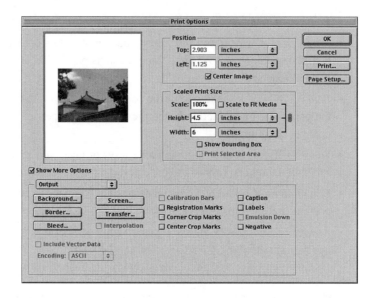

Here are some of the options and what they mean:

- *Background*—Want to print a background color around your image? Click the Background button and you'll be greeted by the standard Color Picker. Whichever color you pick is used for printing only and does not alter your actual image file. (If you're printing from Windows, be sure to turn this off after you use it. Otherwise, you'll print the background around the next picture as well.) Be careful about using this feature. It eats up a lot of ink!

- *Border*—Similarly, if you'd like a border around your printed image, click the Border button. In the resulting dialog box, you can set the width of the printed border in inches, millimeters, or points. The border is always black; you can't change the color. (Like Background, using this feature doesn't affect the actual image file.)

- *Bleed*—*Bleeding* means that part of the image runs right off the edge of the paper. There isn't any border or empty space between the image and the edge of the page. (Note that this feature won't work on every printer. Some printers are incapable of printing to the very edge of a page.)

  Click the Bleed button to define the bleed area of an image in inches, millimeters, or points. Higher values move the crop marks within the boundaries of the image so that less of the image gets printed. You can't bleed an image more than an eighth of an inch.

- *Caption*—Check this box, and on the printed page you'll see the text that appears in the Caption area of the File Info dialog box for that file. (To get to this dialog box, choose File→File Info and make sure Caption is selected in the top pull-down menu.) This can be helpful for providing contact info or details next to your image.

- *Calibration Bars*—Check this box to print Calibration and Color bars next to your image. A Calibration bar is a row of 11 gray squares of different values, and a Color bar is a row of 11 colors. These bars can help when you're trying to calibrate to a specific printer or to see how a specific printer prints. (This option is available only if you're using a PostScript printer.)

- *Registration Marks*—Activate this feature to print a variety of registration marks around the image. Depending on your printer, you'll get bull's-eyes (which look like what you'd expect), star targets (two crossed lines within a circle), and/or precise pinpoint marks (two simple crossed lines). These marks can be helpful for aligning color separations.

- *Corner Crop Marks*—Corner crop marks appear around each corner of your image, defining where it should be trimmed. They're simply horizontal and vertical lines.

- *Center Crop Marks*—These crop marks are centered along each side of the image, defining the exact center of the image. They look like two crossed lines. Figure 23.4 shows the registration marks and crop marks added to the image.

- *Labels*—This check box prints the filename next to the image. If you're printing color separations, the name of the appropriate color channel is also printed on each color plate.

- *Negative*—With this option checked, the printer reverses the values of the image. That is, the whites become black, the blacks become white, and everything in-between changes accordingly. You end up with a negative image. This option is useful if you're printing to film for commercial offset printing because these images usually need to be negatives.

- *Emulsion Down*—This setting prints your image as a horizontal mirror image of the original. Everything gets flipped left-to-right. Your print shop will tell you whether you need to print this way for some reason.

- *Interpolation*—*Interpolation* refers to some printers' capability to resample an image as they print it. That is, any PostScript Level 2 printer can take a low-resolution image and resample it on-the-fly, improving the resolution so the print-out is of better quality. This is valuable only if you're dealing with low-resolution images. Interpolation is available only on PostScript printers.

23

- *Screen*—Use Printer's Default Screens is checked by default, and you won't be able to change anything else. Uncheck this option if you want to customize the other halftone options. Most of the time, Photoshop's default settings work fine.

Figure 23.3 shows the additional options I've selected in the print options dialog box. Figure 23.4 shows the resulting output.

FIGURE 23.3

Now we're ready to print with the desired features.

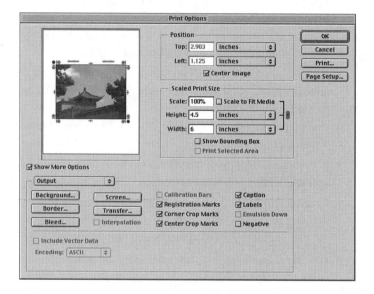

FIGURE 23.4

A printout showing various crop marks, registration marks, and a caption.

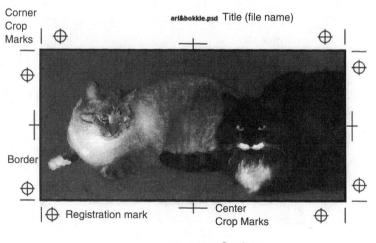

Before you continue, make sure that whatever you want to print is currently visible on the screen. By default, Photoshop prints all visible layers and channels. If you want to print just certain layers or channels, make them the only ones that are visible.

Printing the Page

Okay, now we're finally getting around to printing the image. I told you there were a lot of printing variables, didn't I?

Pull up the Print dialog box by choosing File→Print (see Figure 23.5). The first thing you should notice is that this dialog box also looks different depending on what printer you have, what platform you're running on, and the mode of the image. However, they all ask for the same information.

23

FIGURE 23.5

The ultimate dialog box: Print.

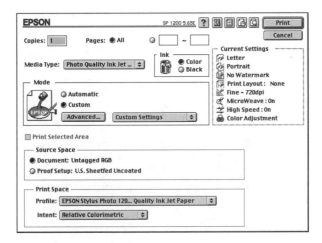

Let's look at all the Print fields and options:

- *Copies*—How many copies of the document do you want to print? Enter a number here.
- *Pages*—This area (called Print Range in the Windows version) specifies the range of pages to be printed. This setting is usually irrelevant in Photoshop because most documents consist of only one page.
- *Media Type*—Here you enter what kind of paper or transparency film you're printing on. This setting actually determines how much ink is applied because different kinds of paper are more or less absorbent.
- *Ink*—Choose Color or Black.

- *Print Quality (also called Mode)*—Windows users can often specify a printer resolution here, such as 300 or 600 dpi. Macintosh users can often specify Best, Normal, Econofast, or some variation on this theme, or a specific dpi setting. In this case, it's done by choosing Custom and then the quality.

- *Destination*—You can print to the printer, obviously, but you can also print to a file. This means saving the printed output as a PostScript or EPS file or an Adobe Acrobat PDF. (This option only works if you've selected a PostScript-compatible printer.)

  When you select File, the Print button says Save. Click it to bring up the Save dialog box, where you can name the file and select the file format you want (see Figure 23.6). You can also choose an encoding scheme. (ASCII is best for PostScript files, and Binary can speed things up on printers that accept binary data.) Level 1 Compatibility means that the file prints on all PostScript printers, whereas Level 2 Only files work only on PostScript Level 2 printers. The PDF options are shown in Figure 23.6. Finally, you can specify whether you want font information to be embedded in the file, and for which fonts.

FIGURE 23.6

Printing to a file.

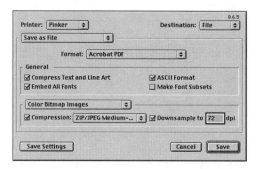

- *Print Selected Area*—When this box (simply called Selection in Windows) is checked and you have a rectangular area currently selected in your Photoshop image, you can print just that area. This works only with rectangular selections created with the Marquee Tool. Also, it doesn't work for feathered selections.

- *Encoding* (May also be simply a check box for ASCII format)—Here you tell Photoshop which encoding method to use when it sends the image data to the printer. ASCII is understood by all PostScript printers, so it's a safe bet. Binary encoding is more compressed and thus can be faster, but it doesn't work on all printers. JPEG encoding is even faster, but it results in some loss of data because it's a lossy compression scheme. JPEG encoding works only with PostScript Level 2 printers.

- *Print In*—Here you can decide how to print the image: in grayscale, in RGB colors, or in CMYK colors. For some desktop printers, RGB gives better results. (If you're unsure, try both and see which looks better to you.)

- *Print Separations*—This option appears in place of the Print In option, but *only* if the image is currently in CMYK or Duotone mode and the composite color channel is active. When you check this option, Photoshop prints each channel as a separate color plate. For example, a CMYK document would print as four separate pages, one for all the cyan data in the image, one for magenta, one for yellow, and one for black.

- *Options*—Strangely enough, Options isn't always one of your options. On a non-PostScript printer, such as the HP DeskJet series, you'll see the Options button as one of your choices in the Print dialog box. Options lets you select Intensity, Halftoning, and Color Matching. Leave all three at Auto unless you're printing a photograph. If you are, choose Photographic from the Color Matching menu to get the best possible color reproduction.

At long last, when everything's set to your satisfaction, click Print to print it!

> Each printer is slightly different, as are its dialog boxes. I have attempted to cover the most common ones. Be sure to read your printer manual before you start printing. It's your best source for printing info.

So that's how to print from Photoshop. But as you'll probably discover, printing directly from Photoshop doesn't happen as often as you might expect. Most of the time, images created in Photoshop are brought into another application for final placement and output. Most often these are page layout applications, such as PageMaker and Quark XPress. Photoshop images can even be brought into other image-editing applications, such as Painter and Illustrator, and printed from there.

The main thing to watch for when you're printing Photoshop images from other applications is the format of your file. Make sure it's compatible with the program you're bringing it into. If it's not, believe me, you'll know! Other than that, any settings related to the image, such as custom colors or halftone screens, are brought with the image automatically.

Preparing the Image

Here's the best strategy if you know you'll want to print your final Photoshop image: Keep the printer in mind throughout the entire process! Different printers output differently, so knowing your printer enables you to adjust your image for its particular behavior and, thus, guarantees the best possible image on the final printed page. This is particularly true for full-color images.

With that in mind, always configure Photoshop for the monitor and printer you'll be using, and do this before even considering printing anything important! This configuration involves several different areas: setting up monitors, printing inks, separations, and separation tables.

Color management capabilities have been changed in Photoshop 6, which provides a collection of predefined settings. Each setting includes a corresponding color profile and conversion options, which should give you consistent color for a particular kind of printer under typical conditions. Color management is most helpful if you output your work to several different printers or different kinds of printers, such as laser and imagesetter, or if images will appear on the Web as well as in print.

What's Color Management?

Color management is what lets you move color information from one device (such as a monitor) to another (such as a printer) in a predictable and measurable manner. This is what's meant by WYSIWYG color: What You See (on the monitor) Is What You Get (when the image is printed). It's not automatic.

For high-end printers, scanners, and monitors, color management is handled by ICC profiles. These are made by measuring each device in accordance with a language agreed upon by the ICC (a consortium of color management professionals and vendors). To create an ICC profile for a printer, the software includes a target chart with many small squares of color. The target is printed on the printer being profiled. Then, a measuring tool is placed over each of the color squares and a measurement is taken. The data goes back to the computer, which compares the printed colors against the theoretically perfect colors of the software target and defines the differences. These are all assembled and calculated, and an ICC profile for that printer, ink, and paper combination is produced. The profile is actually a set of numbers that tells the computer how to adjust the color information it sends to that particular printer to compensate for any differences it finds. Scanner profiles are produced by scanning a known color chart, and monitor profiles are created by displaying the chart and measuring the color squares with a tool similar to the one used for the printed chart.

ColorSync is color management software developed jointly by Apple and Linotype-Hell. ICM is a similar program for Windows. They are used to correct color spaces for both display and print. ColorSync and ICM include profiles of many different kinds of monitors, so you can select yours or at least one close to it. They compensate on the monitor so that printer color space (CMYK) will be displayed correctly.

What does all this mean to the novice user with a home-quality inkjet printer? Here are a few suggestions:

Do your work in RGB color. If you have ColorSync available, be sure you've set it to your own monitor. If you don't have it, use Adobe Gamma setup. It's a control panel that comes with Photoshop to let you adjust your monitor according to how it displays colors.

If you're printing to a low-end printer, don't convert the color to CMYK. Photoshop will make the conversion as it sends the data to the printer. It actually does this quite well.

If you'll be printing on a machine that has an ICC profile, change the file color space to CMYK when you're ready to save it for printing, and apply the ICC profile. (Be sure to save an RGB copy too.)

Figure 23.7 shows the Color Settings dialog box. You can find it on the Edit menu, or you can type Command+Shift+K (Mac) or Ctrl+Shift+K (Windows) to open it. Be sure to notice the descriptions window at the bottom of the dialog box. It can be very helpful when you're not sure what to use.

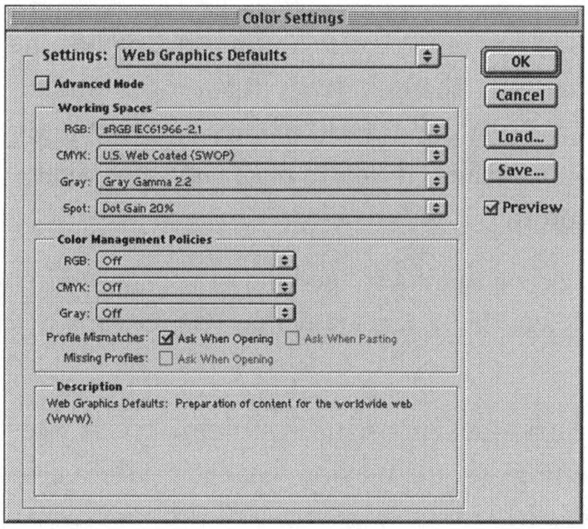

FIGURE 23.7

The default color *settings are for Web use.*

As you can see, there are several decisions you need to make, even without shifting to the Advanced mode. First, you need to use the Settings pop-up menu, shown in Figure 23.8. You need to decide whether Color Management should be on or off. If you turn it off, you're not left colorless. Photoshop will still apply minimum color management standards to make the color onscreen match that of non–color-managed documents. It's most useful for onscreen presentations.

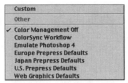

FIGURE 23.8

Choose an appropriate setting.

If you know that your work will be printed on standard printing presses (not a home inkjet), apply either the US, European, or Japanese standard prepress defaults according to where your printing company is. (It's not uncommon for some artists and ad agencies in the USA to send high-quality print jobs to another country where they can be done less expensively.)

> You can also save and load various settings you create via the Save and Load buttons.

Working Spaces

The Working Spaces settings in the Color Settings dialog box are *less* complicated than they look (which is nice for a change). RGB asks for the kind of monitor you're looking at. You can choose it from the pop-up list, or choose the monitor profile you made using the Adobe Gamma control panel. If you're really not sure what you should choose, go for the Generic RGB profile. It will be close.

The CMYK field wants you to choose the kind of printer you're using. Again, if it's all Greek to you, choose Generic. If you know that you're using a home inkjet, try U.S. Sheetfed Uncoated.

Gray is easy. If you use a Mac, choose Gray Gamma 1.8. If you have a PC, choose 2.2. These are the basic settings for the method that each system uses to display grayscale images.

Spot refers to pages printed with black and one or two spot colors, such as duotones, or illustrations done with black and white and limited PANTONE colors. The standard setting is Dot Gain 20%.

Color Management Policies

The Color Management Policies refer to how Photoshop handles files created in another application or in an earlier version of Photoshop. Your choices are to preserve the color management profiles embedded in the file, convert to your active mode, or turn off color management. This last choice lets Photoshop display the file in Active mode, while keeping the embedded profile, until you resave it with the new color management information. You can also direct Photoshop to warn you when a color management mismatch occurs as you open a file and ask what to do about it. Figure 23.9 shows a warning message.

FIGURE 23.9

This happened because I bought a new monitor and changed the profile.

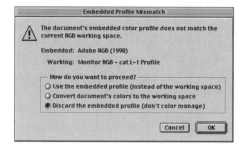

Conversion Options

If you check Advanced mode, you'll have additional choices to make. The first of these is Engine, which refers to the color conversion engine that Photoshop uses to send your file to the printer. Even if you're using a Mac, ignore the Apple ColorSync option and choose Adobe (ACE). It's designed specifically to work with Photoshop and other Adobe graphics applications. For Intent, I suggest you use Perceptual. It will give you the most pleasing colors, rather than the most mechanically accurate ones. It also allows you to print a wider range of colors than, for example, Absolute Colorimetric. Check both Blackpoint Compensation and Dither, unless your print shop or service bureau tells you not to. Again, you'll see better-looking color.

However, you can usually ignore the Advanced Controls panel. You don't want to desaturate your monitor or change the color-blending gamma except under rare circumstances, which is something only an expert user is likely to encounter.

Papers

What you print on makes almost as much difference as how you do the printing. You can get various types and weights of paper for all kinds of printers. There are special papers for ink jet and for laser. If you want your picture to resemble a photograph, consider investing in a pack of "photo weight" glossy paper. It's a much thicker paper with a glossy surface that really does help make your inkjet or laser printed picture look like something that came out of a real darkroom rather than a computer.

You can get coated papers for printing color on inkjet printers. These give you photo-quality prints with a matte surface, rather than the glossy one just mentioned. Transparency paper is clear acetate film, specially treated to accept the inks. Use it to make overhead projection slides and overlays.

You can also get "art" papers for some kinds of inkjet printers. These are heavy rag papers, much like artist's watercolor paper. Find these at www.inkjetmall.com/store. I've had very good luck printing on Somerset Smooth and Somerset Velvet with the Epson Photo 750 and 1200 printers. These fine-art papers are ideally suited to printing pictures that you've converted to imitation watercolors, pastel drawings, and so on. This is because they are the same papers generally used for those techniques. If you use a heavy art paper, feed in one sheet at a time and set the printer for thicker paper (if it has such an option).

Label stocks come in all kinds of sizes and shapes, and literally hundreds, if not thousands, of different kinds and weights of paper for both inkjet and laser printers.

Finally, you can buy packs of iron-on transfer paper (for color laser or inkjet printers), which let you put your images on T-shirts, aprons, tote bags, or anything else onto which you can iron. Follow the instructions with the paper and don't forget to flip your image before you print it so it reads correctly.

I used to use inexpensive photocopying paper for most of my work. It's fine for printing a quick proof to see how a picture comes out. For serious proofing, though, you need to use the same paper that you'll use for the final print. Otherwise, you aren't proving that the combination works. For work that a client will see, I use a coated inkjet paper like Epson Photo Quality Ink Jet paper because the colors are brighter and don't bleed into each other. If I want the picture to look more like a darkroom photo, I'll pay the dollar per sheet to print it on special glossy paper.

Summary

Printing Photoshop images isn't difficult; there are just a lot of decisions to make along the way. This hour discussed those choices, from initially preparing an image for printing, to setting up the page, and finally setting the Print options. The wonderful thing about printing is that if you don't get a gorgeous printout the first time, you can simply change settings and try again, provided you have enough paper and ink, of course.

Q&A

Q I love the idea of putting pictures on T-shirts and so on. What should I know before I start?

A Iron-on transfer paper works best with white or light colored cotton or cotton/polyester blends. Transfer with a household iron on its highest setting or in a professional heat press. Iron the fabric first and be sure it's cooled before you place the transfer on it. Also back up the single layer of fabric you're ironing onto with a sheet of cardboard. This prevents the dye from bleeding through and giving you a second image on the back of the T-shirt. Press firmly and expect to iron a large, full-page image for two to three minutes. Keep the iron moving enough so you don't scorch the fabric. Small images are easier to manage and take less ironing time. To avoid fading the transfer, wash shirts inside out and do not bleach.

Q How can I print my company logo on a hat? I only need one.

A Use the iron-on paper and make your logo the right size for the space where it's going. Since you can't iron it directly onto your hat, put it on a piece of white cloth, and sew or glue it in place.

Q I'd love to have a really big print of one of my pictures. Where can I find out about Iris printing?

A Start on the Web. Do a search for giclée and Iris. With more than 16,000 matches, you're bound to find an affordable Iris printer close to you.

Q I want to print pictures at the top of the page that my kids can write their stories under, but Photoshop insists on centering the images. Is there any way around it?

A Easy. Use the Print Options dialog box to move your pictures wherever you want them on the page.

Quiz

1. Dye-sublimation printers need special paper.

    a. True

    b. False

2. Registration marks look like

    a. The letter R in a circle

    b. A cross in a circle

    c. Four concentric circles in CMY and K

3. RGB stands for

    a. The initials of Roy G. Biv, inventor of ColorSync

    b. Raster, Gray, Black

    c. Red, Green, Blue

Quiz Answers

1. a. It can be expensive.

2. b. These marks make it easy to see when a color's out of register.

3. c. Those are the colors your monitor uses.

Exercises

PaperDirect is a company that sells more different kinds of papers for more purposes than you can possibly imagine. Visit its Web site (www.paperdirect.com) to see how to get a sample kit of their papers and envelopes.

Take a field trip to your local computer store or to a really good office supply store to see what kinds of papers they have for your printer. Also, check out art supply stores for unusual papers, such as canvas-textured, silk, and watercolor. Treat yourself to a package of high-quality paper and try printing some of your best work.

HOUR 24

Photoshop for the Web

Wow! You're almost finished; this is the last hour. You've learned enough to work effectively with Photoshop, even if you haven't yet mastered all the tricks and timesaving features. The rest will come as you do more work with the program. This final hour is devoted to one of the newest and best uses for Photoshop—putting your work on the World Wide Web.

You've "surfed" the Web with your favorite browser, Internet Explorer or Netscape Navigator. You probably have email and maybe even your own home page. But, do you know what's really going on out there in cyber-space? First of all, although the Web is what you might call a *virtual space,* meaning that it creates the illusion of space and distance, it also exists in a physical space. It is comprised of computers called *servers* that serve files across networks that stretch around the world. The computers can be anything from supercharged SPARC stations to minis and mainframes—or a machine not unlike the one sitting on your desktop. These machines run software that can *talk* with your machine via what are known as *protocols*.

Thus, when you type a URL (Uniform Resource Locator) into your browser to access a Web site, a message, made up of electronic pieces of information called *packets*, goes out to these remote machines. These machines then send back the files for which you have asked. The files that make up all the sounds, pic-tures, and text of the Web then have to travel across phone lines or down a cable TV line.

This creates a problem that you have to keep in mind as you create graphics for your Web site. Phone lines are slow, and there is only so much information that can travel at a time. If you are lucky enough to have a cable modem or an ISDN, DSL, or T1 connec-tion, you are doing okay speed-wise. A 28.8Kbps (kilobits per second) modem is moder-ately fast. A 56Kbps modem is fairly fast. A 14.4 modem is pretty slow. We used to be satisfied with 2400bps modems, but those were the pre-Web days, when we only used our modems for email and perhaps accessing chats on CompuServe or America Online.

The most popular language used to publish documents on the Web is HTML (Hypertext Markup Language). HTML isn't really a computer *programming* language, so relax. It is, as its name suggests, a *markup* language. A series of relatively simple *tags* enables you to specify how text appears in the browser, images, and links to other sites. HTML isn't difficult to learn, but you really don't need to. (If you decide to get into it, look for *Sams Teach Yourself HTML4 in 24 Hours*. It's an excellent reference.)

There are programs, including desktop publishing programs, Web browsers, and word processors you might already own, that can translate your pages into HTML with just a couple of mouse clicks. All you need to do is lay out the page the way you'd like it to look with your Photoshop pictures pasted in. You do have to make sure they're in a com-patible format, though. Because Web pages can be viewed on all kinds of computers, the graphics have to be in a format that's common to as many as possible.

Jumping into ImageReady

NEW TO VERSION 6 One of the best features of Photoshop 6 is the program that comes along with it, ImageReady 3.0. This is the latest and greatest (to date) version of this web graphics program. You can shift back and forth between Photoshop and ImageReady just by clicking the icon at the bottom of the toolbar.

ImageReady is Adobe's Web graphics program. ImageReady includes many of the basic color correction, painting, and selection tools that you've already learned in Photoshop, plus a powerful set of Web tools for optimizing and previewing images and creating GIF animations and rollovers.

Figure 24.1 shows the ImageReady toolbox. As you can see, many of the icons are famil-iar. A few of the new ones let you create and view image maps, rollovers, and slices. (You'll learn about these interesting terms later on this hour.) The last icon in that set is perhaps the most important. It's the one that shows two pages with an arrow between them. This lets you view your Web creations within your browser so you can see what works and what doesn't.

FIGURE 24.1

Click the arrow at the bottom of the toolbar or type Command+ Shift+M (Mac) or Control+Shift+M (Windows) to switch between ImageReady and Photoshop.

Toggle image map visibility   Toggle slices visibility
Rollover preview   Preview

Jump to Photoshop

24

If Photoshop and ImageReady have the same tools, and both can save images in GIF, JPEG, and PNG formats, how do you know when to use which one? If you're just dealing with one picture, you can use either. If you want to optimize several pictures so they'll display well while using as little memory as possible, use ImageReady to do the optimization. You can edit, apply filters and type, and color correct in either program.

File Formats and File Size

The first thing you need to learn about preparing Web graphics is the type of file format to use. There are two standard choices: GIF (Graphics Interchange Format) and JPEG (Joint Photographic Experts Group). There's also a third, newer format known as PNG (Portable Network Graphics). It promises to be the best choice of all three, but it is not supported by older browsers. Use it if you like it, but be aware that there might still be a few folks out there whose software can't read PNG files.

The most important thing to remember, regardless of the file format you decide to use, is that the Web has limited bandwidth. This means that if you create an absolutely beautiful image and it weighs in at something like four megabytes, it will take forever to download on a 28.8 modem. This is not to say that you *can't* create images with as large a file size as you want. I am just suggesting that few Web surfers out there will have the patience to sit and wait while your 4MB image downloads. If you know that your primary audience is surfing from home with slower modems, you might want to keep your Web pages well under 30KB apiece. This is an area where ImageReady can be a big help. It lets you decide how small you can save a file without sacrificing quality.

If you have some big files that you want to publish on the Web, don't fret. There are ways around the big file issue. Most surfers won't mind the wait for a big file if they have a warning. Give them a thumbnail version of the image and tell them how big the file is. This way, they can decide for themselves whether they want to spend the time waiting for the download. A little courtesy, as in all aspects of life, goes a long way on the Web.

JPEG (Joint Photographic Experts Group)

Depending on your needs, JPEG could be the best file format for you. It is great for photographs and other continuous tone (full-color) images, primarily because it lets you use 16 million different colors. (Of course, some Web browser programs can't handle that color depth. Instead, they display a "reasonable approximation" of your artwork.) JPEG maintains color information but does, however, employ a *lossy* compression scheme, which means that you can adjust and reduce the file size—at the expense of the image quality.

To save as a JPEG, you need to work in RGB mode within Photoshop. This is reasonable because RGB is the "monitor" viewing mode, and Web images are going to be seen on, guess what—an RGB monitor. ImageReady only has one mode, RGB, which is all it needs. (You can't print from ImageReady.)

When you're working in Photoshop, choosing File→Save for Web will open the window shown in Figure 24.2. I selected JPEG Low Quality from the Settings pop-up menu in the upper-right corner. I could have chosen GIF or PNG, as well. After a short calculation, and because I'd clicked the 4-Up tab at the top of the window, I can see my original image, plus the image with three different JPEG settings. The file size and download time are displayed for each image.

The original image was 801KB. As a low-quality JPEG, it's 11.27KB and will take about 5 seconds to download on a fast modem. At medium quality, the file size increases to 20.25KB and the download time increases to 8 seconds. At high quality, it's a 47.4KB file and loads in 18 seconds. Is the quality difference worth the upload time?

On the other hand, we've gone from 800KB down to 11KB. That's a tremendous difference with a relatively small loss of quality.

FIGURE 24.2
As a JPEG in High, Medium, or Low quality.

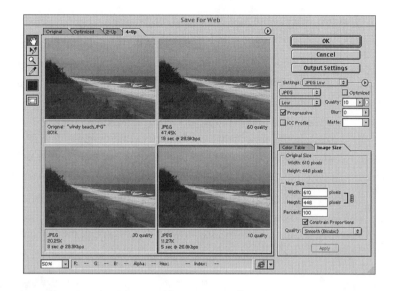

Each time you save the file as a JPEG, you lose some data to compression. This can create *artifacts*, blocky areas or color bands in your picture. Never save a file as a JPEG a second time. If you make a conversion to JPEG, and then decide to make changes, go back to the original Photoshop file. Don't make changes and resave the previously saved JPEG.

To save your file, click OK. The usual Save As dialog box will open, letting you name your document and save it where you want it, presumably in the same folder with other Web page items.

If you are saving a JPEG file directly from Photoshop with the File→Save As... command, you will open a second dialog box, like the one in Figure 24.3.

FIGURE 24.3
The JPEG Options box lets you choose image quality and how the picture is loaded into a browser.

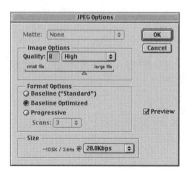

This box will prompt you for format options:

- *Baseline ("Standard")*—This is the default option, if you leave the others unchecked.

- *Baseline (Optimized)*—This option optimizes the colors in the file. It creates a smaller file.

- *Progressive*—Except for very small JPEGs, this is almost a must for Web work. Progressive means that your file is visible within a Web browser faster and it is then refined by subsequent passes, or *scans,* as more file information is downloaded. If you select a progressive JPEG, it will automatically be optimized.

Saving your file as a JPEG in ImageReady opens a similar window and optimization palette (see Figure 24.4). After you've selected a JPEG quality and your other settings, click the version of the image you want to save. Click the OK button in the Save Optimized dialog box.

FIGURE 24.4

You have the same options in ImageReady as in Photoshop.

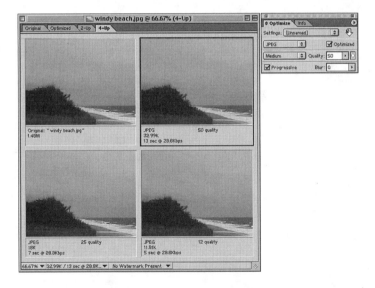

Always keep your Web browser open when you are creating Web graphics. This allows you to take a look at them in context.

Don't be fooled by how quickly File→Open File in your browser opens one of your files. These files are on your hard drive—they're *local.* When a viewer has to go out on the Web to get your pages, the process is slowed down quite a bit.

GIF (Graphics Interchange Format)

GIFs are another option for Web file formats. Because they're limited to 256 colors (with a Web browser limit of 216), they're not as good as JPEG for continuous tone art, but they're great for line art, logos, and anything with limited color. The GIF format also lets you save files with transparent backgrounds, which is extremely useful when you are creating buttons and other round graphics. Furthermore, you can animate a GIF.

24

A good way to select the file format that's right for you is to visit Web sites that have graphics similar to what you want to publish. To find out what kind of file format an image is, simply click the image. On a Macintosh, click and hold the image until a dialog box appears. On a Windows machine, click the image with the right mouse button.

In the dialog box, choose to save the image. When you are prompted for where you want to save the image, note the file extension—.jpg for JPEG, .png for PNG, or .gif for GIF. Click OK to save the file or click Cancel if you are just looking.

In Figure 24.5, I've created a simple button that I'll be saving as a GIF. Notice how much the file shrinks when I limit the colors in the GIF.

FIGURE 24.5

You can set the GIF colors according to what's needed for your image. For this button (shown in ImageReady), I only needed a few shades of purple, plus black and white.

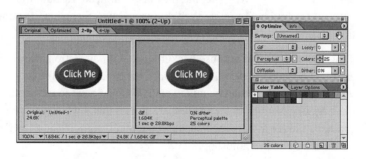

PNG (Portable Network Graphics)

There are two kinds of PNG, 8-bit and 24-bit. The PNG-8 format uses 8-bit color. Like the GIF format, PNG-8 compresses solid areas of color very well while preserving sharp detail, such as that in line art, logos, or illustrations with type. Because PNG-8 is not supported by older browsers, it might be a good idea to avoid this format for situations in which your image must be accessible to as much of the Web viewing audience as possible. The PNG-8 format uses a lossless compression method, with no data discarded during compression. However, because PNG-8 files are 8-bit color, optimizing an original 24-bit image as a PNG-8 will degrade image quality. PNG-8 files use more advanced compression schemes than GIF, and can be 10%–30% smaller than GIF files of the same image, depending on the image's color patterns.

PNG-24 file format uses 24-bit color and is suitable for continuous-tone images. PNG-24 uses a lossless compression scheme. However, PNG-24 files can be much larger than JPEG files of the same image. PNG-24 format is recommended only when working with a continuous-tone image that includes multilevel or variable transparency, such as you'd have in an anti-aliased image on a transparent layer. (Multilevel transparency is supported by the PNG-24 format but not the JPEG format.)

Bottom line: If you'd consider GIF for an image, consider PNG-8 as well. It might give you a smaller file, and can do the job well. If you're thinking about JPEG, consider PNG-24 if your picture has multi-level transparency. If it's a straight image, JPEG will probably give you a smaller, more efficient file.

Preparing Backgrounds

I admit that I have mixed feelings about backgrounds on Web pages. These can really add personality to a Web site, but they also can make reading the text of your site difficult and frustrating. To quote Web designer David Siegel, "Gift-wrap makes poor stationery."

That said, however, if you use backgrounds with discretion, they can add to a site's presence and look. Because HTML includes the capability to tile any image as a background, your background file can be quite small. You just have to make sure it doesn't have obvious edges or pictures that end abruptly, unless that's what you want. In Figure 24.6, I've created a tile for a Web page background, and I'm saving it as a GIF using the Save for Web dialog box in Photoshop.

FIGURE 24.6

This tile combines several filters placed over a plain white background.

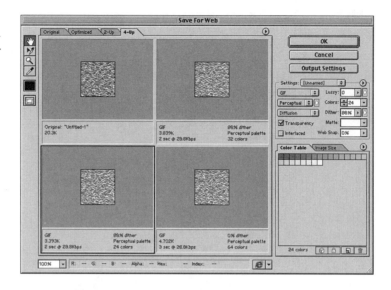

To turn the tile into a background, all I have to do is open my page creation program and place it. Using Netscape Composer to build my pages, that's what I'm doing in Figure 24.7. To convert the image into a tiled background, all I need to do is to check the Page Background box. The rest happens automatically.

FIGURE 24.7

This tile could also have been a JPEG or PNG image, but GIF gave me the smallest file.

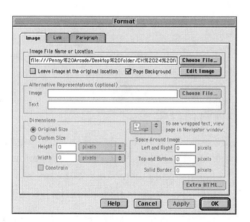

Now, all you have to do is to be sure that when you upload your page to the Web, the background image goes into the same folder as the page itself. Figure 24.8 shows the tiled background with some type placed over it.

24

FIGURE **24.8**

The background looks even, and the tiling hardly shows at all.

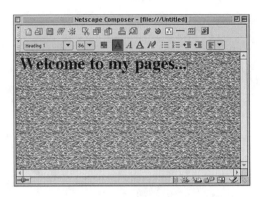

Here's a trick for placing a stripe down one side of your page. Make a single tile that's the width of the screen by as few pixels high as needed. Place your color and/or texture on it, and then save it as a GIF or JPEG. The file will probably look something like Figure 24.9.

FIGURE **24.9**

Note that this is reduced, so you can see the whole strip.

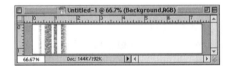

When you place this file as a background, it will be tiled vertically but not horizontally, because it's already as wide as the screen. You'll end up with a nice stripe, as wide as you care to make it, in the color and texture of your choice. It makes a good accent for a plain page, especially if you then place buttons on it.

Building Animations

GIF animations are commonplace on Web pages, and you'll probably see dogs wagging their tails endlessly, cats catching mice, balls bouncing. It's enough to make you dizzy. Photoshop and ImageReady can create the graphic elements and add motion to any of these goodies.

Creating animated GIFs, however, is really way beyond the scope of this book. The manual that came with Photoshop and ImageReady can get you started. If you want to get serious about Web page design and using HTML, run to your local bookstore or computer store and look for Hayden's *Photoshop Web Magic*. It's a great source for tips and tricks to spiff up your Web site.

Many Web design programs even come with buttons and other goodies you can apply to your page, as well as instructions on how to put your own graphics onto their buttons. Nothing could be easier. After you're done playing, the software makes the conversion to HTML in the background for you and gives you files ready to upload to your Web page provider.

Web Photo Gallery

Want to put your art on a Web page? Sure. So do I, but those files can be huge. Wouldn't it be better to put up thumbnail images, and then let interested viewers click those thumbnails to see the large versions? Of course it would. But creating all those thumbnails, and then making the page and linking the images to it… well, that sounds like hard work.

Fortunately, there's a better way. Photoshop's Web Photo Gallery does the job for you. You have a choice of layouts: a simple page of thumbnails, which you can click to open a new window with a full-size view; table-format, again with thumbnails; or all the thumbnails in a frame that scrolls vertically or horizontally. For this last format, you open the thumbnails in a second frame on the right. Figure 24.10 shows the Web Photo Gallery dialog box.

24

FIGURE 24.10

I've chosen to use Horizontal Frame rather than the Simple or Table layouts.

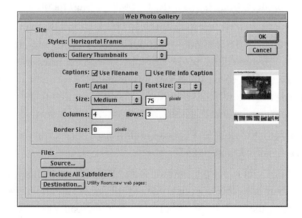

To Do: Making a Gallery Page

Let's practice making a gallery page:

1. Before you begin, make sure all the images you want to include are in one folder. Then open File→Automate→Web Gallery.

2. The first pop-up menu lets you choose how the pictures will be displayed. Choose Frame (Horizontal or Vertical), Simple, or Table, as described previously.

▼   3. The second pop-up, Options, lets you set up a title banner for your work, determine
       the sizes of thumbnails and images, and set text and background colors. Open
       Banner Options, as shown in Figure 24.11.

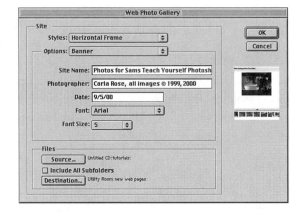

   4. Enter a name for your page, as well as your own name if you want. I always add a
      copyright notice to anything I am putting on the Web, in addition to watermarking
      the individual images. Choose a font and size to display your type.

   5. Choose Gallery Images from the Options pop-up menu and set a size and quality
      for the large display images. Add a border if you wish.

   6. Choose Gallery Thumbnails from the Options menu and choose whether to use no
      captions, use the filenames as captions, or add captions in the File Info window for
      each image. You can also choose a font and size for the captions, and decide
      whether or not they'll have borders. If you're using table or simple layout, you
      might select the number of photos in rows and columns.

   7. Open Custom Colors and choose appropriate colors for your page's background,
      banner, headline, and links.

   8. In the Files section at the bottom of the Web Photo Gallery dialog box, use the
      Source button to locate your folder of pictures, and choose a destination where
▲   you'll save the Web page. When everything's ready, click OK.

Photoshop will assemble the page according to your specifications. When it's complete,
it will automatically open in your default browser. Figure 24.12 shows the Web page I
am creating for this book. (See it at www.graphicalcat.com/TYPS6.)

FIGURE 24.12
*My Web gallery,
viewed in Netscape.*

Photoshop lists the images alphabetically. If you aren't happy with the type size or font, the background color, or any of the other settings you've made, now is the time to go back and change them. Changes will be applied to your page automatically.

Creating Slices

Slices are not the easiest concept to grasp, but they can save you a lot of file space, after you figure out what they are about. Simply put, *slices* divide a document into smaller files. Each slice is an independent file, containing its own optimization settings, color palettes, URLs, rollover effects, and animation effects. Slices can give you increased image quality when you are working with documents that contain more than one kind of image, or text and images. They can make pages seem to load faster because each slice becomes visible as soon as it's loaded, giving the viewer something to look at while the rest of the image loads. Slices also let you create image maps that do useful things when you click part of an image. They can take you to new pages, show an enlarged view of the slice, or anything else you care to program them to do.

Slices are assembled in an HTML table in the document's HTML file. By default, the document starts with one slice that comprises the entire document. You can then create more slices in the document. ImageReady will automatically make additional slices to complete the full table in the HTML file.

Slices are created by dragging the Slice Tool, which looks like a drawing of an Exacto knife. Select it from the ImageReady toolbox, the Photoshop toolbox, or simply type **K** to activate it. Drag a selection box across the area you are slicing. If you make a slice across the middle of an image, by default, you have defined three slices—one above and one below where you have sliced. Slices that you create are called *user-slices*. Slices that Photoshop generates are called *auto-slices*. If you place a slice across the middle of a picture, Photoshop will place auto-slices above and below it. Slices can be vertical as well as horizontal. There are also subslices created when you overlap two or more user-slices. Figure 24.13 shows a sliced image and the Slice palette.

Figure 24.13

The numbers in the upper-left corner of the sections are their slice numbers.

Creating a Rollover Effect

Rollover effects are one of the most powerful features of ImageReady, allowing you to create effects that are triggered when the mouse is moved in relation to part of the image within a slice. For example, if the mouse is moved over an image, or if the mouse button is clicked on the image, these can activate an effect. A button is actually a kind of rollover effect, in that, when you click the affected piece of the screen, something happens. You're taken to another page or to some different Web site.

The action that takes place when you move over a rollover is called a *rollover state*. The first state, by default, is always the *Normal state*, with no mouse action performed. When you create a new rollover state, you can select the mouse action that activates the state from a pop-up menu that appears when you choose New State from the Rollover window's menu. You can also activate it by clicking the new State button at the bottom of the Rollover palette. (It looks just like the New Layer icon.) The State pop-up menu is shown in Figure 24.14.

FIGURE 24.14

Choose a rollover state to apply.

The rollover states will be assigned by default if you don't choose one. In order of appearance, they are Normal, Over, Down, Click, Out, Up, Custom, and None.

- *Over* defines the rollover state when the viewer rolls a mouse over the slice with the mouse button up or hovers over the slice or button. (Over is automatically selected for the second rollover state.)

- *Down* is the rollover state when the viewer presses the mouse button while on the slice. (This state appears as long as the viewer keeps the mouse button pressed while staying on the slice.)

- *Click* defines the rollover state when a viewer clicks the mouse on the slice. (This state appears after the viewer clicks the mouse, and remains until the viewer activates another rollover state, even if the mouse moves off the target slice.)

- *Out* is the rollover state when the viewer rolls the mouse out of the slice. Usually, this is used to return to Normal.

- *Up* is seldom used. It defines the rollover state when the viewer releases the mouse button over the slice. (The Over state usually serves this purpose.)

- Select *Custom* to define a new rollover state. (To define a state other than those listed, you must create JavaScript code and add it to the HTML file for the document Custom rollover option to function. Consult a JavaScript manual for more information.)

- *None* will preserve the current state of the image for later use as a rollover state. (A state designated as None will not be shown on the Web page.)

What happens when you activate a rollover state depends on what you've defined it to do. The easiest way to change an image with a rollover is to add a layer to the existing image and put the changes on it. When the rollover is activated, the new layer will be displayed. Otherwise, it remains hidden. For instance, if I wanted to change the sky in a photo from midday to sunset, I'd make a new layer that masked the midday blue sky and covered it with a sunset sky. Until the viewer rolled over the picture with a mouse, he'd see blue sky. As soon as the mouse rolled over the sky, it would change to sunset, and would change back to Normal when the mouse rolled off the image. Figures 24.15 and 24.16 show these states. Notice the position of the mouse pointer in each frame.

24

FIGURE **24.15**

*In the Normal state,
the sky is blue.*

FIGURE **24.16**

*When I move the
pointer over the slice,
the sky changes to a
sunset.*

When you save an optimized image that has rollover states, each rollover state gets saved
as a separate file. By default, rollover states are named using the corresponding slice
name plus the mouse action that triggers the rollover state. If you change the name of a
slice, rollover states in the slice are correspondingly renamed. Because rollover states are
saved separately, they add to the size of your page and lengthen the download time.
Apply them carefully. As with every other possible Web page toy, they can be, and often
are, overused.

That's a very brief look at rollovers. To learn more, consult the manual that came with your software.

Preparing Text for the Web

HTML Web standards include a handful of different type sizes and fonts, some for headings, some for text, and some for "emphasis." Uh-huh. "Bo-ring," to quote the kids. However, you're not necessarily limited to what HTML has to offer. If you want an elaborate title for your page, create it in Photoshop, using filled letters, filters, drop shadows, glows, or whatever other special effects you like. Crop it tightly and save it as either a GIF or JPEG. Figure 24.17 shows one that I created for my page. Compressed, the file is only 6.3KB.

FIGURE 24.17

I used Eyecandy 4.0's Bevelboss filter to create the three-dimensional effect.

You have the option of converting your file to JPEG or to GIF. One good thing about text is that it usually, but not always, is applied to a white background. If this is the case with your Web site, there is no need to go through the trouble of exporting a transparent GIF89a file. Just make sure that your background is white and save it as a plain GIF file.

There's one "rule of thumb" that professional Web page designers apply to choosing formats. With line art, or anything with a limited palette (fewer than 216 colors), choose GIF. With photos or full-color art, choose JPEG or PNG.

Making Pages Load Faster

The bottom line for making Web pages load faster is—you can't. The page will load as fast as the server can send it and the recipient can receive it. Those are both factors beyond your control.

What you can do, though, is make sure that your page is arranged so there's something to see while the graphic loads. Bring up a Welcome headline first, and then add the background. If there's a graphic that will take some time to load, bring up a block of text before the graphic appears. The load time for the picture will seem much shorter if the person waiting has something else to read or think about.

Keep your images small or put up a thumbnail and link the full-sized picture to it, so visitors have the option of waiting to see the big picture. Remember that a few diehards still use text-based Web browsers and don't see images at all. If the content of your picture is important, put a text description of it on the page, too. If you learn HTML, you can use ALT to place an image description in place of the image. (This also helps make your Web site handicapped-accessible, which is important to do for the estimated two million visually impaired Web users.)

Summary

In this final hour, we looked at putting your work on the Web. We examined what file formats the Web uses and how you might best choose the right formats for your own work.

So what comes next? You've finished your 24th hour, and you know a lot more about Photoshop than you did when you began. That doesn't mean you know it all, but you now have the tools—your imagination, creativity, and a basic understanding of Photoshop. There is still plenty out there to learn and with which to experiment. I've personally been using Photoshop ever since it first came out, and I'm still learning new tricks and techniques. You can spend years with this program and still not try everything it can do.

Above all else, have fun!

Q&A

Q **Can I mix the kinds of images I use on a Web page—some JPEGs, some GIFs, a PNG—or will that cause everything to crash?**

A There is no reason not to mix image types. Choose the type depending on the content of the image. Realistic photos look best as JPEG or PNG files. Graphics with limited color are most efficiently stored as GIFs.

Q **What's the trick for using a picture as a page background?**

A Keep it small and apply the picture as a tiled background. If you keep the edges blurry, they blend smoothly, avoiding that floor tile look. Save your file as either a

GIF or JPEG with the name background. Your Web page creator program should be able to insert it automatically, but if not, use the HTML tag <body background = "background.gif"> (or .jpg, if appropriate).

Another effect that uses the whole photo once is to make the image nearly transparent so it looks really toned down. Use it as a non-tiled background, or *watermark*.

Q If I want to put my pictures on the Web, but only for my friends to see, can I protect them?

A There are lots of ways to do this. The easiest is to put them on a "hidden" page. This is a second page on your site, not linked to the first. Instead it has a separate address, such as home.myservice.net/mypage/hidden.htm. Give your friends the direct URL to this page. No one who doesn't know it's there will be able to reach it. However, "security through obscurity" is never a recommended policy for truly sensitive information or images. If you want to be more secure, you can learn enough JavaScript to password-protect the site. Look for *Pure JavaScript* by Sams. It's a good way to learn JavaScript.

24

Quiz

1. What do I have to do to a Photoshop .psd file before I can put it on the Web?

    a. Attach a copyright notice.

    b. Flatten the image and save as a .jpg, .gif, or .png file.

    c. Get a model release on any recognizable people.

2. HTML stands for

    a. Hypertext Markup Language

    b. Hand-coded Type Meta Language

    c. Has Trouble Making Lines

3. What's the most important thing to remember about Photoshop?

    a. Experiment

    b. Experiment

    c. Experiment

Quiz Answers

1. b., but a. and c. are good ideas, too.

2. a. It's the language that defines Web pages.

3. The most important thing is that there's no wrong answer. Keep trying new things, new combinations, and new approaches. Photoshop is a wonderful tool, but, without *your* creativity and imagination, it's just software.

Exercises

After you've chosen some of your best Photoshop work and put it on your own Web page, send me an email (author@graphicalcat.com) with your page location, and I'll give you a critique of your work. No Web page? Attach no more than three JPEGs to your email. Expect a response within five to seven days or sooner, unless I am swamped with requests.

APPENDIX A

Photoshop 6 Palette
Quick Reference

Navigator Palette

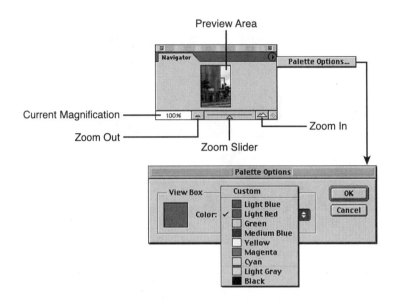

Info Palette

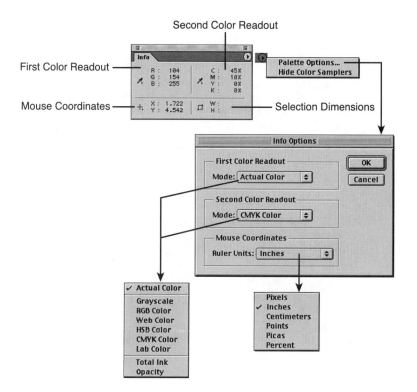

Second Color Readout

First Color Readout

Mouse Coordinates

Selection Dimensions

Palette Options...
Hide Color Samplers

Info

R : 104
G : 154
B : 255

C : 45%
M : 10%
Y : 0%
K : 0%

X : 1.722
Y : 4.542

W :
H :

Info Options

First Color Readout

Mode: Actual Color

OK
Cancel

Second Color Readout

Mode: CMYK Color

Mouse Coordinates

Ruler Units: Inches

✓ **Actual Color**

Grayscale
RGB Color
Web Color
HSB Color
CMYK Color
Lab Color

Total Ink
Opacity

Pixels
✓ Inches
Centimeters
Points
Picas
Percent

A

Color Palette

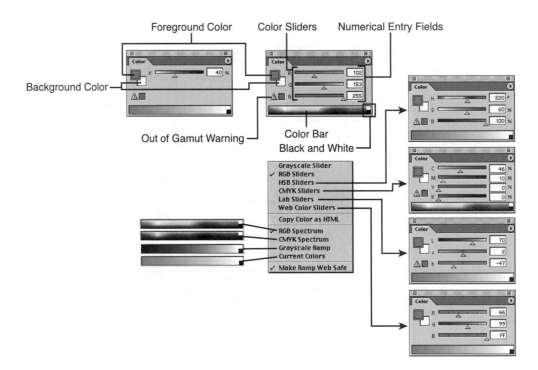

Foreground Color   Color Sliders   Numerical Entry Fields

Background Color

Out of Gamut Warning

Color Bar

Black and White

Swatches Palette

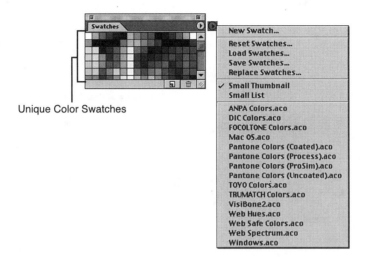

Unique Color Swatches

Styles Palette

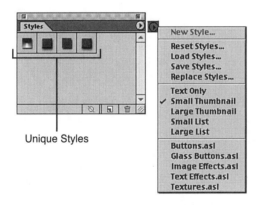

Unique Styles

A

History Palette

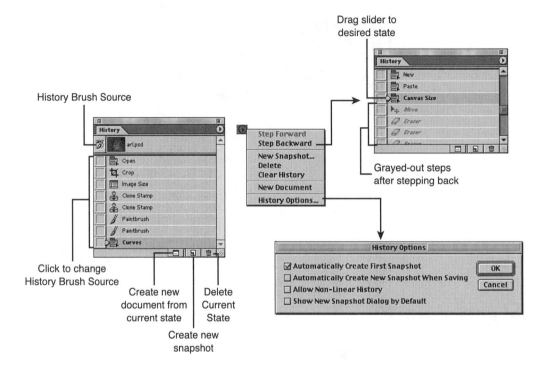

Drag slider to
desired state

History Brush Source

Grayed-out steps
after stepping back

Click to change
History Brush Source

Create new
document from
current state

Delete
Current
State

Create new
snapshot

Actions Palette

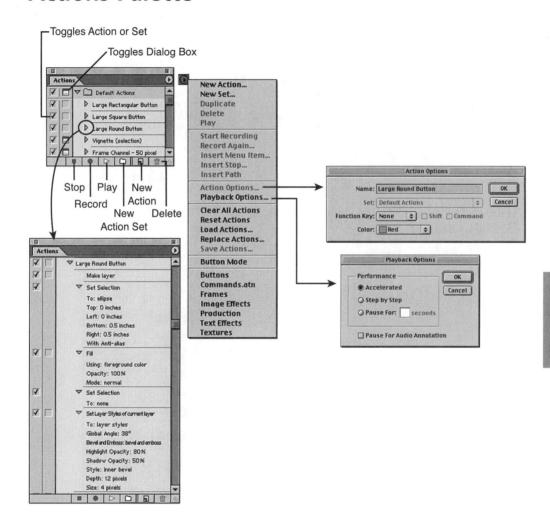

Layers Palette

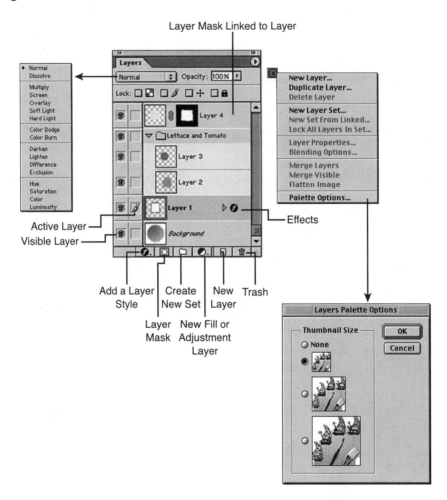

Layer Mask Linked to Layer

Normal
Dissolve

Multiply
Screen
Overlay
Soft Light
Hard Light

Color Dodge
Color Burn

Darken
Lighten
Difference
Exclusion

Hue
Saturation
Color
Luminosity

Layers

Normal   Opacity: 100%

Lock:

Layer 4

Lettuce and Tomato

Layer 3

Layer 2

Layer 1

Background

New Layer...
Duplicate Layer...
Delete Layer

New Layer Set...
New Set From Linked...
Lock All Layers In Set...

Layer Properties...
Blending Options...

Merge Layers
Merge Visible
Flatten Image

Palette Options...

Active Layer

Visible Layer

Effects

Add a Layer
Style

Create
New Set

New
Layer

Trash

Layer
Mask

New Fill or
Adjustment
Layer

Layers Palette Options

Thumbnail Size

None

OK

Cancel

Channels Palette

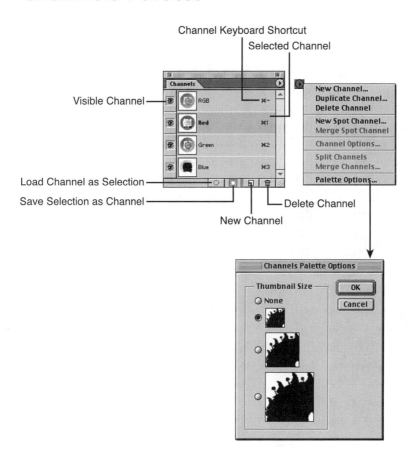

Channel Keyboard Shortcut

Selected Channel

Visible Channel

Load Channel as Selection

Save Selection as Channel

New Channel

Delete Channel

A

Paths Palette

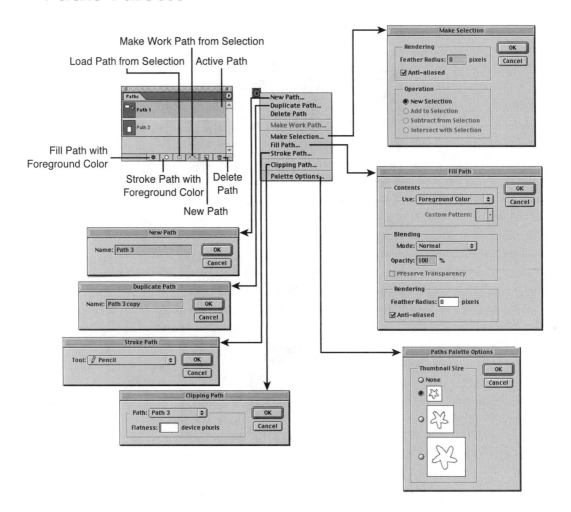

INDEX

Q-R